P372 Mzi

D0468543

INTERMEDIATE

The **MAILBOX** — IDEA MAGAZINE FOR TEACHERS®

2006–2007
YEARBOOK

The Education Center, Inc.
Greensboro, North Carolina

The Mailbox® 2006–2007 Intermediate Yearbook

Managing Editor, *The Mailbox* Magazine: Peggy W. Hambright

Editorial Team: Becky S. Andrews, Kimberley Bruck, Diane Badden, Debra Liverman, Karen A. Brudnak, Sharon Murphy, Hope Rodgers, Dorothy C. McKinney

Production Team: Lori Z. Henry, Margaret Freed (COVER ARTIST), Pam Crane, Rebecca Saunders, Chris Curry, Sarah Foreman, Theresa Lewis Goode, Greg D. Rieves, Eliseo De Jesus Santos II, Barry Slate, Donna K. Teal, Zane Williard, Tazmen Carlisle, Kathy Coop, Marsha Heim, Lynette Dickerson, Mark Rainey

ISBN10 1-56234-813-2
ISBN13 978-156234-813-7
ISSN 1088-5552

Printed in the United States of America.

The Education Center, Inc.
P.O. Box 9753
Greensboro, NC 27429-0753

Look for *The Mailbox® 2007–2008 Intermediate Yearbook* in the summer of 2008. The Education Center, Inc., is the publisher of *The Mailbox*®, *Teacher's Helper*®, *The Mailbox*® BOOKBAG®, and *Learning*® magazines, as well as other fine products. Look for these wherever quality teacher materials are sold, call 1-800-714-7991, or visit www.themailbox.com.

Contents

Seasonal ideas
&
Reproducibles

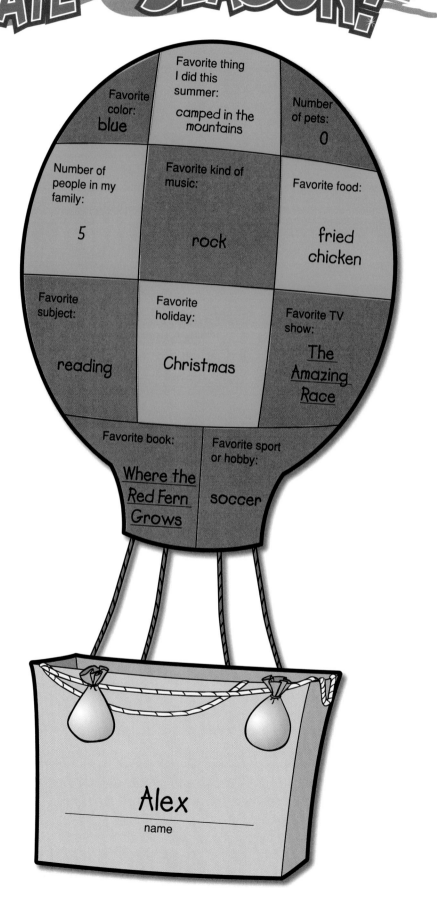

Favorite color: blue

Favorite thing I did this summer: camped in the mountains

Number of pets: 0

Number of people in my family: 5

Favorite kind of music: rock

Favorite food: fried chicken

Favorite subject: reading

Favorite holiday: Christmas

Favorite TV show: The Amazing Race

Favorite book: Where the Red Fern Grows

Favorite sport or hobby: soccer

Alex
name

Soaring Into a Great Year!

Getting acquainted

For a back-to-school activity that helps students get to know one another, give each child a copy of the hot-air balloon patterns on page 9. Instruct him to follow the directions on the page to label, color, and assemble the parts. Then invite him to share his completed project with the class before displaying it on a bulletin board with colorful cutouts of clouds and a larger hot-air balloon. To extend the activity, have each child write an uplifting story about a time he did something that cheered someone up and post it on the board next to his balloon.

Elizabeth Loeser, Jacksonville, FL

Putting Pencil to Paper
Taking notes, summarizing

Celebrate Constitution Day (September 17) with an activity that simulates the Constitutional Convention. If possible, obtain Jean Fritz's book *Shh! We're Writing the Constitution*. Or flag pages in a social studies text related to topics debated during the convention. Next, give each child a brown paper towel. Have her trim the towel to resemble a scroll of parchment paper. Have her also transform her pencil into a quill pen by drawing a feather shape on colorful paper, cutting out the shape, and taping it to her pencil. Select from Fritz's book one or more hot topics that convention delegates debated (see the suggested topics). Read those portions of the book aloud. As you do, have students use their quills to take notes about what is read and then write a paragraph summarizing their notes. To add excitement, post a sign outside your classroom door that says, "Shh! We're Writing the Constitution!"

adapted from an idea by Keen Niedzwiecki, Knowlton Elementary, San Antonio, TX

Hot Topics
division of power
state representatives
The Bill of Rights
taxes
slavery

Slavery

The northern states wanted to make the slave trade against the law. The southern states did not want to give Congress this power.

We're a Team!
Getting-acquainted activity

Help students get to know one another with a first-day activity that culminates with opening a time capsule at the end of the year! Give each child a copy of the trading card pattern at the bottom of page 8. Have him fill in the requested information, draw a self-portrait in the box provided, and then color the card using his favorite colors. After students share their work with the class, display the cards on a board titled "We Make a Great Team!" When the display is taken down, place the trading cards in a container labeled "Time Capsule." Open it on the last day of school so students can see whether their lists of favorite things changed during the year!

Lisa M. Mellon, Southwest Elementary, Waterford, CT

Birthday Bash!
Graphing

This back-to-school math activity is not only educational but also makes it easier for you to remember student birthdays! Have each child write his birthday on a colorful sticky note or cupcake cutout and affix it to a whiteboard or a length of bulletin board paper labeled as shown. Use the resulting graph to review the parts of a graph as well as range, median, mean, and mode. Then remove the sticky notes and affix them each month to the appropriate classroom calendar!

Michele Wilbur, Nelson Elementary, Dover, FL

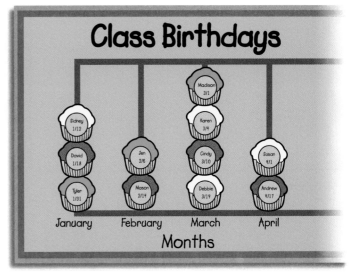

Seasonal Journal Prompts

September Topics

- Imagine that you have been asked to make sure all the new kids at your school know where to go and what to do on the first day of school. What will be your plan of action?

- Pretend that every time you open your textbook, all of the answers magically appear. List all the good and bad things that could happen because of this.

- September is College Savings Month. Which college would you like to attend one day? Why?

- If you could travel to any planet in the solar system, which one would you choose? Use your five senses to describe what it might be like to live there.

- Suppose that one day all the food items in the cafeteria started singing and dancing. What songs did they sing? What type of dancing did they do?

- How would life change if people hibernated six months out of the year?

- Which would you prefer: going to a school where only math and science are taught or one where only language arts and social studies are taught? Explain.

- Pretend that your school requires all school work to be done on laptop computers. Just as you are about to save a week's worth of assignments, the computer crashes. What will you do?

The reproducible on page 10 was written by Jacqueline Beaudry of Getzville, NY.

- -

Trading Card Pattern
Use with "We're a Team!" on page 7.

Name: _____

My Favorite...

Food: _____

Board Game: _____

TV Show: _____

_____

Movie: _____

_____

Book: _____

_____

Song: _____

_____

TEC44026

Hot-Air Balloon Patterns

Use with "Soaring Into a Great Year!" on page 6.

Directions:
1. Cut out the balloon and basket.
2. Fill in the information on the balloon. Write your name on the basket.
3. Color the balloon and basket.
4. Connect the basket to the balloon using tape and lengths of yarn.

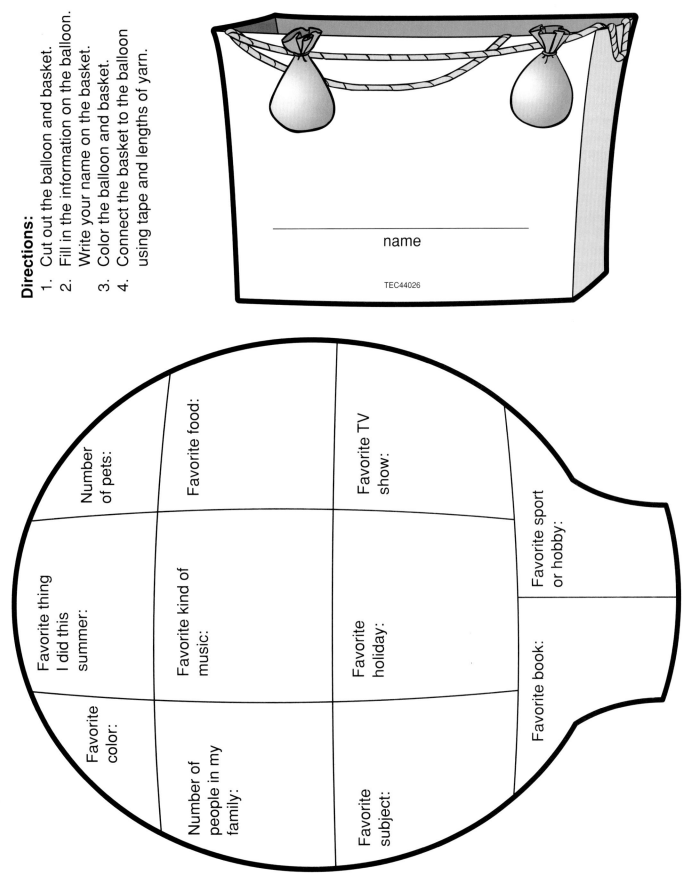

name

TEC44026

Favorite thing I did this summer:

Number of pets:

Favorite food:

Favorite color:

Favorite kind of music:

Favorite TV show:

Number of people in my family:

Favorite holiday:

Favorite sport or hobby:

Favorite subject:

Favorite book:

A Sentence Convention

Read each sentence. Write the number of each sentence on the correct document below.

1. Why is the Constitution needed?

2. The Constitution of the United States lists the basic rights of all American citizens.

3. The U.S. Constitution was signed on September 17, 1787.

4. Learn about our Founding Fathers.

5. What wise men they were!

6. How does the Constitution balance our government's power?

7. Tell which branch of government creates our laws.

8. Who chooses the members of the U.S. Congress?

9. Respect the head of the executive branch.

10. The judicial branch explains the Constitution and our laws.

11. The Constitution makes our government strong!

12. The first ten amendments are called the Bill of Rights.

13. Which amendment gives us the freedom of speech?

14. Hooray for the Constitution of the United States!

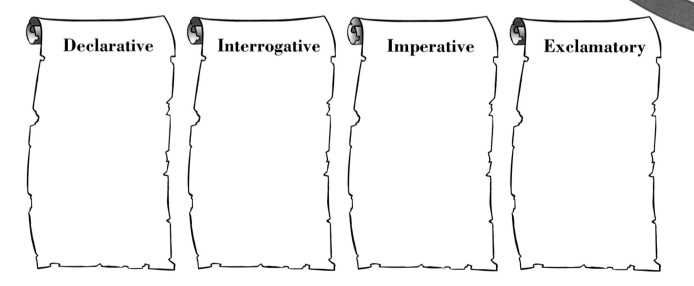

Declarative	Interrogative	Imperative	Exclamatory

Bonus Box: Why do you think Constitution Day (September 17) is celebrated every year? Write your answer on the back of this page.

 ©The Mailbox® • TEC44026 • Aug./Sept. 2006 • Key p. 308

LET'S GET STARTED!

Use each pair of numbers in the number bank to complete the problems.

Number Bank

72 and 4	160 and 10
55 and 89	257 and 413
67 and 6	99 and 912
65 and 47	4 and 367
84 and 78	20 and 500

Welcome!
Please find
your seat.

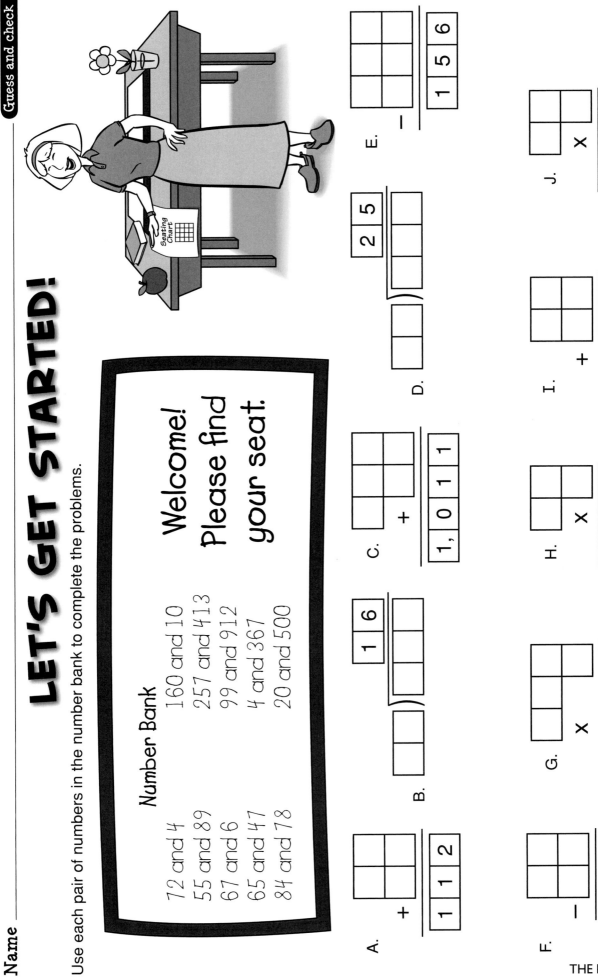

A.
```
    ☐ ☐
  + ☐ ☐
  ───────
  1 1 2
```

B.
```
  ☐ ) 1 6
```

C.
```
    ☐ ☐
  + ☐ ☐ ☐
  ─────────
  1 , 0 1 1
```

D.
```
  ☐ ☐ ) 2 5
```

E.
```
    ☐ ☐
  − ☐ ☐
  ───────
  1 5 6
```

F.
```
    ☐ ☐
  − ☐ ☐
  ───────
    3 4
```

G.
```
    ☐ ☐
  ×   ☐
  ───────
  1 , 4 6 8
```

H.
```
    ☐ ☐
  ×   ☐
  ───────
    2 8 8
```

I.
```
    ☐ ☐
  + ☐ ☐
  ───────
  1 6 2
```

J.
```
    ☐ ☐
  ×   ☐
  ───────
  4 0 2
```

©The Mailbox® • TEC44026 • Aug./Sept. 2006 • Key p. 308

Guess and check

The turkey has tail feathers labeled with the following equations:

$6 \times (12 \div 3)$

$(6 \times 6) - 12$

$12 + 12$

8×3

$48 \div 2$

$18 + 6$

The turkey body is labeled: 24

The small turkey has a feather labeled $48 \div 2$ and a body labeled 24.

Pass the Turkey, Please!
Writing equations

Gobble up great math practice this Thanksgiving by dividing students into small groups. Have each group cut out a turkey body from brown construction paper and then label it with a number from 1 to 25. Next, the group cuts out the same number of tail feather shapes from colorful construction paper as there are student groups. Each group takes a minute to write on one feather a math problem whose answer matches the number written on its turkey. The group then glues the feather to the back of the turkey and passes it to another group. That group writes a different problem with the same answer on one of its feather cutouts and glues it to the turkey. The process continues until every group has added a math problem to each turkey and all the turkeys have the same number of feathers.

Jennifer Otter, Oak Ridge, NC

Falling for Words
Vocabulary development

Celebrate the colorful changes of autumn with improved word skills!
Have each child write a five-word sentence in which the first word is
a vocabulary word from a unit currently being studied. Then challenge
him to write a different sentence of the same length, advancing his
vocabulary word one space. Have him continue this pattern
until the vocabulary word is the last word in the sentence. To
complete the activity, have the student copy his sentences onto a large, colorful
leaf cutout and display it on a board with a tree that's losing its leaves.

Isobel Livingstone, Rahway, NJ

Pioneers traveled in covered wagons.
The pioneers were very brave.
Many strong pioneers traveled west.
How did the pioneers succeed?
We thank those courageous pioneers!

The Call
It was a few days before

Web of Wonder
Descriptive writing, art project

Spin spooky stories with this unique creepy-crawly writing
prop! Draw a spiderweb on a sheet of paper, laminate it,
and then place it at a center with white school glue, black
construction paper, chalk, and notebook paper. Have each
child use a generous amount of glue to trace the web. When
the glue is completely dry, she carefully peels the web of glue
off the laminated paper, glues it to black paper, and writes
seasonal adjectives and phrases on the web with chalk. Then
she uses the web's descriptive words to write a seasonal
story and glues it to the other side of her web. To display all
the "spider-ific" projects, hang them from the ceiling!

Courtney Rasmussen, Shore Acres Elementary, St. Petersburg, FL

Set the Table!
Poetry project

These festive, personalized table runners are sure to brighten students' Thanksgiving
meals! Give each child a long, narrow rectangle cut from an inexpensive plastic tablecloth.
Have him use permanent markers to draw colorful leaf shapes on the plastic and to write
an original Thanksgiving poem around the edge. Then have him roll up the completed
table runner, tie it with ribbon, and take it home to present to his family as a gift!

Cindy Barber, Fredonia, WI

I am thankful for food and clothes, a house and a home, and a room of my own. But most of all, I am thankful for my family and friends. ~ Joseph

Seasonal Journal Prompts

October Topics

- Imagine that bad weather is predicted for Halloween. How will this change your costume and plans?

- Daylight savings time ends in October. Why do you think most states observe daylight savings time?

- What is your favorite fun-to-say phrase? Explain.

- What do you think the proverb "No pain, no gain" means?

- In honor of National Pajama Month, write a letter convincing your principal to let you wear pajamas to school all month long.

- Imagine that your teacher has decided to broadcast all of her lessons over the Internet, allowing you to learn at home instead of at school. List the pros and cons of this decision.

I GET AN EXTRA HOUR?

Why did the turkey cross the road?

November Topics

- Write an original joke to tell at Thanksgiving dinner.

- Why do you think some people won't eat turkey without cranberry sauce?

- Write a recipe for a happy Thanksgiving at a turkey's house.

- If you were the teacher, how would you have taught your last science or social studies lesson?

- Pretend you will be traveling over 500 miles and must pack something that is very fragile and expensive. What is the item and how will you pack it?

- Describe two simple games that can be played in a car on a long trip to a relative's house.

The reproducible on page 17 was written by Colleen Dabney of Williamsburg, VA.

Name

Making the Rounds at the Farmer's Market

Estimate the cost of each item to the nearest dime.
Then find the exact cost.

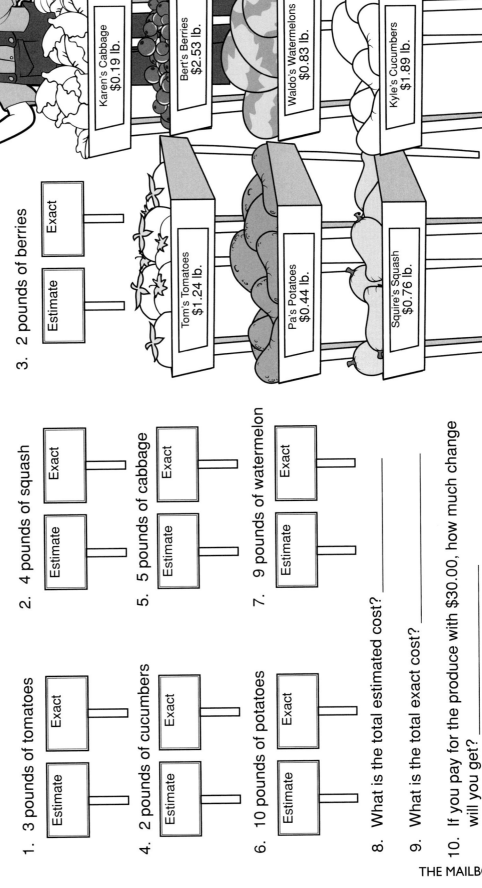

Karen's Cabbage
$0.19 lb.

Bert's Berries
$2.53 lb.

Waldo's Watermelons
$0.83 lb.

Kyle's Cucumbers
$1.89 lb.

Tom's Tomatoes
$1.24 lb.

Pa's Potatoes
$0.44 lb.

Squire's Squash
$0.76 lb.

1. 3 pounds of tomatoes

Estimate _____   Exact _____

2. 4 pounds of squash

Estimate _____   Exact _____

3. 2 pounds of berries

Estimate _____   Exact _____

4. 2 pounds of cucumbers

Estimate _____   Exact _____

5. 5 pounds of cabbage

Estimate _____   Exact _____

6. 10 pounds of potatoes

Estimate _____   Exact _____

7. 9 pounds of watermelon

Estimate _____   Exact _____

8. What is the total estimated cost? _____

9. What is the total exact cost? _____

10. If you pay for the produce with $30.00, how much change
will you get? _____

©The Mailbox® · TEC44027 · Oct./Nov. 2006 · written by Jennifer Otter, Oak Ridge, NC · Key p. 308

Monster Meanings

Write a synonym for each word in parentheses.

An ant and a spider met one morning. It was really _____
(cool)

outside. The ant began to _____ to the spider. "You are a really
(sing)

_____ singer!" exclaimed the spider. The _____ spider
(good)   (big)

smiled in a _____ way. "Why are you so _____?" asked
(funny)   (happy)

the ant. "Because I will have a _____ breakfast," answered the
(good)

spider. "Oops! I hope I am not the _____ breakfast!" cried the
(good)

_____ ant.
(nervous)

Write an antonym for each word in parentheses.

There once was a _____ monster named Monty. He had three
(big)

eyes, a _____ nose, and _____ feet. He was really
(big)   (small)

_____. All of the _____ girl monsters in town wanted to go
(cute)   (pretty)

to the Monster Ball with him. Molly Monster bought a(n) _____
(expensive)

dress to wear to the party. She also bought a hat with _____
(hard)

green feathers. When Monty saw Molly, it was love at first sight. They had a

_____ wedding and had a(n) _____ life together.
(cheerful)   (interesting)

 ©The Mailbox® · TEC44027 · Oct./Nov. 2006 · written by Mary Maxey, Orange Grove, TX

ONE CONFUSED SHOPPER

Use the chart to find the weight of each turkey.

	1	2	3	4	5	6	7	8	9	10
English	one	two	three	four	five	six	seven	eight	nine	ten
Spanish	uno	dos	tres	cuatro	cinco	seis	siete	ocho	nueve	diez
German	eins	zwei	drei	vier	fünf	sechs	sieben	acht	neun	zehn
French	un	deux	trois	quatre	cinq	six	sept	huit	neuf	dix

1	2	3
siete x tres =	trois^3 =	(dos x cuatro) + tres =

4	5	6
(neun x vier) ÷ zwei =	(nueve − uno) + (dos x tres) =	(sept x dix) − (six x huit) =

7	8	9
(three x six) ÷ two =	(zehn + acht) − fünf =	(huit x neuf) ÷ trois =

10	11	12
cuatro x cinco =	(trois + neuf) − deux =	cinco + (seis + ocho) =

Ho, Ho, Ho! It's Mexico!
Geography

See if your students can find St. Nick in Mexico! Provide each child with a copy of page 21. Have her complete the page as directed and then cut out the map and punch a hole near Guerrero, Mexico. Once she threads a length of yarn through the hole and ties the ends together, she has an ornament that's ready to hang as a holiday decoration!

Linda Paul, Wolf Lake Elementary, Albion, IN

Capturing Conversations
Punctuating dialogue

For this partner activity, mix one cup of elbow macaroni with at least two teaspoons of rubbing alcohol and a few drops of red food coloring in a large resealable bag. Repeat, using a second cup of macaroni and green food coloring. Spread the pasta on a paper towel to dry.

After a review of quotation marks, have each child talk with a classmate about a seasonal topic and record what her partner says as they go along. When the conversation ends, the duo proofreads the sentences for correct punctuation. The partners then rewrite their sentences on poster board, gluing the colorful pasta in place of all the commas and quotation marks. 'Tis the season for festive chats!

Paula Epker, Hannibal Middle School, Hannibal, MO

"Paula exclaimed, I can't wait until Christmas vacation!"
"Me neither," said Kelly. "I really like to sleep late!"

$$
\begin{array}{r}
32\;15 \\
-18\;20 \\
\hline
13\;95
\end{array}
$$

Buttons, Buttons
Adding and subtracting decimals

Use this creative winter project to help students align decimal points. Provide each child with a snowman-shaped cutout and three buttons. Allow the student to decorate his snowman and glue the buttons down the center as shown. Next, have him program the cutout with an addition or a subtraction problem, using the buttons as decimal points. Have him solve his problem and record the answer so that the third button is the decimal point of the sum or difference. Then display the math-smart snowmen on a wintry board!

Emily George, P.S. 101, New York, NY

He's a happy elf, old St. Nick.

He really is the best.

He's as pudgy as a chef

And as jolly as the rest.

We love him so much, our St. Nick!

Colorful Caroling
Identifying adjectives

Provide each small group with the lyrics of a popular seasonal song. Have the group highlight all of the descriptive words. Then have the group change the words to write a unique holiday song to share with the class. Students can even write the new lyrics on blank staff paper and display them on a board next to the original carol. To extend the activity, use another favorite song, such as "Up on the Housetop," and have students focus on prepositional phrases instead!

adapted from an idea by Julie Clark, Paradise Canyon School, La Canada, CA

Seasonal Journal Prompts

December Topics

- If you could create your own holiday, what would it be called and how would it be celebrated?

- Imagine that everything you touch turns red or green. Describe what you see.

- Pretend that you have a billion dollars to give away this holiday season. Who will get the money and why?

- Each year on December 10, the Nobel Peace Prize is given to those who strive to improve life. If there were an award named after you, what would it be called? What would someone have to do to receive it?

- In honor of Underdog Day (December 15), describe a way to salute a person who does not get the attention he or she deserves for helping someone else achieve something great.

- Some of the words used in the first crossword puzzle ever published were *rule, fun, receipt, farm, rail, lion, sand, evening, dove,* and *trading.* What ten words would you use to create a crossword puzzle? Explain.

January Topics

- Imagine that babies are born only on January 1 each year. What effect would this have on the world?

- Make a top five countdown list of your favorite songs or books from last year. Explain why these titles are on your list.

- The first radio broadcast was in January 1910. The first scheduled TV broadcast was in 1941. Twenty years from now, what do you think will be our biggest source of entertainment? Why?

- In honor of the new session of Congress, write a letter to your local member of Congress about an important issue you think lawmakers should discuss.

- Imagine that you are a famous sculptor. What kind of statue would you create out of snow? Describe it.

- January is named for the Roman mythological god of the doorway and beginnings. Why do you think the first month of the year is named for this god?

Name _____

Ho, Ho, Ho! It's Mexico!

Follow the directions below.

1. Outline the country of Mexico in black.

2. Color the four U.S. states red.

3. Make a black dot at the city of Tepic in Nayarit.

4. Color the Mexican state of Nayarit either pink or light brown. Then outline it in black.

5. Draw a black line from Puerto Vallarta to Tampico.

6. Draw a black line from Cihuatlán to the city of Veracruz.

7. Draw a black line from Celestún to Chetumal.

8. Color the area between the lines drawn in Steps 6 and 7 red.

9. Turn the map upside down. Who is pictured?

_____

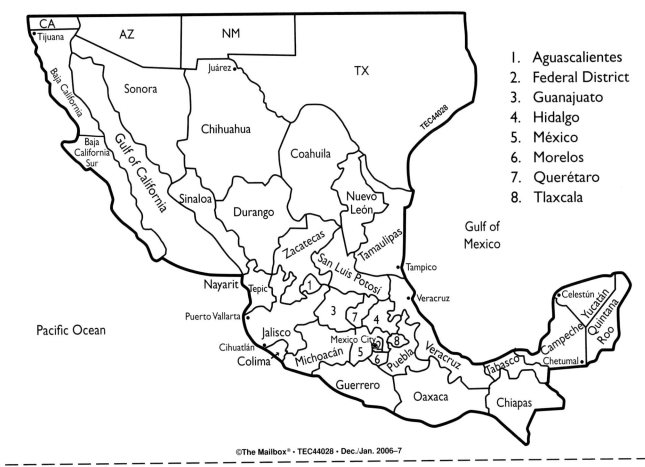

1. Aguascalientes
2. Federal District
3. Guanajuato
4. Hidalgo
5. México
6. Morelos
7. Querétaro
8. Tlaxcala

©The Mailbox® • TEC44028 • Dec./Jan. 2006–7

Hanukkah Happenings

Correct the mistake in each sentence. Then record the sentence number on a candle flame to tell the type of correction you made.

Family and Fun

(1) Hanukkah is celebrated by liting a menorah.
(2) This candleholder had places for nine candles.
(3) Eight of the candles stand for the number of daze the oil burned. (4) The ninth candle, or shammes is used to light the other eight candles. (5) *Shammes* means "servant" in yiddish. (6) Many familys celebrate by gathering to eat foods made with oil. (7) Kids play with dreidels, and presents is exchanged. (8) Some kids receive gelt, or Money. (9) If only the celebrations could be lasted longer than eight days!

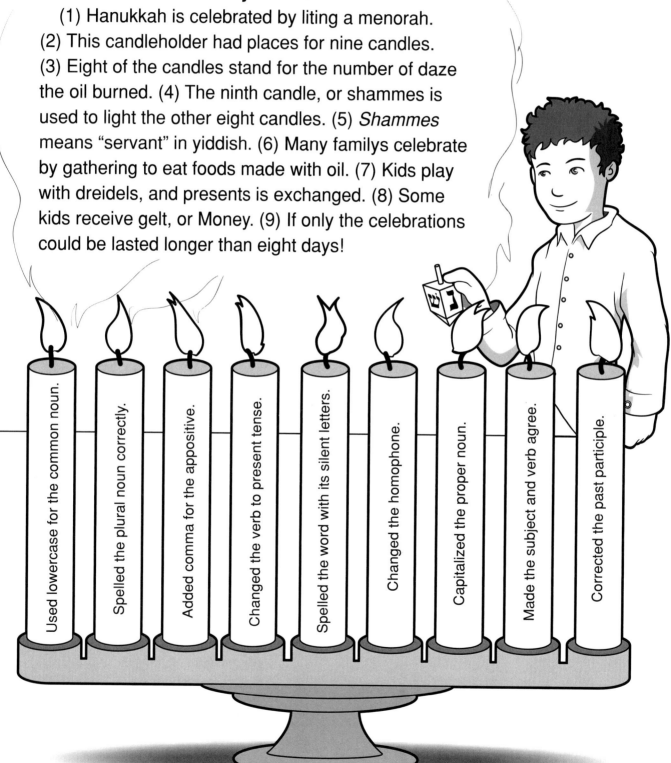

Used lowercase for the common noun.

Spelled the plural noun correctly.

Added comma for the appositive.

Changed the verb to present tense.

Spelled the word with its silent letters.

Changed the homophone.

Capitalized the proper noun.

Made the subject and verb agree.

Corrected the past participle.

©The Mailbox® • TEC44028 • Dec./Jan. 2006 • Key p. 308

Name _____

Poinsettias for Sale

Use the map to complete each sentence.
Then color the poinsettia leaves by the code.

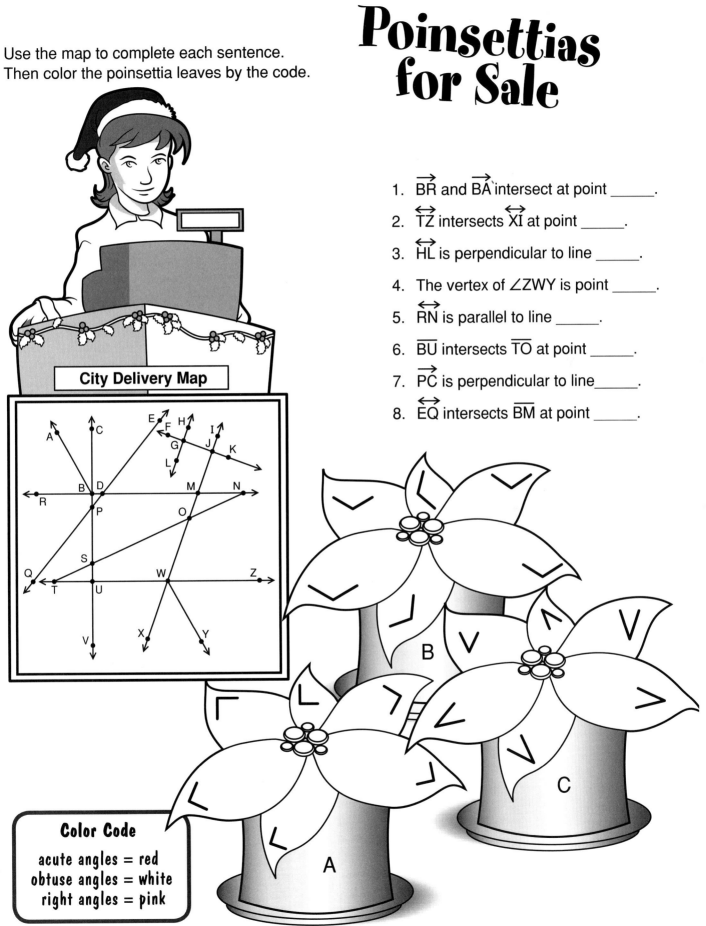

City Delivery Map

1. $\overrightarrow{BR}$ and $\overrightarrow{BA}$ intersect at point _____.
2. $\overleftrightarrow{TZ}$ intersects $\overleftrightarrow{XI}$ at point _____.
3. $\overleftrightarrow{HL}$ is perpendicular to line _____.
4. The vertex of ∠ZWY is point _____.
5. $\overleftrightarrow{RN}$ is parallel to line _____.
6. $\overline{BU}$ intersects $\overline{TO}$ at point _____.
7. $\overrightarrow{PC}$ is perpendicular to line_____.
8. $\overleftrightarrow{EQ}$ intersects $\overline{BM}$ at point _____.

Color Code
acute angles = red
obtuse angles = white
right angles = pink

I HAVE A DREAM

Divide to answer each question about Martin Luther King Jr.

O. When was he born? 3858 ÷ 2 = _____

F. At what age did he go to college? 165 ÷ 11 = _____

H. When did he marry Coretta Scott? 7812 ÷ 4 = _____

T. When did he publish his first book? 7832 ÷ 4 = _____

E. How many books did he write? 410 ÷ 82 = _____

N. In what year did he give his "I have a dream" speech? 5889 ÷ 3 = _____

A. In what year did he win the Nobel Peace Prize? 3928 ÷ 2 = _____

C. At what age did he die? 975 ÷ 25 = _____

I. In what year was he shot? 3936 ÷ 2 = _____

R. In what year was Martin Luther King Jr. Day first observed? 5958 ÷ 3 = _____

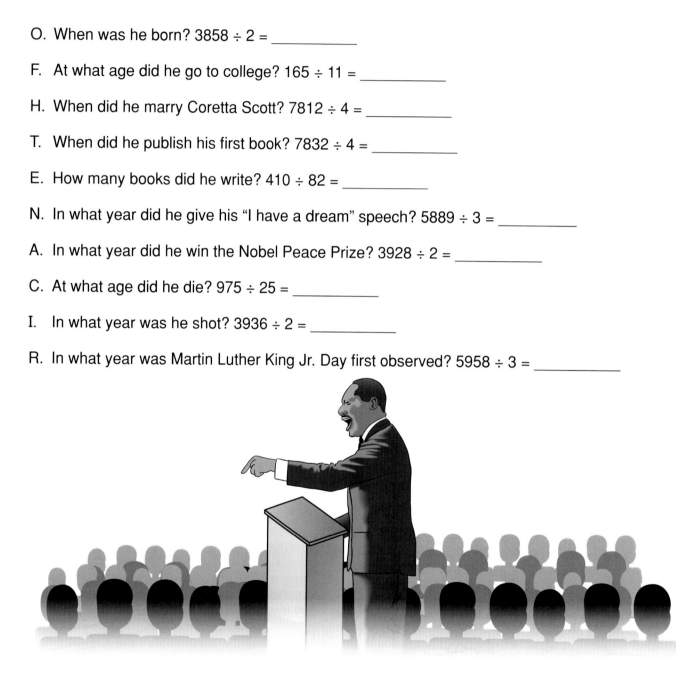

What did Martin Luther King Jr. want his children to be known for?
To answer this question, write the letters above on the matching numbered lines below.

$\overline{1958}$ $\overline{1953}$ $\overline{5}$ $\overline{39}$ $\overline{1929}$ $\overline{1963}$ $\overline{1958}$ $\overline{5}$ $\overline{1963}$ $\overline{1958}$ $\overline{1929}$ $\overline{15}$ $\overline{1958}$ $\overline{1953}$ $\overline{5}$ $\overline{1968}$ $\overline{1986}$

$\overline{39}$ $\overline{1953}$ $\overline{1964}$ $\overline{1986}$ $\overline{1964}$ $\overline{39}$ $\overline{1958}$ $\overline{5}$ $\overline{1986}$

       ©The Mailbox® • TEC44028 • Dec./Jan. 2006 • Key p. 308

Which president's face is on the front of pennies?

In God We Trust

LIBERTY

Penny-Wise Explorations

Presidents' Day

For this cross-curricular activity, give each child a penny and a magnifying lens. Have him examine both sides of the coin. Discuss with students the details that can be seen. Then have him draw two circles on paper and sketch each side of the coin. To follow up, choose from the following activities:

- Have each child research pennies and show what he learned by writing questions and answers for a booklet. His sketches of the penny serve as the front and back covers, and each page has a question written on one side and the answer on the back.

- Discuss what the letter and year on the front of most pennies means. Then have each child write an adventurous story about the states his penny traveled through to get from its mint to your state.

- Have students order the years the pennies were minted and find the sum. Or have students estimate and then find actual answers for the following: the weight of all the pennies, the pennies' length when aligned, and the number of pennies in a yard or a meter.

Diane Coffman, Lawrence, KS

History-Making Events
Black History Month

To make this self-checking center, write on large index cards the years and events shown. Puzzle-cut the cards and place them in a bag at a center. Then introduce the center by discussing with students each event's significance. To use the center, a child arranges the years in chronological order to form a timeline and matches each event to a year. When all the cards are matched, she records the correct year for each event on a copy of a timeline like the one shown.

adapted from an idea by Simone Lepine, Fayetteville, NY

1955

Rosa Parks refuses to go to the back of the bus.

Name_____ Timeline

History-Making Events

1955	Rosa Parks refuses to go to the back of the bus.
1957	Nine African American students attend an all-white high school in Little Rock, Arkansas.
1960	Four African American college students begin sit-ins at a lunch counter in Greensboro, North Carolina.
1963	During the March on Washington, Martin Luther King Jr. makes his famous "I Have a Dream" speech.
1964	Martin Luther King Jr. receives the Nobel Peace Prize.
1966	Edward Brooke of Massachusetts becomes the first elected African American U.S. senator.
1967	Thurgood Marshall becomes the first African American Supreme Court judge.
1973	Maynard Jackson becomes the first elected African American mayor of a major southern U.S. city.
1983	Martin Luther King Jr. Day becomes a federal holiday.
1989	L. Douglas Wilder of Virginia becomes the first elected African American governor.

Heartfelt Conversations
Fractions, decimals, and percents

Begin this sweet activity by having each student divide a sheet of paper into five columns and label them as shown. Next, give him a box of conversation hearts and a calculator. Have him count the candies, record the total on his paper, and then group the candies according to their messages. In the chart's first column, he lists the different messages. In the second column, he lists the number of candies with each message. He writes a fraction to show what part of all the candies are labeled with each message, plus the decimal and percent forms of those fractions. After his work has been checked, allow him to eat the candies as a treat!

Christy Noble, Franklin Elementary, Salt Lake City, UT

Eddie   Total candies: 24

Message	Number of Candies	Fraction	Decimal	Percent
Kiss Me	2	$\frac{2}{24}$	0.08	8%

Kiss Me

Tri-Word Shamrocks
Vocabulary

Instead of searching for pots of gold this St. Patrick's Day, challenge students to use dictionaries to find as many words beginning with the prefix *tri-* as they can. When a student finds three words, have her cut out four green shamrocks—one large and three small. (For patterns, go to themailboxcompanion.com.) She writes "*Tri-* Words" on the large cutout and a different one of her *tri-* words and its definition on each of the remaining cutouts. Once she attaches the small shamrocks to the large one with yarn, her project is ready to display. To follow up, have her use her three new words to write a poem or story about a leprechaun!

Judith Shutter, Elmira, NY

Tri- Words

triangle

tricycle

trifoliate

Seasonal Journal Prompts

February Topics

- What makes you happier: getting a compliment or giving a compliment? Explain.

- If you saw your best friend cheating on a test, what would you do? Explain.

- If valentine cards could not be red, pink, or white, what color would you want them to be? Why?

- How could you help a friend have more confidence at sports, with school work, or when speaking in front of the class? Explain.

- Do you like it when someone takes a photograph of you? Why or why not?

- Would you rather eat ice cream in a bowl, in a cone, or on a stick? Why?

I don't eat broccoli.

March Topics

- March is National Nutrition Month. How could you convince the pickiest eater in your family to eat a vegetable?

- Daylight Saving Time now begins for most of the United States in March instead of April. Do you like this earlier starting time? Why or why not?

- Are you afraid of thunderstorms? Why or why not?

- Suppose that you found something made of gold on St. Patrick's Day. What would you think? What would you do? Explain.

- Which do you think is more important: getting a task done quickly or getting it done well? Explain.

- If you had three hours to do anything you wished, what would you choose to do? Explain.

The reproducible on page 28 was written by Ann Fisher of Toledo, OH.
The reproducible on page 29 was written by Jacqueline Beaudry of Getzville, NY.
The reproducible on page 30 was written by Caroline Chapman of Vineland, NJ.

THE MAILBOX 27

Marshall "Major" Taylor

Read each sentence.
Use context clues to circle the meaning of the boldfaced word.

1. Taylor was given the nickname Major because he wore a soldier's **uniform.**

   E. clothing   F. badge   G. armor

2. Major was thought to be one of the fastest **cyclists** in the world.

   G. runners   H. bike riders   I. drivers

3. He **forfeited** many races because of being fouled by other cyclists.

   B. won   C. lost   D. did not ride in

4. He refused to be upset by the **mind-set** of people who did not approve of his being in the contests.

   R. brains   S. sight   T. beliefs

5. He had to overcome many **barriers.**

   M. rivers   N. sounds   O. troubles

6. In 1899 this **capable** athlete set seven world records!

   E. talented   F. lazy   G. lucky

7. That same year he **conquered** the World Sprint Championship.

   W. lost   X. tied   Y. won

8. Major once rode in a **grueling** six-day race in New York.

   K. easy   L. tough   M. windy

9. After riding 1,732 miles over 142 hours, he must have been **fatigued.**

   B. scared   C. tired   D. smart

10. Some people have said Taylor's success is **comparable** to that of Lance Armstrong's.

    N. similar to   O. better than   P. different from

What did the newspapers call Marshall Taylor?
To answer the question, match the letter of each circled answer
above to a numbered line below.

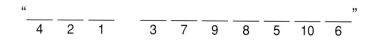

" __ __ __   __ __ __ __ __ __ __ "
  4 2 1   3 7 9 8 5 10 6

©The Mailbox® • TEC44029 • Feb./Mar. 2007 • Key p. 308

Name _____

Presidential Ratios

Using the information in the chart, circle the letter of each correct ratio. All fraction ratios are written in simplest terms.

	President	Year He Took Office	Approximate Years of Service
1st	George Washington	1789	8 years
3rd	Thomas Jefferson	1801	8 years
12th	Zachary Taylor	1849	1 year
16th	Abraham Lincoln	1861	4 years
32nd	Franklin D. Roosevelt	1933	12 years
35th	John F. Kennedy	1961	3 years
38th	Gerald R. Ford	1974	2 years

RATIOS

1. Ratio of years Zachary Taylor served to the years Thomas Jefferson served
   A. 1:8   B. 8:1   S. $\frac{1}{4}$ Y. $\frac{1}{2}$

2. Years Abraham Lincoln served to the years George Washington served
   M. 3:2   O. 3:4

3. Years John F. Kennedy served to the years Gerald R. Ford served
   A. 8 to 1   B. 8 to 8

4. Ratio of years George Washington served to the years Thomas Jefferson served
   C. $\frac{1}{4}$ U. $\frac{1}{6}$

5. Number of years the 38th president served to the number of years the 32nd president served
   O. 2:1   T. 3:1

6. Number of presidents to serve eight years to the number of presidents to serve four years
   K. $\frac{1}{3}$ E. $\frac{3}{1}$

7. Number of presidents who served in the 1800s to the number of presidents who served in the 1700s
   Y. 3:3   Z. 3:2

8. Number of presidents who served in the 1800s to the number of presidents who served in the 1900s
   T. $\frac{1}{1}$ S. $\frac{1}{2}$

9. Number of presidents with 16-letter names to the number of presidents with 12-letter names
   A. 2:4   I. 3:2

10. Number of presidents with six-letter first names to the number of presidents with seven-letter first names

Who might be a future president?
To answer the question, match each circled letter above to a numbered line below.

___ ___ ___ ___ ___ ___ ___ ___ ___ ___!
10 9   3   1   2   4   7   8   6   5

Snakes Alive!

Use reference materials to decide whether each statement is true for all snakes, some snakes, or no snakes. Color a snake to show your answer.

	All	Some	None
1. Snakes have fangs.			
2. Snakes use their tongues to help them sense odors.			
3. Snakes can survive where the ground is frozen year-round.			
4. Snakes molt.			
5. Snakes spit to defend themselves.			
6. Snakes have long, thin, cylinder-shaped bodies.			
7. Snakes are a dull brown color.			
8. Snakes can swim.			
9. Female snakes lay eggs.			
10. Snakes eat other snakes.			
11. Snakes chew their food before swallowing.			
12. Snakes keep their body temperature steady by panting.			

According to legend, St. Patrick drove all of the snakes out of Ireland!

Circle the word in each set that does not belong. Then explain why it does not belong.

13. pythons   lizard   vipers   rattlesnakes   cobras

_____

_____

14. hissing   escaping   playing dead   biting   offensive odor

_____

_____

15. fangs   scales   forked tongue   fur   tail rattle

_____

_____

©The Mailbox® • TEC44029 • Feb./Mar. 2007 • Key p. 309

You make my favorite foods.

You help me with homework.

Mom

Include a Little Gratitude

Mother's Day gift

Make Mother's Day extra special with a keepsake flower that lets Mom know she is appreciated for all she does. Give each child a colorful copy of page 34 to cut out. Have him write "Mom" (or the name of someone who is a mother figure) on the circular piece and glue it to the center of the flower. Have him also record under each flower petal something he is grateful that his mom does for him. Once he tucks the edge of each petal under the center part of the flower and tapes a chenille stem with leaves to the back, the gift is ready to present to his mom for some well-deserved thanks.

Jennifer Otter, Oak Ridge, NC

Springtime Creations
Descriptive-writing project

A little imagination goes a long way, especially if students use a vivid vocabulary! Each child folds a sheet of paper in half, draws an egg so that the top of the egg touches the fold, and cuts out the shape, leaving it uncut along the fold. She decorates the outside of the cutout to look like the exterior surface of an egg. Inside the cutout, she draws an imaginary creature that is nestled and waiting to hatch. Then she writes a paragraph describing the egg and the creature inside it to post alongside her cutout on an " 'Egg-ceptional' Descriptions" display.

Terry Healy, Marlatt Elementary, Manhattan, KS

e red-speckled surface of val object helps hide it from w. Even its enemies have trouble eeing it since it is buried in red dirt. The growing lizard is safe inside the egg, but it is ready to leave its cramped space. The baby reptile begins to use its tiny horns, sharp claws, and pointed teeth to chip through the fragile shell. Before long, its scaly green body will crawl out into a new world.

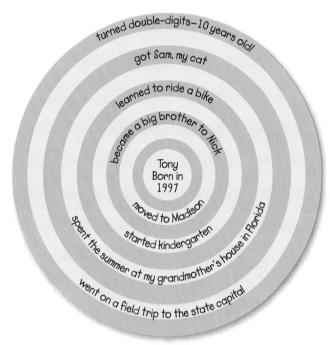

turned double-digits—10 years old!
got Sam, my cat
learned to ride a bike
became a big brother to Nick
Tony
Born in
1997
moved to Madison
started kindergarten
spent the summer at my grandmother's house in Florida
went on a field trip to the state capital

Personal Growth Rings
Timeline

Celebrate National Arbor Day with an activity that links the annual growth rings of a tree to the key events of a child's life. First, share a picture of a cross section of a tree from an encyclopedia or a science text. Explain that each tree ring represents one year of growth. Next, have each child choose two colors of paper. Instruct him to cut out concentric circles, alternating the colors, until the total number of circles equals his age. Have him glue the circles atop one another, beginning with the largest and ending with the smallest in the center. Then have him write his name and birth year on the center circle and label some or all of the rings in chronological order with different memorable events from his life. When he's finished, he'll have his own timeline in the round!

Deanna Bolden, LaValle School, Fairfield, OH

A Card for the Librarian
Showing appreciation

April is School Library Media Month, so it's the perfect time for students to thank the school librarian for all she does. Have each child fold a sheet of paper in half to make a card. On the front, have her illustrate the cover of a book that the librarian helped her select or draw a book character who reminds her of the librarian's caring ways. Inside the card, have her write a message of thanks or one that briefly explains how the librarian and the character on the front of the card are alike. For an added personal touch, allow students to hand deliver their cards on their next trip to the library!

Julia Ring Alarie, Williston, VT

ette,
anks for read-
oks to us. You
the captain
ned Stone by
burg. Even
like a bunch
and say we
read on our
p on reading
til we get
eading again.

Seasonal Journal Prompts

April Topics

- Are you more likely to spring-clean your room or get a flower bed ready for spring planting? Explain.

- April 5 is National Fun at Work Day. Should teachers have fun at work? Why or why not?

- It has been said that every cloud has a silver lining. What do you think this means?

- Suppose that time leaped forward ten years. Where would you like to be? What would you be doing? Explain.

- Jane Goodall, a zoologist who has studied chimpanzees for many years, celebrates her birthday on April 3. If you had the chance to study an animal, which animal would you choose? Why?

- Which are you more like: a bicycle or a motorcycle? Explain.

May Topics

- Suppose that you opened your closet door and found an opening to another world. Would you walk through to this world? Why or why not?

- No Homework Day is in May. Should your school observe this holiday? Why or why not?

- The Greek philosopher Aristotle once said, "Well begun is half done." What do you think this means? Explain.

- If you invented a new cereal, what would it be named, how would it look, and what ingredients would it have? Explain.

- National Backyard Games Week is in May. What is your favorite backyard game? Explain how the game is played.

- Are you more like an ocean or a lake? Explain.

The reproducibles on pages 35–37 were written by Jacqueline Beaudry of Getzville, NY.

Flower and Flower Center Patterns

Use with "Include a Little Gratitude" on page 31.

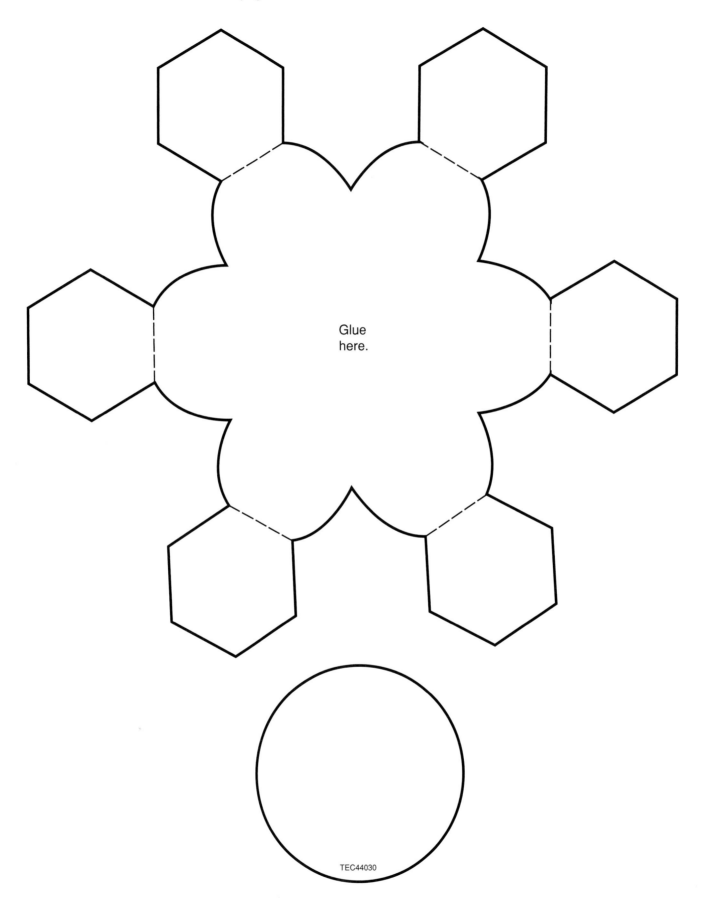

Glue here.

TEC44030

Earth Day Every Day!

Convert each measurement. Then write the letter of each answer on the correct recycling bin.

A. 96 in. of newspaper = _____ ft.

B. 27 ft. of aluminum cans = _____ yd.

C. 7 yd. of colorful paper = _____ ft.

D. 2 ft. of telephone books = _____ in.

E. 5 yd. of mixed-paper egg cartons = _____ in.

F. 112 oz. of paper bags = _____ lb.

G. 6 lb. of milk jugs = _____ oz.

H. 4,000 lb. of green glass bottles = _____ tn.

I. 5 lb. of Styrofoam containers = _____ oz.

J. 2 tn. of wooden pallets = _____ oz.

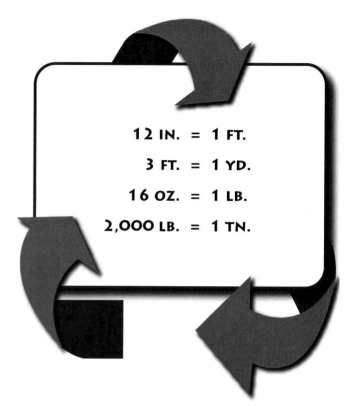

12 IN. = 1 FT.

3 FT. = 1 YD.

16 OZ. = 1 LB.

2,000 LB. = 1 TN.

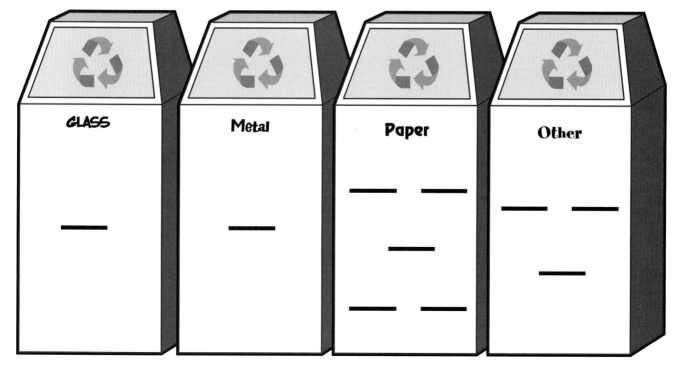

GLASS

Metal

Paper

Other

We Love Her!

Use a pronoun to complete each sentence.
Then color the flower part of each word used.
Some words will not be used.

1. My friends and _____ made Mother's Day cards for our moms.

2. _____ wanted the cards to be special because of what our moms do for us.

3. I'm thankful for all of the times that my mom has driven my friends and _____ to the movies.

4. My cousins and I are going to bring flowers to _____ grandmother.

5. I am going to help my brother and sisters buy Mom _____ favorite perfume.

6. I have saved _____ allowance for weeks to buy this special gift.

7. For Grandma's Mother's Day gift, my mom, her sisters, and all of _____ children had a group portrait made.

8. When Mom got her gift, she looked at my dad and gave _____ a kiss.

9. Dad said _____ is proud of all of us.

10. We gave both of _____ hugs.

yours
her
its hers
us
we them him
you she his

my our
ours their
mine
he it
me I

©The Mailbox® • TEC44030 • April/May 2007 • Key p. 309

Name _____

Salute Our Finest

Circle the answer that makes each sentence correct.

1. On Memorial Day, my family took a trip to Arlington, Virginia, to see the second (A. largest, B. larger) national cemetery in the United States.

2. This trip was the (C. longer, D. longest) we had ever taken on Memorial Day.

3. My brother and I were (E. more excited, F. the most excited) than we have ever been about a trip.

4. My parents had just bought a (H. newest, I. newer) van than the one we had before.

5. I got to travel all the way there in the (M. better, N. best) seat in the whole van—the one in the back.

6. We arrived in Virginia (O. earlier, P. earliest) than we had planned.

7. At the Tomb of the Unknowns, we got to see the (R. most beautiful, S. beautifulest) wreath that we'd ever seen.

8. My dad said that our soldiers are the (T. bravest, U. most bravest) of all because they fought for freedom.

9. Later that day, we watched a parade with bands that were (B. loudest, C. louder) than the ones we have in our town.

10. When we got home that night, my brother and I were the (X. sleepier, Y. sleepiest) that we have been in a long time.

What was Memorial Day called in 1868?
To answer the question, write the letter of each circled answer above on the matching numbered line below.

___ ___ ___ ___ ___ ___ ___ ___ ___ ___   ___ ___ ___
 2   3   9   6   7   1   8   4   6   5   2   1   10

Celebrate the Season!

Bookmark Themes
Different genres the new student
    will read
A favorite genre
A favorite book read independently
    this year
Reading strategies the new student
    will need to use
A preview of a book the new student
    will read

HOORAY
for
Historical Fiction!

Set in the past

Sometimes includes real historic
events and people

My Historical Fiction Favorites

The Sign of the Beaver

Skylark

Across Five Aprils

Allows reader to learn
about the past

Bookmark Gifts
Reading review, end of year

For this end-of-school project, have each student create a bookmark for a child who will be in your class next year. Each student chooses a theme from those shown and makes a rough draft of his bookmark (front and back), including words, phrases, and pictures that support his theme. After editing his draft and showing it to you, the student uses available art materials to create the bookmark. Laminate each bookmark, adding yarn or ribbon as a finishing touch, and store them to distribute to your new class in the fall. If desired, have each child make a card to go with his bookmark. In the card, have the student introduce himself, explain why he chose the bookmark's theme, and describe what the recipient can look forward to in the new school year.

Teralyn Rizzuto, Hebron Elementary, Hebron, CT

Great Goodbyes
End of the year

Poster Topics
The Most Challenging Part of This Year
The Best Activity of the Year
Top Advice for Next Year's [Grade Level]-Graders
What I'll Always Remember About This Year
What I Learned in [Subject] This Year

Cap off a great year with activities that help students reflect on their accomplishments and celebrate them together.

• Label each of several poster boards with a topic about the school year, such as the ones shown. After mounting the posters around your classroom, divide students into groups (one group per poster). Give each group a marker and turn on some quiet, reflective music. Then rotate groups from poster to poster, having each student sign each poster and write his personal reflection about the poster's topic. When everyone has signed all posters, review together the thoughts expressed on each one.

• For several days prior to the last week of school, post on the board a top-ten topic, such as one of the ones shown. As a class or in small groups, have students brainstorm items to place on each list. Then select together the top ten items. After several lists have been created, present them to the upcoming grade in a special newsletter, on posters placed in the hallway, or in a special presentation.

Brooke Beverly, Dudley Elementary, Dudley, MA

THE BEST ACTIVITY OF THE YEAR

My favorite was the map activity where we created our own island nation. Carrie

I loved the math activity when we got to build our own gingerbread houses. Max

Making pottery was the best! Megan

I really liked making the piñata for our holiday party. Sam

I loved when we read Number the Stars for social studies. Millie

TOP 10 LISTS

Top Ten Ways to Be Organized in [Grade Level] Grade

Top Ten Things You'll Learn in [Subject] This Year

Top Ten Reasons to Turn In Homework on Time

Top Ten Activities You'll Love Doing Next Year

Top Ten Ways to Succeed in [Grade Level] Grade

Top Ten Reasons to Read This Summer

Ugly Tie Talk
Father's Day, descriptive writing

Introduce this writing activity by explaining that many dads are given ties—often ugly ones—as gifts on Father's Day. Then give each student a copy of the tie pattern on page 40. Direct students to decorate their ties to make the ties contenders for the title of World's Ugliest Tie. After each student has designed, colored, and cut out his tie, have him post it on a bulletin board. Number the ties using sticky notes. Then have each student choose a tie other than his own to describe in a paragraph. Collect the finished paragraphs. Then read each description aloud and challenge the class to identify the tie being described.

Colleen Dabney, Williamsburg-JCC Schools
Williamsburg, VA

The world has never seen such an ugly tie! The first thing one notices are the bright, wavy orange and pink stripes. They are so brilliant they are almost blinding. Between the stripes are tiny shapes that appear to be miniature purple dog bones. Surrounding each itty-bitty bone is a colorful swirl that resembles a whirling tornado. The tip of the tie is decorated with a yucky face that looks like it hates the tie as much as the rest of the world does!

Seasonal Journal Prompts

June Topics

- On the first day of summer vacation, you could either stay home and sleep late or get up early to go to an amusement park. Which would you choose? Why?

- June is Dairy Month. Explain why you would or would not like to learn how to milk a cow.

- June 14 is Flag Day. What four symbols would be on a flag that honors you? Explain what each symbol would represent about you.

- On June 15, 1752, Benjamin Franklin flew a kite during a storm. He proved that lightning is an electrical charge. Tell about how the first two hours of today would have been different for you if there were no electricity.

- The first erasable ballpoint pen was patented on June 27, 1978. If you could erase one big problem from the world today, what problem would you choose? Why?

- Father's Day is always the third Sunday in June. Do you want to be a parent when you grow up? Why or why not?

The reproducibles on pages 42–44 were written by Ann Fisher of Toledo, OH.

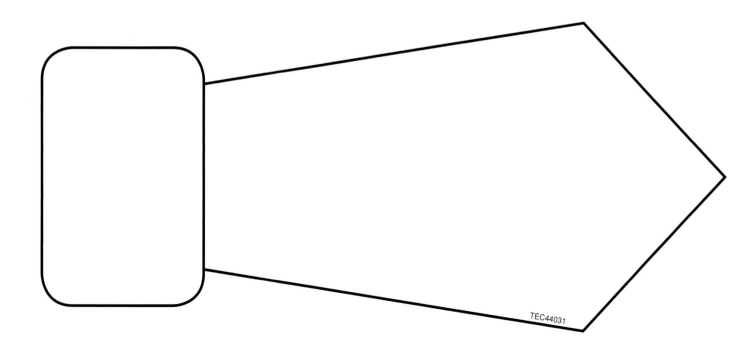

Tie Pattern
Use with "Ugly Tie Talk" on page 39.

TEC44031

©The Mailbox® • TEC44031 • June/July 2007

Flag Day

Cut out the effect boxes below. Then glue each effect next to its matching cause.

Cause   ## Effect

1 George Washington, Robert Morris, and George Ross asked Betsy Ross to sew a flag for the United States.

2 At the time, the United States had 13 colonies that needed to be symbolized on the flag.

3 On June 14, 1777, the Continental Congress passed the first Flag Act, which told how official flags should look.

4 One hundred years later, Congress asked that flags be flown at all public buildings on June 14, 1877.

5 In 1949, President Truman signed a bill stating that Flag Day will be observed on the same date each year.

6 Over the years, Congress passed laws that allowed one star to be added to the flag each time a new state joined the union.

©The Mailbox® • TEC44031 • June/July 2007 • Key p. 309

Some people began to think this day should be observed every year.	Today our flag has 50 stars.
The American flag with 13 white stars on a blue field and 13 alternating red and white stripes became official.	Betsy Ross had the chance to create the first American flag.
Flag Day is observed on June 14 every year.	The flag Betsy Ross created had 13 stars and 13 stripes.

Name _____

Father's Day Fashions

Complete the tree diagram to show all the possible clothing combinations.

SHORTS	striped	polka-dotted
SHIRTS	pink	plaid
SHOES	sneakers	flip-flops

SHORTS   **SHIRTS**   **SHOES**

striped

polka-dotted

1. How many different combinations are there in all? _____

2. List the combinations.

_____   _____

_____   _____

©The Mailbox® • TEC44031 • June/July 2007 • Key p. 309

What a Trip!

Write the correct word in each blank to complete the passage.

The first day of the Wilson _____ (family's, families) vacation

was finally here. Jan, Jerry, Jim, Jill, and Jack had been waiting many

_____ (month's, months) to go on this trip. They had packed two

_____ (weeks', weeks) worth of clothes. Each _____

(persons, person's) clothes had filled two _____ (suitcases',

suitcases).

Soon the Wilson _____ (family's, family) loaded into a van.

There was barely enough room to squeeze in the luggage around all the people!

Jim asked, "Dad, where are we going?"

"Please tell us!" exclaimed all the _____ (kid's, kids) at once.

"We are driving to the airport," Dad answered. "Then we are going to get on one of

those big _____ (airplane's, airplanes) and fly to London!"

_____ (Squeals', Squeals) of joy erupted.

"I have just one question," said Jill. "Will the airplane be big enough to hold all our

_____ (suitcases', suitcases)?"

CHINA

LONDON

Wilson Family

Firework Hot Spots

Study the circle graphs. Then answer the questions.

1. Where is the most popular fireworks display west of the Mississippi River? _____

2. Where is the most popular display in the country? _____

3. What two spots, when their votes are combined, equal the number of votes for Pike's Peak? _____

4. What three spots together total exactly 50% of the votes for their side of the Mississippi? _____ _____

5. How many more people prefer Disneyland's fireworks to Austin's? _____

6. Where is the second most popular fireworks display east of the Mississippi River? _____ _____

7. Which fireworks display received two more votes than the one at Colonial Williamsburg? _____

8. Which two spots received a total of 44 votes? _____

9. If 42 people voted for Walt Disney World's fireworks, how many did not vote for it? _____

10. How many more people voted for New York City's display than for the one at Pike's Peak? _____

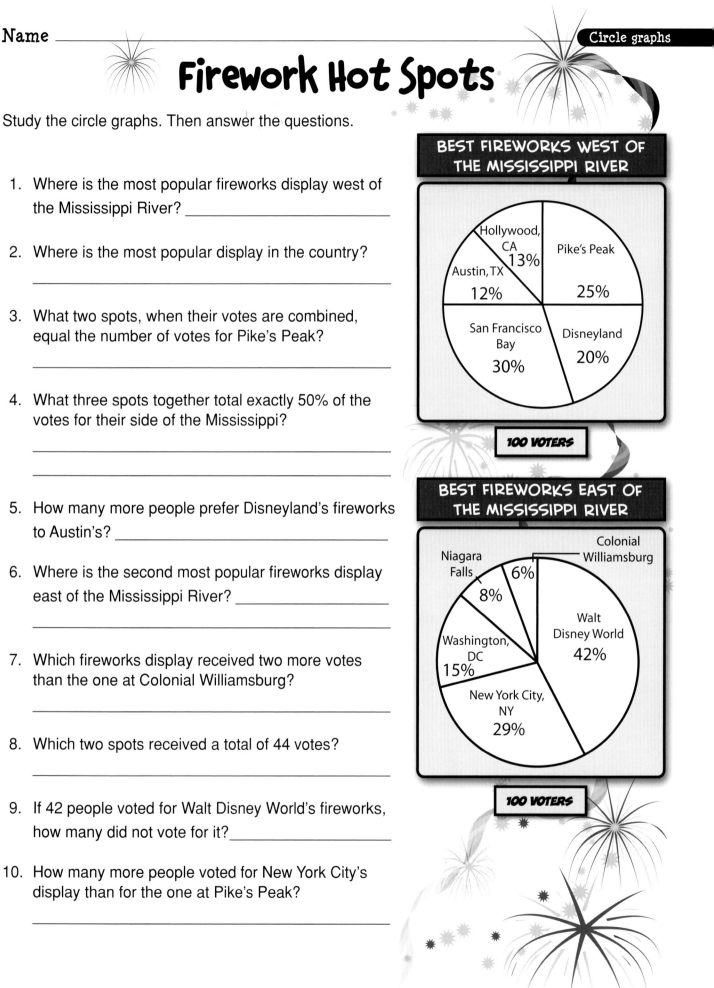

BEST FIREWORKS WEST OF THE MISSISSIPPI RIVER

Hollywood, CA 13%
Pike's Peak 25%
Austin, TX 12%
San Francisco Bay 30%
Disneyland 20%

100 VOTERS

BEST FIREWORKS EAST OF THE MISSISSIPPI RIVER

Colonial Williamsburg 6%
Niagara Falls 8%
Walt Disney World 42%
Washington, DC 15%
New York City, NY 29%

100 VOTERS

©The Mailbox® • TEC44031 • June/July 2007 • Key p. 310

CLASSROOM DISPLAYS

Classroom DISPLAYS

"WHEEL" HAVE A GREAT YEAR!

Display this versatile organizer to remember students' birthdays, assign groups or classroom jobs, and more! Cut a large circle from white poster board. Divide the cutout into a few more sections than the number of students in your class. Next, draw a concentric circle for each category you wish to include. After coloring the sections, laminate the cutout for durability and program it accordingly with a wipe-off marker. Add a spinner by attaching an arrow and a brad. Then post the wheel in a prominent place on the wall where it can be quickly cleaned and reprogrammed as needed!

Kim Minafo, Dillard Drive Elementary
Raleigh, NC

At Your Service

Keep your classroom helpers fueled up with this rotational job display! Make enough copies of the gas pump and racecar patterns on page 58 to have a gas pump for each job and a car for each child. Program each gas pump with a different classroom job. Write each student's name on a different car. Post the gas pumps along a paper road. Then attach a different car next to each gas pump using self-adhesive Velcro strips. Set the extra cars aside. To change job assignments, advance each car to the next gas pump. When a child has performed all the jobs, replace his car with one that is waiting to join the rotation!

Lynne Viapiano, Maryvale Intermediate, Cheektowaga, NY

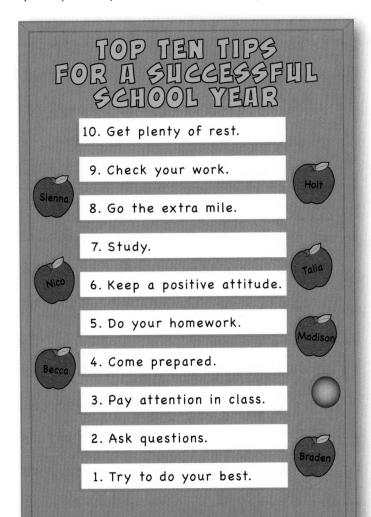

Count down the ways to transform your students into top-notch learners! Program ten sentence strips with the suggestions shown and display them on a wall, bulletin board, or door. Each time you spot a child exhibiting one of the listed ideas, write his name on a seasonal cutout and display it around the list. Revise the suggestions periodically to keep students on their toes!

Kim Brown, Longfellow Middle School, Indianapolis, IN

"Bat's" a Great Book!

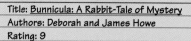

Title: <u>Bunnicula: A Rabbit-Tale of Mystery</u>
Authors: Deborah and James Howe
Rating: 9
Reason for Rating: This book appealed to me because it was a mystery that also included animals and humor. I didn't read it to my younger brother, though, because it might scare him to think a rabbit could be a vampire.
Evaluator: Abbie

This October display could cause quite a flutter! Each time a child finishes a book, invite her to rate it from 1 to 10 on an index card that uses the format shown. Then have her attach the card to a colored cutout of the bat pattern on page 59. By the end of the month, the display could be the home of a large colony of bats!

Terry Healy, Marlatt Elementary, Manhattan, KS

Weaving a Word Web

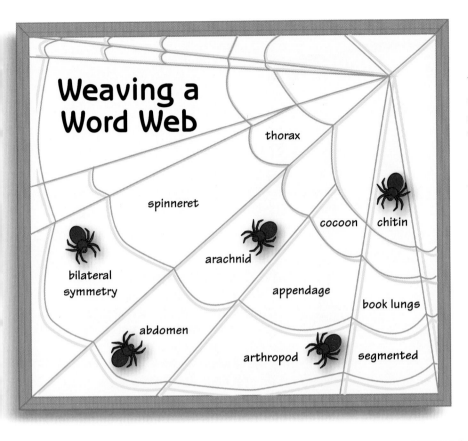

thorax

spinneret

cocoon chitin

arachnid

bilateral
symmetry

appendage

book lungs

abdomen

arthropod segmented

Vocabulary words from *any* content area can get caught in this spiderweb! Prepare a board as shown. In each section of the web, write a word you want students to learn. Next to the display, place a container of spider shapes. As students demonstrate their understanding of each new word, pin a spider in the appropriate section. If all of the words are mastered by Halloween, reward each child with a small treat!

Colleen Dabney, Williamsburg, VA

Allow this perky turkey to showcase your students' knowledge of an important skill. Give each child two copies of the feather pattern on page 59. He writes on one feather a fact about a story or a nonfiction selection the class has read and then colors it orange. He writes on the other feather an opinion about that story or selection and then colors it yellow. Once the bird's colorful tail feathers are attached, it'll really have something to strut about!

Amber Barbee, Wharton, TX

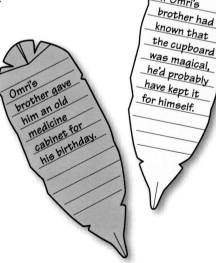

Omri's brother gave him an old medicine cabinet for his birthday.

If Omri's brother had known that the cupboard was magical, he'd probably have kept it for himself.

Gobblin' About Facts and Opinions

The Indian in the Cupboard

by
Lynne Reid Banks

Classroom DISPLAYS

Celebrate students' reading with this tree-trimming door display. Give each child a copy of the ornament pattern on page 60 to cut out and label with the title, the author, and a brief recommendation of a book she has recently read. Have her add an illustration of a character, a symbol, or an event from the story and then decorate the cutout with various craft materials. After she shares her ornament, she can add it to a paper Christmas tree attached to the door.

Pamela Paige Cromer, Whitmire Elementary
Whitmire, SC

Season's
Readings

Title **The Polar Express**

Author **Chris Van Allsburg**

Recommendation **Ride the Polar Express and discover the spirit of Christmas!**

Recommended by **Olivia**

"S-mitten" With Glyphs

Personality Code

red = energetic, likes a challenge

yellow = loves animals

blue = enjoys reading and quiet times

green = adventurous

Felipe

I have so much energy that I ride around on my bike every day and speak to the neighbors. I play with my dog, cat, and gerbil. I also like to hike in the mountains.

This mitten-drying display uses glyphs to inspire expository paragraphs that will help students learn something new about their classmates. Each child traces his hands on white paper, mitten-style, and cuts out the tracings. He decorates the cutouts by the code, leaving room on the right-hand mitten for his name and space on the left-hand mitten to explain his color choices. Then he hangs his mittens on the board's clothesline with clothespins.

Stephanie Roelke, Whispering Meadows School, Fort Wayne, IN

To create this holiday display, each small group of students is assigned a different fraction. The group lists equivalent fractions for its assigned fraction and then cuts out an equal number of gift box shapes from holiday gift wrap. The students divide each cutout into the correct number of parts. Then they cut out and discard one part, adding a piece of construction paper in its place and labeling it accordingly. Once they trace the dividing lines with a marker and add a bow to each gift, their set of packages is ready to mount on the board!

Unlock the Details

Donna G. Pawloski, Springfield, PA

Showcase paragraph-writing skills by making a colorful copy of the lock and key patterns on page 61 for each child. Each student then writes a topic of his choice across the lock's shackle and a supporting detail on each key. He uses the details to help him write a paragraph; then he copies it onto the lock. Next, he cuts out the lock and keys and hole-punches the keys. He threads the keys onto a short length of yarn to form a key ring and attaches it to his lock. After he shares his paragraph with the class, he adds his lock and keys to a display.

spend more time with family

exercise more after school

participate in activities, such as scouts and choir

Homework for all elementary students should be limited to 30 minutes per night.

Every school should limit homework to 30 minutes per night.

Use this display to promote helpfulness. Brainstorm with students different ways they could provide a service to their school, neighborhoods, or community. Next, have each child fold a piece of construction paper in half and draw a heart on it so that the top of the heart touches the fold. Have her cut out the shape, leaving it uncut in two places along the fold as shown. Then have her label the outside with the recipient's name and her name and record on the inside the service she will perform. After she decorates the cutout, have her display it on the board until it's time to present it to the beneficiary of her giving spirit.

adapted from an idea by Donna Hall, Fairview Elementary, Jennings, MO

Soar into spring with this good work display! Have each child design a colorful kite. Then have him select a piece of work he'd like to show off and attach his kite and work sample to the board.

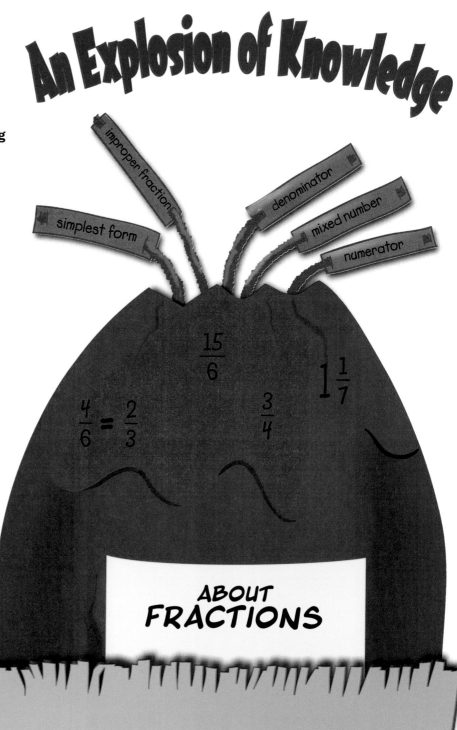

An Explosion of Knowledge

This fiery display is bursting with vocabulary words and is easy to adapt! Glue a laminated cutout of flowing lava to the top of an oversize volcano cutout and a laminated rectangle to its base. Label the rectangle with the topic of a current unit of study. Next, write key words from the unit on separate paper strips. Glue (or thread) each strip onto a chenille stem and insert the stems in the volcano's opening. Then label the lava flow with examples of the words on the stems. When you begin a new unit of study, just change the labels.

Natalie McGregor, Grenada Upper Elementary, Grenada, MS

This bright path offers students options when it comes to responding to literature. Number 11 yellow book cutouts from 2 to 12. Label each cutout with a different book project idea. Then staple the cutouts on background paper to form a path. Each time a child begins a new book, have him trace his shoe on colorful paper, cut out the shape, and label it with his name. To determine which project he will complete, he rolls two dice and then pins his cutout next to the book with the corresponding number.

Jennifer Hukari, Monmouth Elementary
Monmouth, OR

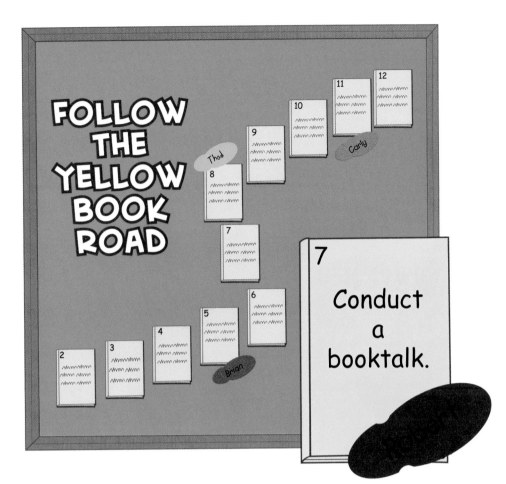

Everybody scores a hole in one with this display! Attach cutouts of a putting green, flag, and hole to background paper. Then invite each child to attach a "tee-rific" paper.

Colleen Dabney, Williamsburg, VA

Classroom DISPLAYS

We've Had a Ball This Year!

We've Had a Ball This Year!
The event that I'll remember most about this school year is
_____
_____
_____

To reminisce about the school year, have each child draw and color his favorite sports ball on a large sheet of construction paper. After he cuts out the shape, have him tape to its center an index card on which he has written a paragraph about his most memorable event or learning experience of the year. There'll be lots of memories to bounce around!

Natalie McGregor, Grenada Upper Elementary
Grenada, MS

Motivate everyone to do "s'more" reading this summer! Have each student summarize on an enlarged copy of the marshmallow pattern on page 62 a favorite book he read this year. Then have him add an illustration. Post the marshmallows on a board with a giant s'more. Encourage summer reading by holding a celebration during which students share their summaries. If desired, serve up a snack of yummy s'mores at the end of the session!

Colleen Dabney, Williamsburg-JCC Schools
Williamsburg, VA

For this reading display, each student colors an enlarged copy of the watermelon slice pattern on page 62 (leaving the seeds uncolored). She cuts out the slice and glues it to a personalized paper plate. Each time she finishes a book, she writes its title in a seed and lightly colors it. Reward each child who colors all of her seeds with a watermelon-flavored treat, such as a fruit snack, a piece of candy, or gum.

Donna G. Pawloski, Springfield, PA

Gas Pump Pattern

Use with "At Your Service" on page 47.

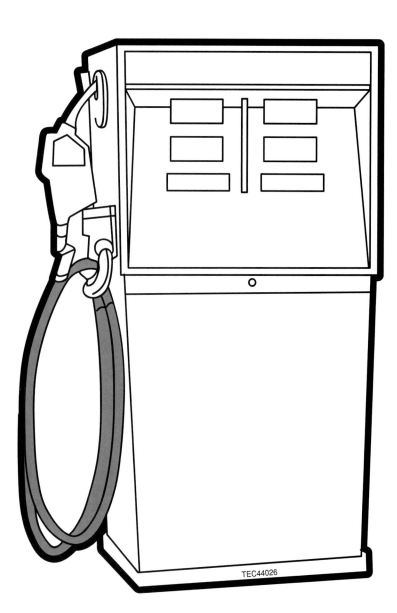

TEC44026

Racecar Pattern

Use with "Writing Racetrack" on page 258 and "At Your Service" on page 47.

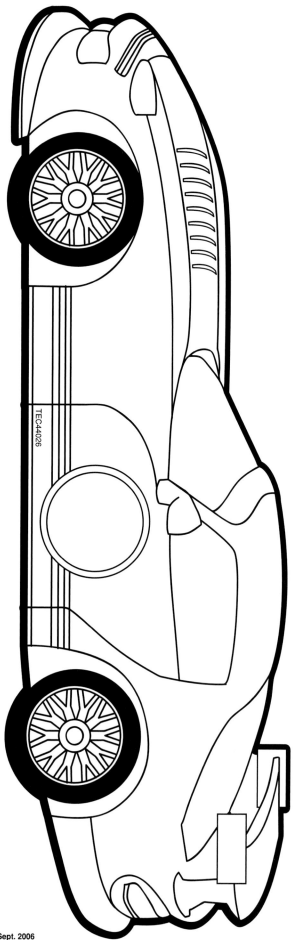

Bat Pattern

Use with "'Bat's' a Great Book!" on page 48.

Feather Pattern

Use with "Gobblin' About Facts and Opinions" on page 49.

TEC44027

Ornament Pattern
Use with "Season's Readings" on page 50.

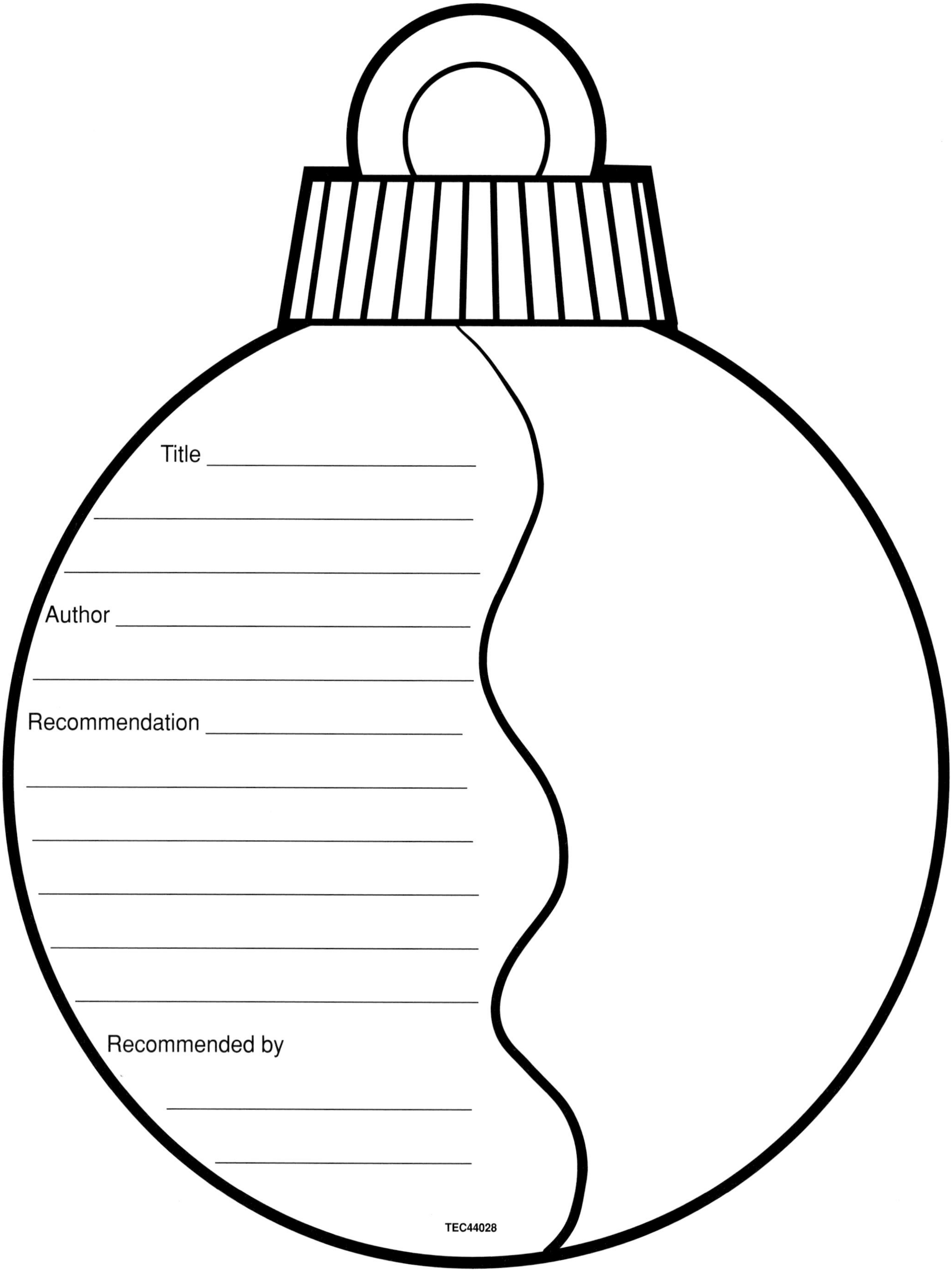

Title _____

_____

_____

Author _____

_____

Recommendation _____

_____

_____

_____

_____

Recommended by

_____

_____

TEC44028

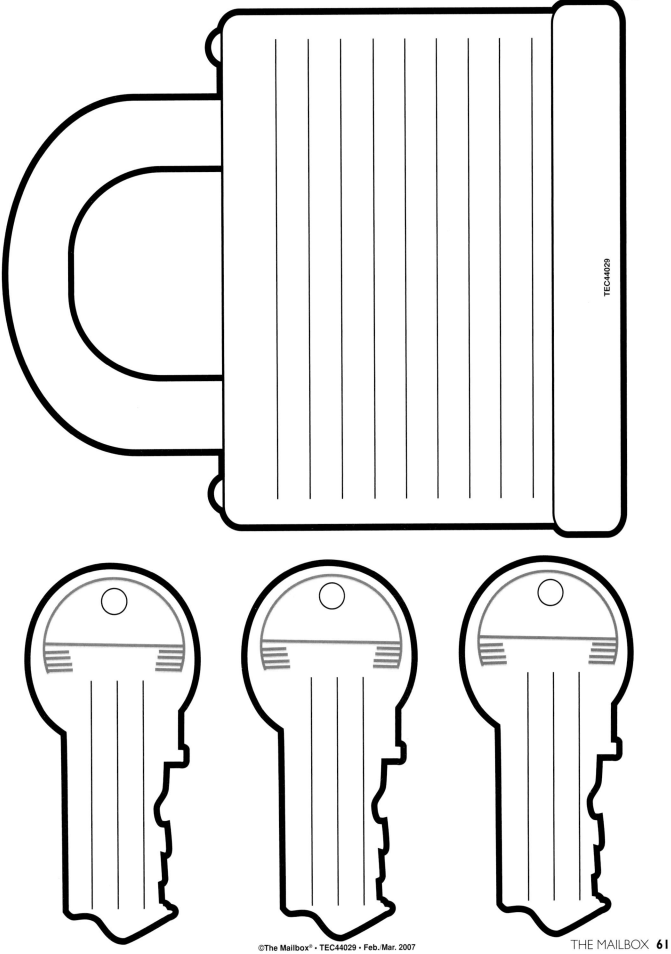

TEC44029

Marshmallow Pattern

Use with "Read 'S'more' Great Books!" on page 57.

Book: _____

Author: _____

Recommended by: _____

TEC44031

Watermelon Slice Pattern

Use with "The Seeds of Reading" on page 57.

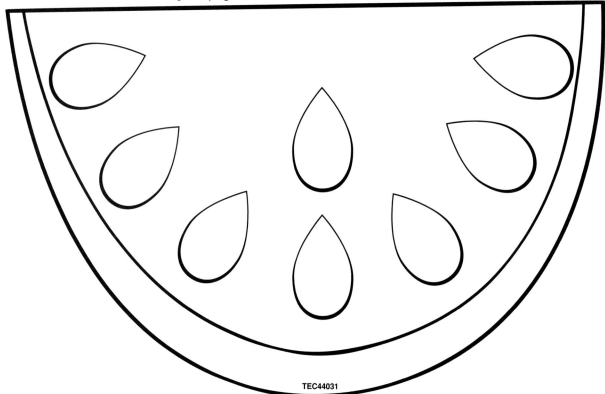

TEC44031

LANGUAGE ARTS UNITS

Ramp It Up!

Exciting Activities for Identifying the Main Idea

DECISIONS, DECISIONS!
Critical thinking

For a self-checking center that provides practice with matching main ideas and supporting details, make a back-to-back copy of the sentence strips on pages 67 and 68. Cut apart the strips and place them in a resealable plastic bag. To use the center, a child sorts the strips into groups by color, with sentences faceup. Then she reads the sentences on each group's strips and decides which one is the main idea and which is a detail that doesn't belong. To check her work, she flips the strips over!

Nobody makes fried chicken like my grandma!

Calzones are ___ food.

___ up to eat.

Greg builds birdhouses.

The city park has six sports fields that are busy all the time.

My brother's football team ___

Baseball games are also played at the park.

Wiping out on the main idea will be a thing of the past with these terrific activities!

with ideas by Teri Nielsen, Deale Elementary, Deale, MD

TREETOP CANOPY
Identifying the main idea and supporting details

This tree analogy and follow-up project could be just what students need to help them determine a selection's chief focus! Discuss how a tree's leaves are its foliage; then compare the leaves to the details in a reading selection. Also discuss how a tree's leaves and branches are connected to its trunk; then compare the trunk to the main idea of a story or a selection of informational text. Next, assign each child a different reading selection. When she's finished reading, have her cut out a brown paper tree trunk and label it with the main idea of her reading selection. Have her also cut out three or four cloud shapes from green paper, label each cutout with a different supporting detail, and then glue the shapes to her tree. As a follow-up, have her complete a copy of page 69 as directed.

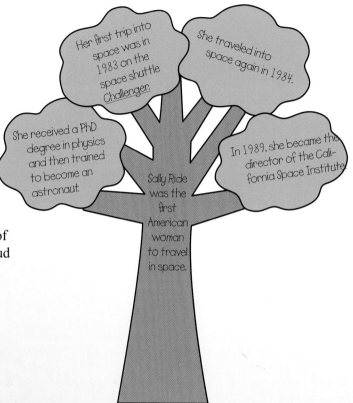

GETTING ON DECK
Distinguishing the main idea from details

To help students visually understand the relationship between a selection's most important idea and the information that supports it, draw a simple skateboard on the board. Explain that just as the deck of a skateboard covers all the wheels and trucks, the main idea of a reading selection covers all the details related to a chief thought or topic. Next, have each child read a different student news magazine article or a selection from a science, social studies, or literature text. When he is finished reading, give him a copy of the skateboard pattern on page 66. Instruct him to label the deck with the main idea of his reading selection and several supporting details as shown. After he decorates his cutout, place it on a display titled "Doing Ollies With Main Ideas!"

Skateboard Pattern

Use with "Getting on Deck" on page 65.

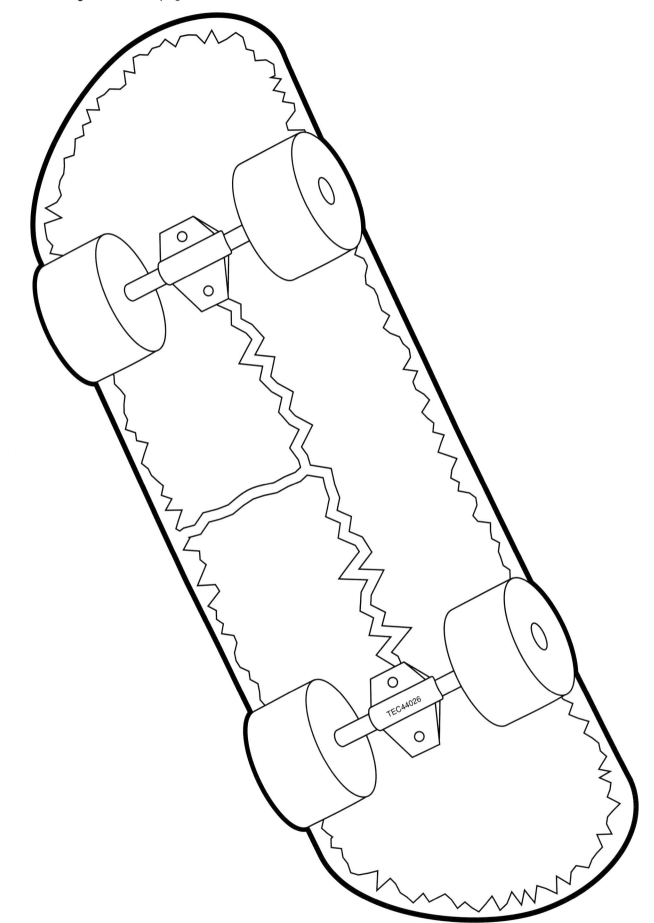

TEC44026

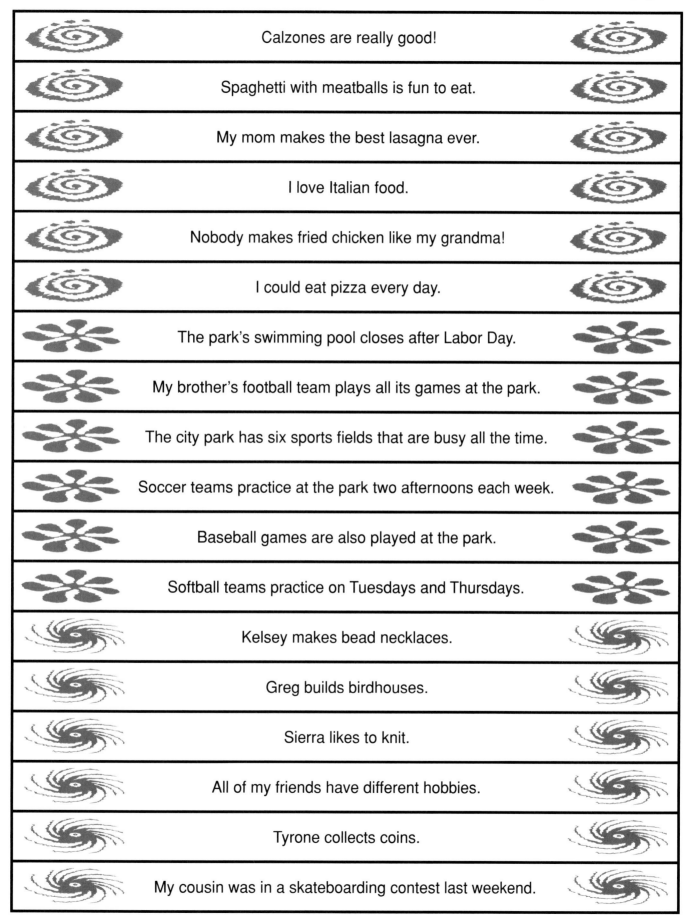

Calzones are really good!

Spaghetti with meatballs is fun to eat.

My mom makes the best lasagna ever.

I love Italian food.

Nobody makes fried chicken like my grandma!

I could eat pizza every day.

The park's swimming pool closes after Labor Day.

My brother's football team plays all its games at the park.

The city park has six sports fields that are busy all the time.

Soccer teams practice at the park two afternoons each week.

Baseball games are also played at the park.

Softball teams practice on Tuesdays and Thursdays.

Kelsey makes bead necklaces.

Greg builds birdhouses.

Sierra likes to knit.

All of my friends have different hobbies.

Tyrone collects coins.

My cousin was in a skateboarding contest last weekend.

supporting detail

TEC44026

supporting detail

TEC44026

supporting detail

TEC44026

main idea

TEC44026

does not belong

TEC44026

supporting detail

TEC44026

does not belong

TEC44026

supporting detail

TEC44026

main idea

TEC44026

supporting detail

TEC44026

supporting detail

TEC44026

supporting detail

TEC44026

supporting detail

TEC44026

supporting detail

TEC44026

supporting detail

TEC44026

main idea

TEC44026

supporting detail

TEC44026

does not belong

TEC44026

Name _____

LARK IN THE PARK

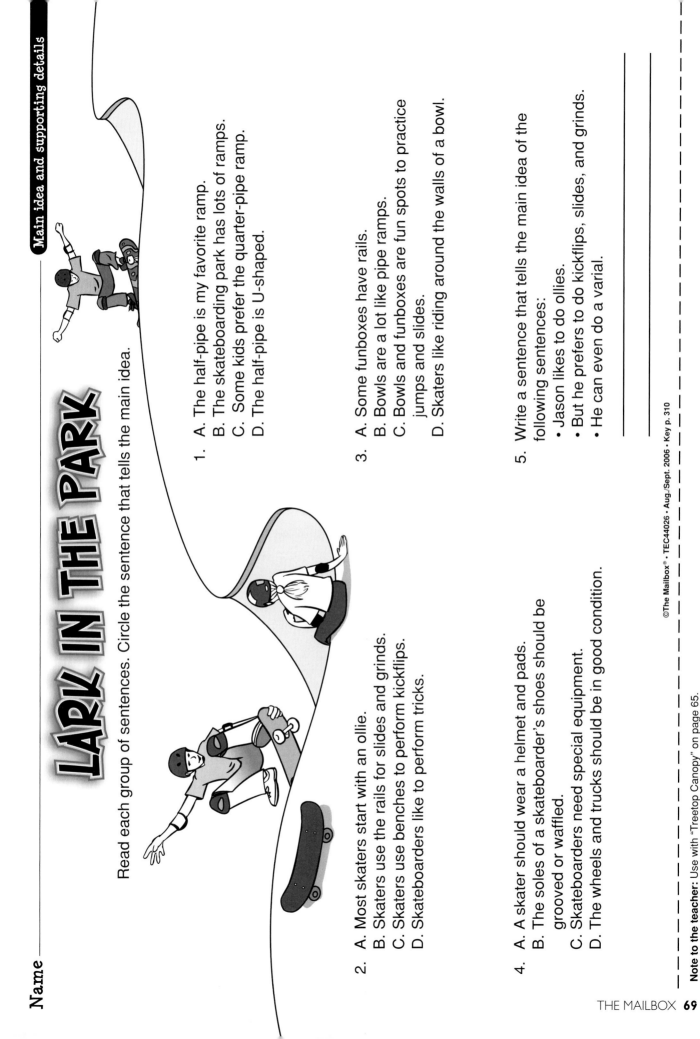

Read each group of sentences. Circle the sentence that tells the main idea.

1. A. The half-pipe is my favorite ramp.
    B. The skateboarding park has lots of ramps.
    C. Some kids prefer the quarter-pipe ramp.
    D. The half-pipe is U-shaped.

2. A. Most skaters start with an ollie.
    B. Skaters use the rails for slides and grinds.
    C. Skaters use benches to perform kickflips.
    D. Skateboarders like to perform tricks.

3. A. Some funboxes have rails.
    B. Bowls are a lot like pipe ramps.
    C. Bowls and funboxes are fun spots to practice jumps and slides.
    D. Skaters like riding around the walls of a bowl.

4. A. A skater should wear a helmet and pads.
    B. The soles of a skateboarder's shoes should be grooved or waffled.
    C. Skateboarders need special equipment.
    D. The wheels and trucks should be in good condition.

5. Write a sentence that tells the main idea of the following sentences:
    • Jason likes to do ollies.
    • But he prefers to do kickflips, slides, and grinds.
    • He can even do a varial.

    _____

©The Mailbox® • TEC44026 • Aug./Sept. 2006 • Key p. 310

Note to the teacher: Use with "Treetop Canopy" on page 65.

Rarin' to Write
Rip-Roaring Narrative-Writing Ideas

TOP *THAT!*
Relating an event or experience

Make writing narratives more interesting by challenging your writers to turn the tables on the plot! If possible, read aloud *Alexander and the Terrible, Horrible, No Good, Very Bad Day* by Judith Viorst. Discuss with students the series of dreadful things that happen to Alexander from the time he awakes until he goes to bed. Then, instead of asking each child to write a story that chronicles awful events, have him write about a unique day in which increasingly wonderful and remarkable things happen to him or to an invented character! Display this issue's narrative-writing poster for students to use as a guide. For a top-notch way to publish the completed stories, guide each writer through the steps shown.

How to Make a Paper Bag Booklet:

1. Fold two paper lunch bags in half. Staple the bags together along the fold with the open ends facing out.
2. Glue a five-inch paper square to the front and back to make a cover; also glue a square to each inside page.
3. Illustrate story scenes on the front and back of two additional five-inch squares. Slide each square into a different pocket. To make the squares easier to remove, staple a short piece of ribbon to each one's right edge.
4. For a finishing touch, tie ribbon through the middle of the booklet next to the spine.

Eddie and the Top-Notch, First-Class, Awesome, Extremely Good Day

by Austin

When Eddie awoke [to f]ind Aladdin's lamp [in] his bed, he knew [it w]as going to be [an] extraordinary day.

Writing a narrative is something students will be thrilled to do when these awesome activities are used for inspiration!

with ideas by Christina Bryant, Huffman Middle School, Humble, TX

FORTUNATELY, UNFORTUNATELY
Relating the ideas of an experience

A mix of good and bad things can happen to a character in a story. To help students understand this concept, have them brainstorm possible positive and negative events that could happen to a singer in a popular band (for example, having an album go platinum and then getting laryngitis right before a big concert). If possible, also read aloud *Fortunately* by Remy Charlip and discuss with students the wonderful and not-so-wonderful things that happen to Ned. Next, have each child label each of three index cards with a different pair of fortunately/unfortunately sentences related to a character of her choice. Invite her to trade cards with a classmate and then write a narrative that integrates the situations on the traded cards.

Unfortunately, the puppy is not housebroken, so I have to clean up every mess it makes.

Fortunately, I got the new puppy I wanted for my birthday.

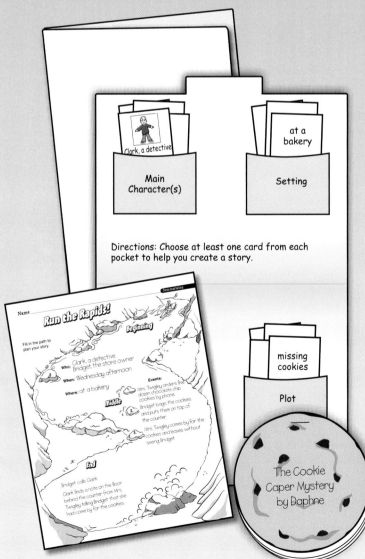

Main Character(s)

Clark, a detective

at a bakery

Setting

Directions: Choose at least one card from each pocket to help you create a story.

Name

Run the Rapids!

Fill in the path to plan your story.

Beginning

Who: Clark, a detective
Bridget, the store owner

When: Wednesday afternoon

Where: at a bakery

Middle

Events:
Mrs. Twigley orders five dozen chocolate chip cookies by phone.

Bridget bags the cookies and puts them on top of the counter.

Mrs. Twigley comes by for the cookies and leaves without seeing Bridget.

End

Bridget calls Clark.

Clark finds a note on the floor behind the counter from Mrs. Twigley telling Bridget that she had come by for the cookies.

missing cookies

Plot

The Cookie Caper Mystery by Daphne

S IS FOR *STORY!*
Planning, writing, and publishing

This cool center helps students remember all of a narrative's components! Glue three labeled library pockets inside a file folder. In the pockets, place index cards labeled with different characters' names and roles, interesting places where a story's action can take place, and a variety of intriguing plots. For even more fun, use famous people as main characters and glue magazine pictures of them to the cards! Laminate the folder and cards for durability and place them at a center along with copies of the planning organizer on page 72. To use the center, a child takes a copy of the organizer and one or more cards from each pocket. Then he uses the materials to plan and write a story he can publish in a clever way.

Amber Barbee, Deaf Smith Elementary, Richmond, TX

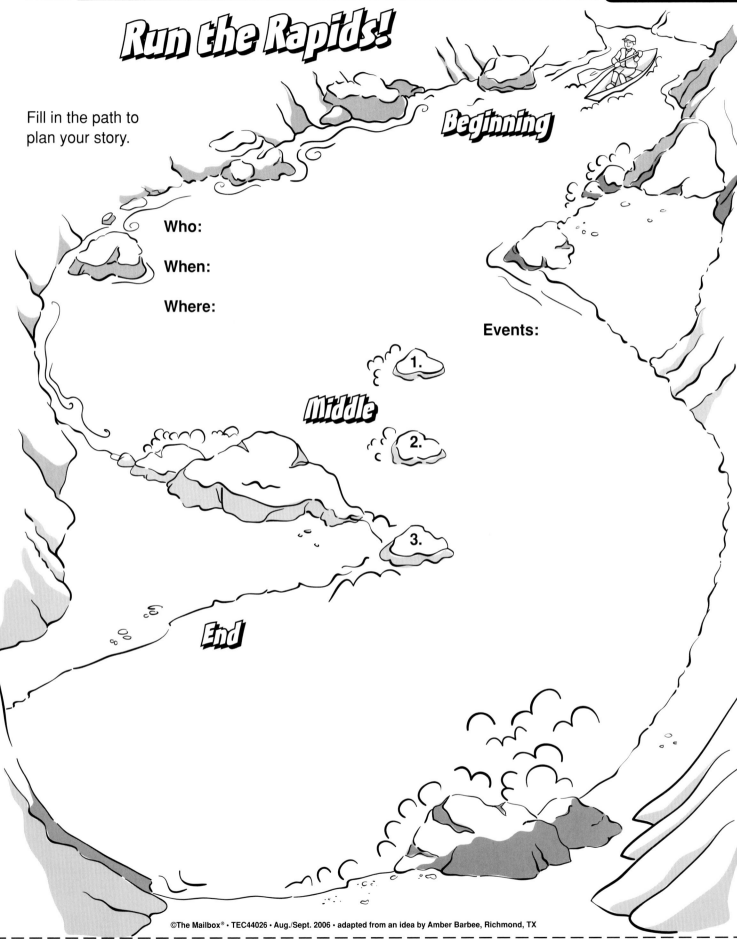

Run the Rapids!

Fill in the path to plan your story.

Beginning

Who:

When:

Where:

Events:

Middle

1.

2.

3.

End

Note to the teacher: Use with "S Is for *Story!*" on page 71.

Face-Off
Winning Activities for Comparing and Contrasting

Raven turns himself into a baby.

p. 18 "It was Raven. Raven had been reborn as a boy child."

Both tales have talking animals

I will search for light.

Carry me!

Coyote by Gerald McDermott

DIFFERENT

ALIKE

DIFFERENT

FLIPPING FOR DISTINCTIONS
Identifying similarities and differences

Determining what's the same or not the same about stories from different cultures is fun when trickster tales are used! Have pairs of students read two tales. Each partner then creates a four-layer booklet by stacking two sheets of paper so that the top edges are about an inch apart. He folds the sheets in half length-wise, staples them along the fold, and draws lines to divide the booklet into three sections. Next, he cuts the top three layers along the lines and writes "Alike" or "Different" on the uncut bottom sections as shown. He also writes each story title on the appropriate top flap and adds an illustration that shows the tale's unique-ness. On the middle top flap, he illustrates something the tales have in common. Then, under each successive flap, he lists an example of how the tales are alike or different, citing page numbers from the text to support each entry. As students share their booklets, there'll be lots of pages being flipped!

Get in the zone! This fantastic field of comparison activities is sure to score points with students!

with ideas by Teri Nielsen, Edinburg Common School, Edinburg, NY

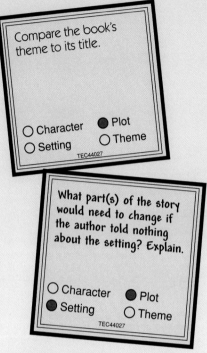

Compare the book's theme to its title.

○ Character ● Plot
○ Setting   ○ Theme

TEC44027

What part(s) of the story would need to change if the author told nothing about the setting? Explain.

○ Character ● Plot
● Setting   ○ Theme

TEC44027

COZY BOOK CLUB
Comparing story elements

Create lively book discussions with this small-group activity. First, have students brainstorm a list of class books read so far this year. Next, each group of students picks one book from the list and cuts apart a copy of the discussion cards on page 75 to stack facedown among them. Each group member takes a turn selecting a card and reading it aloud. She also categorizes the type of question on the card—character, setting, plot, or theme—and colors the appropriate circle(s). Then, while one group member takes notes, the other group members discuss the card's question. Once all the cards have been discussed, students share any unique responses with the class.

TWO HEADS ARE BETTER THAN ONE!
Citing text evidence

This center activity will give student pairs solid practice with comparison skills! Read aloud two brief tales; then place the books at a center along with several copies of page 76. To use the center, the partners write the titles and authors of the tales on a copy of the page. Then they work together to complete the page as directed by identifying the stories' similarities and differences, listing the supportive-text reference(s) for each one, and using the information to summarize what they learned. Students also may illustrate their findings!

A BATTLE BETWEEN TALES

STORY 1
One Grain of Rice
title
by Demi
author

VS.

STORY 2
Clever Beatrice
title
by Margaret Willey
author

ONE WAY THE STORIES ARE ALIKE
Both young girls tricked men out of their money.

Text Evidence From Story 1	Text Evidence From Story 2
p.33 "Rani had received more than one billion grains of rice. The raja had no more rice to give."	p. 26 " Here, here, take the rest," said the giant. He gave her his last ten gold coins in a silver bag."

ONE WAY THE STORIES ARE DIFFERENT
Rani wanted to give the rice to the villagers. Beatrice wanted to give the coins to her mom.

Text Evidence From Story 1	Text Evidence From Story 2
p. 33 "I shall give it to all the hungry people," said Rani. "And I shall leave a basket of rice for you too, if you promise from now on to only take as much rice as you need."	p. 28 "She held up the silver bag with the gold coins inside, waving to her mother."

Use the information above to summarize what you learned.
Both the giant and the king misjudged the girls. They should have been more careful. Both young girls were very clever.

The Write Stuff

	Tale 1: Mufaro's Beautiful Daughters by John Steptoe	Tale 2: The Egyptian Cinderella by Shirley Climo
Character(s)	Manyara and Nyasha	Rhodopis
Plot	The girls have been asked to see the king. He is looking for a wife.	
Setting		
Theme		
Point of View		

Bonus Box: On the back of this page, draw a Venn diagram comparing and contrasting the two tales above.

THE WRITE STUFF!
Using a graphic organizer to write comparatively

Here's a way to strengthen students' essay-writing skills—and you won't need a glass slipper to get it done! In advance, make a transparency of the organizer on page 77. Also make a copy of page 77 for each child. Next, read aloud two Cinderella tales. Using the transparency, model for students how to compare the two stories. As you do, have each child fill in her copy of the organizer. Then have her use the completed organizer to write a detailed essay that compares and contrasts the tales in a royal way!

Christina Bryant, Huffman Middle School, Huffman, TX

Do any of the characters have similar traits? What are they? Describe the traits.

○ Character ○ Plot
○ Setting ○ Theme
TEC44027

Compare the book's theme to its title.

○ Character ○ Plot
○ Setting ○ Theme
TEC44027

Pick one character. How do the character's words match his or her actions?

○ Character ○ Plot
○ Setting ○ Theme
TEC44027

Imagine the story with a different setting. Explain how this would affect the story's theme.

○ Character ○ Plot
○ Setting ○ Theme
TEC44027

Compare and contrast the main events at the beginning, the middle, and the end of the story.

○ Character ○ Plot
○ Setting ○ Theme
TEC44027

Pick one character. Explain how the character's actions support the book's theme.

○ Character ○ Plot
○ Setting ○ Theme
TEC44027

What is the story's climax? Explain how the story might have ended if the climax had not occurred.

○ Character ○ Plot
○ Setting ○ Theme
TEC44027

What part(s) of the story would need to change if the author told nothing about the setting? Explain.

○ Character ○ Plot
○ Setting ○ Theme
TEC44027

Does knowing why a character does something affect how you feel about the character? Explain.

○ Character ○ Plot
○ Setting ○ Theme
TEC44027

Name one character that changes during the story. Describe the difference in this character from the beginning of the story to the end.

○ Character ○ Plot
○ Setting ○ Theme
TEC44027

How would the story change if it were told from another character's point of view?

○ Character ○ Plot
○ Setting ○ Theme
TEC44027

Explain which element of the story you would change if you were the author.

○ Character ○ Plot
○ Setting ○ Theme
TEC44027

A BATTLE BETWEEN TALES

STORY 1

_____ **VS.**
title

STORY 2

_____
author

_____
title

_____
author

ONE WAY THE STORIES ARE ALIKE	
Text Evidence From Story 1	Text Evidence From Story 2
ONE WAY THE STORIES ARE DIFFERENT	
Text Evidence From Story 1	Text Evidence From Story 2

Use the information above to summarize what you learned.

_____

_____

_____

_____

_____

Note to the teacher: Use with "Two Heads Are Better Than One!" on page 74.

Name _____

The Write Stuff

	Tale 1:	Tale 2:
Main Character(s)		
Plot		
Setting		
Theme		
Point of View		

Bonus Box: On the back of this page, draw a Venn diagram comparing and contrasting the two tales.

©The Mailbox® • TEC44027 • Oct./Nov. 2006

Note to the teacher: Use with "The Write Stuff!" on page 74.

Hit the Gym!

Activities for Raising Students' Verb Performance to a Champion Level

The verb is jump!

For a great game on identifying action verbs, helping verbs, and linking verbs, see page 7!

THE HOT SEAT
Action verbs

This charades-inspired game will set your students in motion! Make a copy of the verb cards on page 80 and cut them apart. Divide students into two teams and choose a child from Team 1 to step outside the classroom. To begin, Team 1 chooses a card and reveals it to Team 2. The player who was sent out of the room returns, sits on a stool (the hot seat), and holds a bell. At your signal, players on Team 1 act out the chosen word until the player holding the bell rings it, signaling each child to freeze. Then the hot-seat contestant makes a guess. If she is correct, her team earns a point and a player from Team 2 becomes the next hot-seat player. If she is incorrect, the action continues. If she makes three wrong guesses, the verb is revealed and a player from Team 2 takes the hot seat. Play continues until the actions on all cards have been performed. The team with more points wins. To follow up, have each child complete a copy of page 82 as directed.

Michele Cochran, Benton Elementary, Nicholson, GA

This balanced routine of verb activities is sure to vault students' understanding of this vital part of speech to a new level.

WHEN DID YOU DO IT?
Past- and present-tense verbs

To help students distinguish between these two time-related forms, have each child draw a picture of something he did last night on an index card and label it "Past." Next, instruct him to flip the card over, draw a picture of something he is doing now or wishes he were doing, and label it "Present." Pair students and have them exchange cards. Each child then tells about his drawings and the partner writes a sentence on both sides of the card, using the correct verb tense to explain what her peer did in the past and present. Then, as a class, make a list of the past and present tense verbs used in the sentences, challenging students to notice any patterns that emerge.

Angela Gruner, Angola, IN

Present

Ivan draws a picture playing checkers wit...

Past

Ivan played checkers last night with his dad.

HIT THE MARK!
Irregular verbs

Use this class game to practice the three principal forms of tricky verbs. Create a large target and three arrows from construction paper. Label the target and arrows as shown; then glue each arrow to a clothespin. Also program index cards by writing a different irregular verb phrase on each card. Next, divide the class in half. Team 1 chooses a card and completes each sentence using the correct verb. If the sentence is correct, an arrow is placed on the target and the team earns one point. If all sentences are correct, the team also earns the bonus points. Team 2 then takes a turn and play continues until all cards have been used. The team with more points wins.

Tina Cassidy, Medina, OH

RAPPING FOR A LITTLE ASSISTANCE
Helping verbs

This cool rhyming rap not only motivates students to identify helping verbs in a sentence, but it reminds them not to use *of* as a helping verb as well!

Gloria J. Gancarz, Suwanee, GA

The Helping Verb Rap

Helping verbs all have an attraction
To the main verbs, which show the action.

Please pay attention to what I say;
This helping verb rap will show you the way.

Am, is, are, was, were, and *being*
Are helping verbs you have been seeing.

Have, has, had, did, does, and *do*
Are more helping verbs used by you.

Now I know you're familiar with *can* and *could,*
But do you also remember *should* and *would?*

Don't forget *shall* and *will* or *been* and *be!*
They're as easy to spot as A, B, C!

By now you've learned them all, I trust,
Including *might* and *may* and *must.*

Some additional info for you as well—
Just one more small rule to help you excel.

Never use *of* as a verb—it won't do!
But *should have, could have,* and *would have*
are all great words for you!

Today I bring my lunch.
Yesterday I brought my lunch.
I have brought my lunch many times before.

I have...many times before.

1 point.

Bonus 3 pts.

Today I...

Yesterday I...

Verb Cards

Use with "The Hot Seat" on page 78.

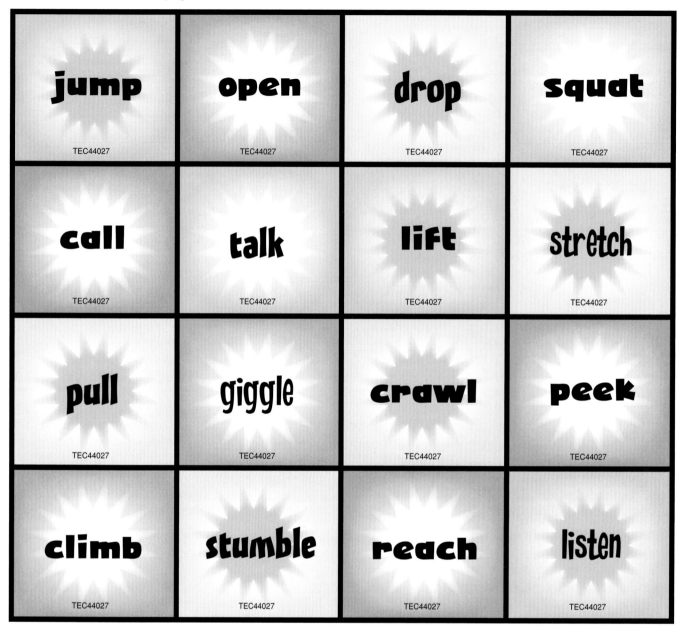

jump	open	drop	squat
TEC44027	TEC44027	TEC44027	TEC44027
call	talk	lift	stretch
TEC44027	TEC44027	TEC44027	TEC44027
pull	giggle	crawl	peek
TEC44027	TEC44027	TEC44027	TEC44027
climb	stumble	reach	listen
TEC44027	TEC44027	TEC44027	TEC44027

Answer Key

Use with "Know Your Verbs!" on page 81.

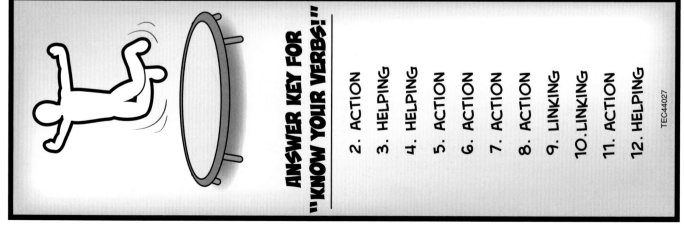

ANSWER KEY FOR "KNOW YOUR VERBS!"

2. ACTION
3. HELPING
4. HELPING
5. ACTION
6. ACTION
7. ACTION
8. ACTION
9. LINKING
10. LINKING
11. ACTION
12. HELPING

TEC44027

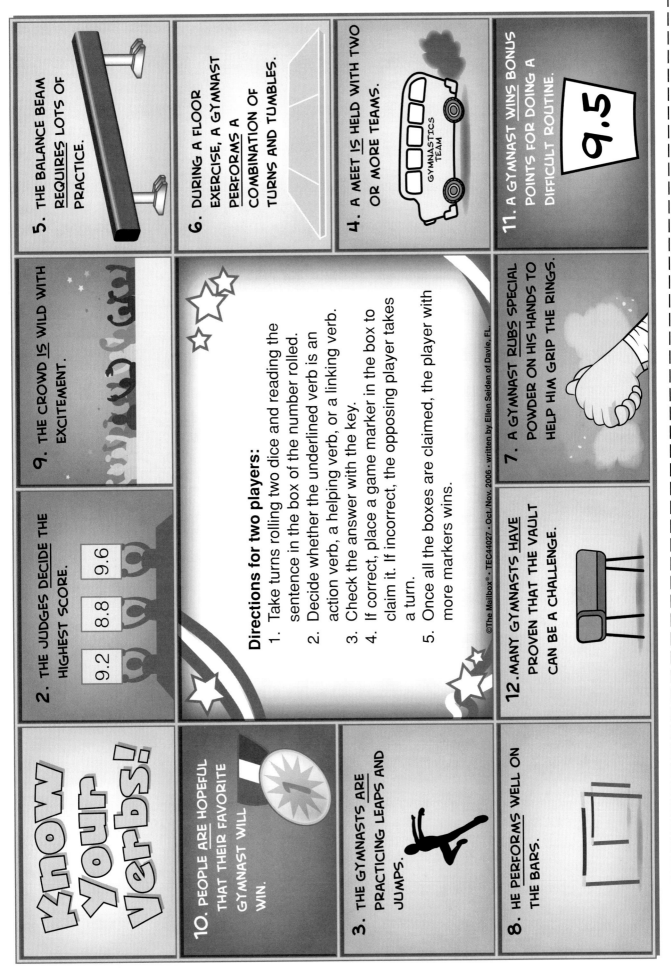

Know Your Verbs!

5. THE BALANCE BEAM REQUIRES LOTS OF PRACTICE.

6. DURING A FLOOR EXERCISE, A GYMNAST PERFORMS A COMBINATION OF TURNS AND TUMBLES.

4. A MEET IS HELD WITH TWO OR MORE TEAMS.

GYMNASTICS TEAM

11. A GYMNAST WINS BONUS POINTS FOR DOING A DIFFICULT ROUTINE.

9.5

9. THE CROWD IS WILD WITH EXCITEMENT.

2. THE JUDGES DECIDE THE HIGHEST SCORE.

9.2 8.8 9.6

Directions for two players:
1. Take turns rolling two dice and reading the sentence in the box of the number rolled.
2. Decide whether the underlined verb is an action verb, a helping verb, or a linking verb.
3. Check the answer with the key.
4. If correct, place a game marker in the box to claim it. If incorrect, the opposing player takes a turn.
5. Once all the boxes are claimed, the player with more markers wins.

©The Mailbox® · TEC44027 · Oct./Nov. 2006 · written by Ellen Seiden of Davie, FL.

7. A GYMNAST RUBS SPECIAL POWDER ON HIS HANDS TO HELP HIM GRIP THE RINGS.

12. MANY GYMNASTS HAVE PROVEN THAT THE VAULT CAN BE A CHALLENGE.

10. PEOPLE ARE HOPEFUL THAT THEIR FAVORITE GYMNAST WILL WIN.

3. THE GYMNASTS ARE PRACTICING LEAPS AND JUMPS.

8. HE PERFORMS WELL ON THE BARS.

Note to the teacher: To play the game, students will need the answer key on page 80, two dice, and 11 game markers.

A Body at Work

List action verbs that tell what each body part can do. One has been done for you.

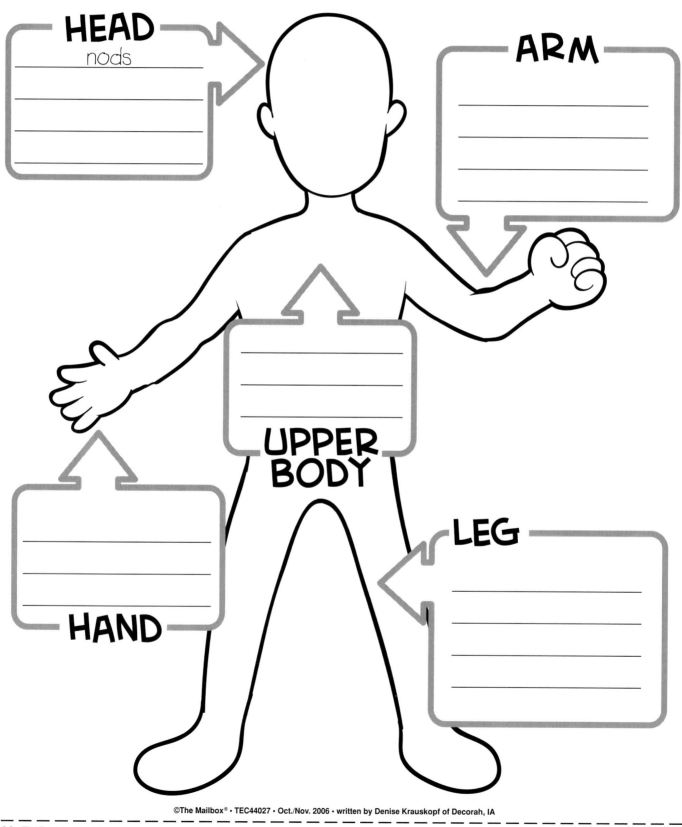

HEAD
nods
_____

ARM
_____
_____
_____

UPPER BODY
_____
_____
_____

HAND
_____
_____

LEG
_____
_____
_____

Note to the teacher: Use with "The Hot Seat" on page 78.

As Easy as Pie

Fun With Figurative Language

À LA MODE
Review project

Provide each student with a copy of the pie pan pattern and six copies of the slice pattern on page 87. Challenge her to find an example of a simile, a metaphor, and personification in each type of literature listed on the pie. When she finds an example, she writes the title, the author, and the example on the front of a pie slice and a brief explanation of its meaning on the back. She then glues the rim of the slice to the matching part of her pie pan as shown. If desired, challenge students to complete the project within a specified amount of time. Then reward those who do with a real slice of pie topped with ice cream!

The blowing wind made a sound like someone whistling.

Personification in Poetry

Simile in Prose

Metaphor in Poetry

Simile in Poetry

Personification in Prose

The BFG by Roald Dahl "The moonbeam was slicing through the room on to her face..."

Are you hungry for figurative language? Then take a bite of these appetizing activities!

with ideas by Teri Nielsen, Edinburg Common School, Edinburg, NY

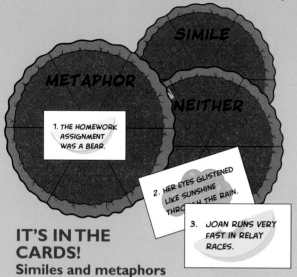

IT'S IN THE CARDS!
Similes and metaphors

Set up this center by making a back-to-back copy of pages 85 and 86. Cut apart the cards and score card on page 85 and place them in a resealable plastic bag. Then place the bag at a center along with three paper pies similar to those shown above. To complete the center, a child reads the sentence on each card and then places it on the correct pie cutout. If desired, challenge him also to write the sentence's meaning on a separate sheet of paper. Once all of the cards have been placed on a cutout, the student checks his work by turning the cards over and reading the answers on the back. Then he scores his performance using the score card.

TOP THAT!
Hyperboles

For this simple class game, have students sit in a circle. Then make an exaggerated statement such as "I'm so fast, I can run a mile in five minutes." Call on any student in the circle to top your statement by adding an exaggeration. Next, have the child at his right exaggerate the statement even more. Continue having students add hyperboles in this manner until the sentence makes it all the way around the circle or until students run out of exaggerations to add. Then introduce a new statement for the next round. Follow up by giving each child a piece of adding machine tape equal in length to his height on which he can write an exaggerated tale that's as tall as he is!

Julia Ring Alarie, Williston, VT

"PERSON-AL" QUALITIES
Personification

To begin this partner activity, draw and label a simple stick figure on the board as shown. Then brainstorm with students different human characteristics related to each body part and list them on the board. Next, choose a classroom object and have pairs of students list human characteristics for it similar to those suggested for the stick figure. Also have the partners write three or four sentences explaining the personifications they assigned to the object. Then invite each duo to share its sentences aloud so students will know just how many different ideas were generated about the same object.

1. THE HOMEWORK ASSIGNMENT WAS A BEAR.

2. HER EYES GLISTENED LIKE SUNSHINE THROUGH THE RAIN.

3. JOAN RUNS VERY FAST IN RELAY RACES.

4. JOSH IS A GIANT COMPARED TO HIS TEAMMATES.

5. STAN'S CAT IS AS LIGHT AS A FEATHER.

6. THE NEIGHBOR'S DOG IS FRIENDLY.

7. THE MOUNTAIN WE CLIMBED WAS A SKYSCRAPER.

8. THAT ATHLETE JUMPS LIKE A FROG.

9. JON IS A GREAT SNOW-SKIER.

10. THIS BISCUIT IS A ROCK.

11. KIM'S VOICE IS LIKE VELVET.

12. THE FRUIT IN THE BASKET WAS RIPE.

13. THEIR ACE BASEBALL PITCHER THREW A ROCKET ACROSS THE PLATE.

14. THE YOUNG TREE SWAYED IN THE WIND LIKE A BALLERINA.

15. THE RACECAR'S ENGINE RUMBLED.

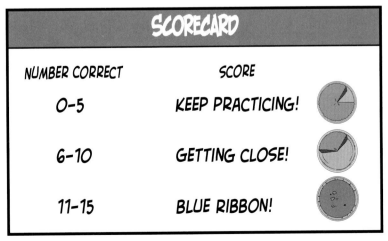

SCORECARD

NUMBER CORRECT	SCORE
0–5	KEEP PRACTICING!
6–10	GETTING CLOSE!
11–15	BLUE RIBBON!

NEITHER	SIMILE	METAPHOR
NEITHER JOAN RUNS FAST. TEC44028	**SIMILE** HER EYES WERE SHINING. TEC44028	**METAPHOR** THE HOMEWORK WAS HARD. TEC44028
NEITHER THE DOG IS NICE. TEC44028	**SIMILE** STAN'S CAT DOES NOT WEIGH MUCH. TEC44028	**METAPHOR** JOSH IS TALL. TEC44028
NEITHER JON SKIS WELL. TEC44028	**SIMILE** THE ATHLETE JUMPS WELL. TEC44028	**METAPHOR** THE MOUNTAIN WAS TALL. TEC44028
NEITHER THE FRUIT WAS READY TO EAT. TEC44028	**SIMILE** KIM'S VOICE IS SOFT AND PLEASANT. TEC44028	**METAPHOR** THE BISCUIT IS HARD. TEC44028
NEITHER THE RACECAR'S ENGINE MADE A LOUD NOISE. TEC44028	**SIMILE** THE TREE SWAYED BACK AND FORTH GRACEFULLY. TEC44028	**METAPHOR** THE PITCHER THREW A FASTBALL. TEC44028

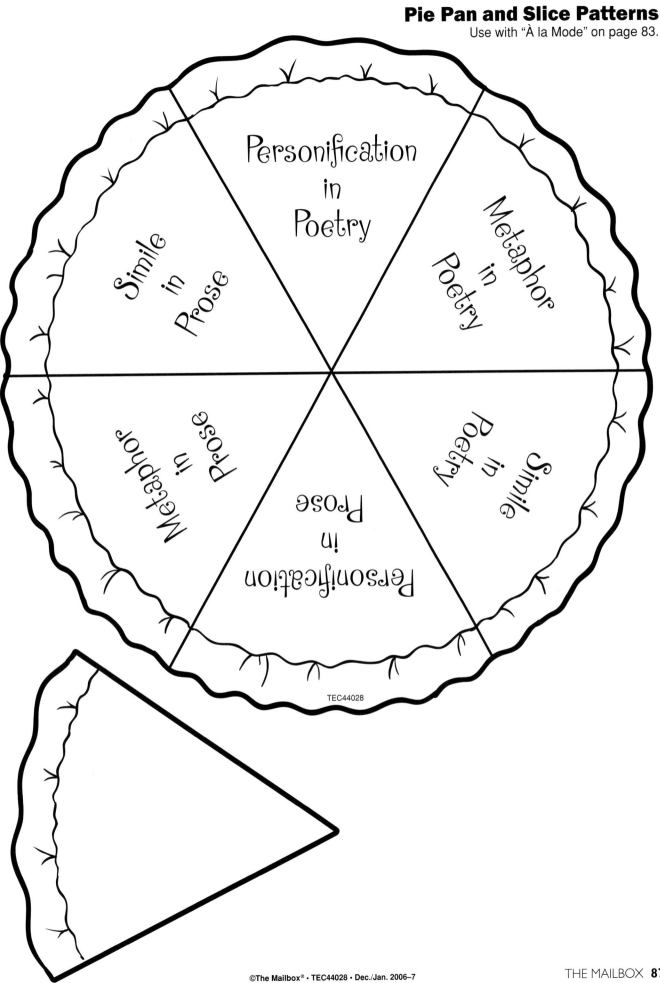

TEC44028

Order, Please!
Organizing and Clarifying Written Work

> CROSS YOUR FINGERS. WRITE YOUR NAME BACKWARD. TAKE OUT A SHEET OF PAPER. PUT YOUR BOOK AWAY. TURN TO PAGE 77. TAKE OUT YOUR SCIENCE BOOKS.

TIME-ORDER WORDS

ABOUT	NOW
AFTER	ONE DAY
A LONG TIME AGO	SECOND
AS SOON AS	SOON
AT	THEN
BEFORE	THIRD
DURING	THIS MORNING
FINALLY	TODAY
FIRST	TOMORROW
LAST	UNTIL
LATER	WHEN
MEANWHILE	YESTERDAY
NEXT	

WHEN TO DO WHAT
Time order

Knowing when to complete a step in a set of directions is important. To illustrate this, quickly give students the directions stated by the character above. Act shocked when students seem confused. Next, quickly mix the order of events of a story they recently read. Expect the same reaction. Then ask what you could have done to make the directions easier to follow or the story events easier to sequence. No doubt students will suggest that you could have used time-order words. Finally, display a list of the time-order words shown. Have pairs of students refer to it to write directions for teaching someone how to do some type of special handshake. As partners share their directions with the class, have listeners identify the time-order words used and then act out each handshake.

Help students judge how to organize and clarify their written work by presenting this full docket of activities!

with ideas by Jacqueline Beaudry, Getzville, NY

LOCATION, LOCATION, LOCATION
Place order

To make the value of using words such as *to the right of, below,* or *above* as clear as a bell, invite one child to the front of the room. Give her any card from a copy of page 90. Direct each of the other students to take out a sheet of paper. Have the volunteer give the class specific oral directions about how to draw the object on the card without identifying it. Encourage her to include geometric terms in her directions. Allow no one to ask the volunteer to be more specific. Once she's finished, invite several children to draw on the board their interpretations of the directions. Repeat the activity with different cards as time allows.

To follow up, display this issue's poster on place-order words and give each child one of the cards copied from page 90. Have him refer to the poster to write directions that would help someone draw the pictured object accurately. Then have him tape the card to the back of his paper. After you check his work, place the directions at a center for more practice.

> To draw this mystery object, First draw a triangle near the upper right corner of your paper. The longest side of the triangle should face the paper's lower left corner.

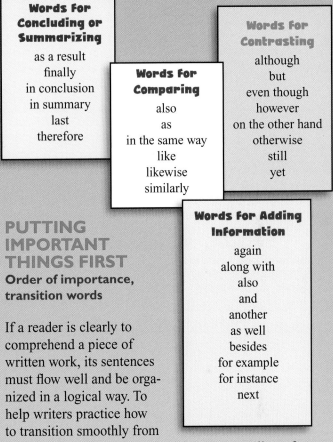

Words For Concluding or Summarizing
as a result
finally
in conclusion
in summary
last
therefore

Words For Comparing
also
as
in the same way
like
likewise
similarly

Words For Contrasting
although
but
even though
however
on the other hand
otherwise
still
yet

Words For Adding Information
again
along with
also
and
another
as well
besides
for example
for instance
next

PUTTING IMPORTANT THINGS FIRST
Order of importance, transition words

If a reader is clearly to comprehend a piece of written work, its sentences must flow well and be organized in a logical way. To help writers practice how to transition smoothly from one sentence and paragraph to the next, post lists of helpful transition words (see the suggested lists above). After discussing the use of each list, assign each child a persuasive or an expository topic to write about. Once he completes the first draft, have him revise and edit his work to see that his sentences are organized and that each one flows sensibly to the next. Remind him to insert transition words as needed to improve clarity and to include an appropriate summary sentence.

FOR PRACTICE USING TRANSITION WORDS IN DESCRIPTIVE WRITING, HAVE EACH CHILD COMPLETE A COPY OF PAGE 91 AS DIRECTED.

Activity Cards

Use with "Location, Location, Location" on page 89.

CAPTURE IT ALL!

Pretend that you have a new bedroom.
Complete the steps to describe what is in the
bedroom so that anyone who reads the description
can picture the room without having to see it.

PREWRITING

Draw a picture of the room in the box below.
Include the main pieces of furniture and other
furnishings. Then color the picture.

**WRITING THE
FIRST DRAFT**

On another sheet of paper, write an interesting topic
sentence about your bedroom. Then describe the bedroom
from top to bottom or from left to right. Tell where all the
furniture and other furnishings are located.

**REVISING AND
EDITING**

Check to see that you have used strong adjectives. Make
sure your sentences are arranged in the correct order. Use
both time-order words and place-order words to make your
description easier to picture.

PUBLISHING

Copy your description neatly on another sheet
of paper. Then staple this sheet behind it.

Find the Clues
Making Inferences to Improve Reading Comprehension

UNCOVER THE EVIDENCE
Comprehension tool

To create this helpful reference, give each child a copy of pages 94 and 95. Have him cut out the magnifying glasses, fold each cutout along the broken line, and glue its back sides together. Next, have him stack the cutouts with the cover on top and use a brad to connect the pieces. Students can slip the magnifying glasses into their reading folders and then pull them out each time they read!

Reading Detective

name

Find the reason a character's actions.

Look for clues about a character's feelings that are not clearly stated.

what you about the get more ing from t you read.

Investigate these activities on making inferences, a comprehension strategy that's sure to keep student sleuths on track!

with ideas by Teri Nielsen, Edinburg Common School, Edinburg, NY

SOLVING "RIDDLE-ISTIC" MYSTERIES
Independent project

This activity has students using prior knowledge and context clues. Give each child a copy of a page of riddles without the answers. Have him choose one riddle. Next, have him fold a sheet of construction paper in half lengthwise, unfold it, and then fold the sides so they meet in the middle. Have him unfold the paper and cut off the top two outer sections. When he's finished, he copies the riddle onto the paper's top portion and then closes the flaps. On the left flap, he lists text clues that can help him solve the riddle. On the right flap, he writes what he knows about the things on the left flap. He writes his answer to the riddle under the flaps. Invite students to share their solutions with the class. Then showcase the projects on a display titled " 'Riddle-istic' Inferences."

Why did the teacher wear sunglasses?

Prior Knowledge
A teacher has students and a classroom, and works in a school. Sunglasses keep out bright light and protect the eyes.

Text Clues
teacher
sunglasses

Why did the teacher wear sunglasses?

Because her students were so bright!

READING DETECTIVES
Incentive

To turn students into real reading pros with their own case files and business cards, give each child a copy of the case file pattern on page 96. Each time you read a story aloud, instruct students to listen for inferences about the setting or the characters' feelings, actions, and experiences. When you finish reading, have students share the examples they heard. Give each child who shares a correct inference a sticker to affix to her case file. When she earns five stickers, allow her to trade the case file for a copy of a business card on page 96.

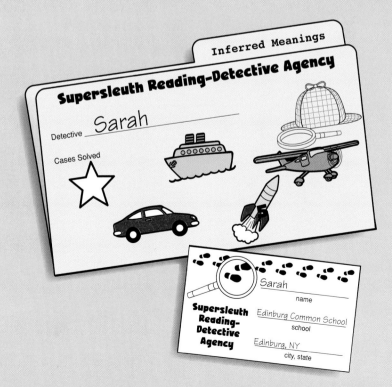

Inferred Meanings

Supersleuth Reading-Detective Agency

Detective ___Sarah___

Cases Solved

Sarah
name
Edinburg Common School
school
Edinburg, NY
city, state

Supersleuth Reading-Detective Agency

Magnifying Glass Patterns

Use with "Uncover the Evidence" on page 92.

Reading Detective

name

TEC44029

Look for clues hidden in a story.

Find the reason for a character's actions.

Look for a possible cause or effect of a character's action.

Look for clues about a character's feelings that are not clearly stated.

Find clues about the story's setting that are not clearly stated.

Use what you know about the topic to get more meaning from what you read.

Ask yourself whether the conclusions you have drawn make sense in the story.

©The Mailbox® • TEC44029 • Feb./Mar. 2007

Case File Pattern and Business Cards

Use with "Reading Detectives" on page 93.

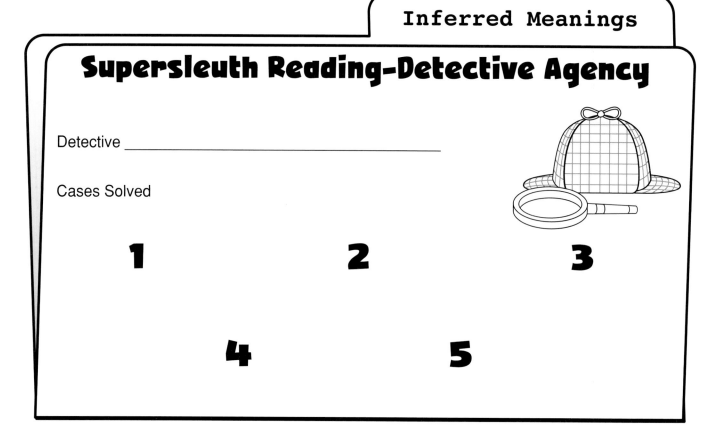

Inferred Meanings

Supersleuth Reading-Detective Agency

Detective _____

Cases Solved

1   **2**   **3**

4   **5**

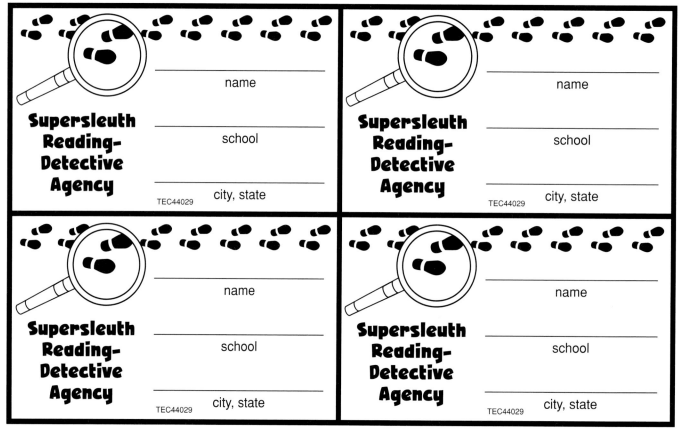

Supersleuth
Reading-
Detective
Agency

name _____

school _____

city, state _____

TEC44029

Supersleuth
Reading-
Detective
Agency

name _____

school _____

city, state _____

TEC44029

Supersleuth
Reading-
Detective
Agency

name _____

school _____

city, state _____

TEC44029

Supersleuth
Reading-
Detective
Agency

name _____

school _____

city, state _____

TEC44029

Clue Finder

Read each paragraph.
Use text clues and what you know about the topic to answer each question.

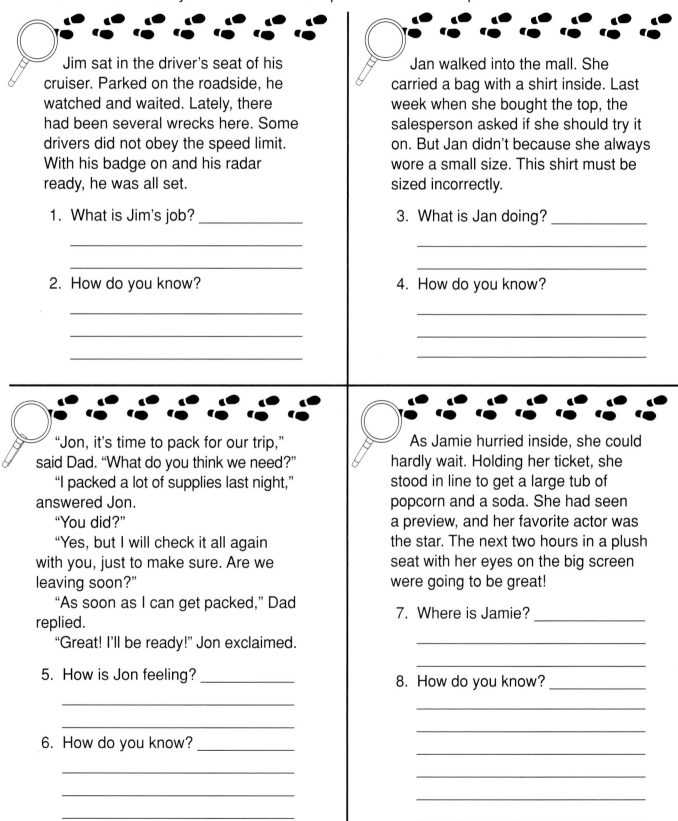

Jim sat in the driver's seat of his cruiser. Parked on the roadside, he watched and waited. Lately, there had been several wrecks here. Some drivers did not obey the speed limit. With his badge on and his radar ready, he was all set.

1. What is Jim's job? _____
   _____
   _____

2. How do you know?
   _____
   _____
   _____

Jan walked into the mall. She carried a bag with a shirt inside. Last week when she bought the top, the salesperson asked if she should try it on. But Jan didn't because she always wore a small size. This shirt must be sized incorrectly.

3. What is Jan doing? _____
   _____
   _____

4. How do you know?
   _____
   _____
   _____

"Jon, it's time to pack for our trip," said Dad. "What do you think we need?"

"I packed a lot of supplies last night," answered Jon.

"You did?"

"Yes, but I will check it all again with you, just to make sure. Are we leaving soon?"

"As soon as I can get packed," Dad replied.

"Great! I'll be ready!" Jon exclaimed.

5. How is Jon feeling? _____
   _____
   _____

6. How do you know? _____
   _____
   _____
   _____

As Jamie hurried inside, she could hardly wait. Holding her ticket, she stood in line to get a large tub of popcorn and a soda. She had seen a preview, and her favorite actor was the star. The next two hours in a plush seat with her eyes on the big screen were going to be great!

7. Where is Jamie? _____
   _____
   _____

8. How do you know? _____
   _____
   _____
   _____
   _____
   _____
   _____

Go Airborne

High-Flying Genre Activities

CLEARED FOR TAKEOFF!
Study aid

To help students recognize the distinguishing features of genres, give each child a colorful copy of page 100. Have him cut out the genre features and glue each one next to the correct genre on the bookmark. When he's finished, have him cut out the bookmark, fold it in half lengthwise, and glue the back sides together, as shown, to complete the bookmark. Also have him fasten a paper clip to the top. Then, each time he reads a different book, have him slide the paper clip up or down to identify the book's genre. This handy tool will not only mark his page in the book, but it will also help him remember a key feature of each listed genre!

GENRE

Memoir

...raphy

...ography

Informational

Realistic Fiction

Fanta...y

Traditional Literature

Historical Fiction

Science Fiction

The Lion, the Witch, and the Wardrobe

by C. S. Lewis

Recognizing the distinguishing features of genres is a destination students can reach if their itineraries include these stops!

with ideas by Kim Minafo, Dillard Drive Elementary, Raleigh, NC

CHECK YOUR BAGS
Small-group activity

In advance, fill each of four paper grocery bags (turned printside in) with library books of the same genre. Next, divide students into four groups and give each group a bag of books. Have the group members review the books together and label the bag with the genre that the books represent. Each group member then writes on the outside of the bag one clue that helped him identify the genre. Invite each group to share its findings with the class before placing its bag of books in a designated area for others to read and enjoy. Repeat the activity periodically, filling the bags with a different genre of books each time.

SOARING WITH SORTING
Self-checking center

Mount a colorful copy of the sorting mat on page 103 onto construction paper and laminate it for durability. Also laminate a back-to-back copy of pages 101 and 102. Next, cut the cards apart and place them in a large resealable bag along with the sorting mat. To use the center, pairs of students turn the cards faceup and then place each card on the mat under the matching genre. To check their work, the partners turn the cards over to reveal the correct answers.

adapted from an idea by Farrah Milby, Weddington Hills Elementary, Concord, NC

Genre Bookmark

Use with "Cleared for Takeoff!" on page 98.

Imaginary story based on a real event or time from the past	Facts and ideas about real topics	True account of a person's life written by someone else	Story about things that could really happen	Story that can include imaginary events and talking animals	Stories—including folktales, fables, fairy tales, myths, and legends—that have been shared from person to person throughout history	Personal record of an event	True story written by a person about his or her own life	Special type of fantasy that includes or is based on scientific principles

GENRE	FEATURE
Memoir	Glue a box here.
Biography	Glue a box here.
Autobiography	Glue a box here.
Informational	Glue a box here.
Realistic Fiction	Glue a box here.
Fantasy	Glue a box here.
Traditional Literature	Glue a box here.
Historical Fiction	Glue a box here.
Science Fiction	Glue a box here.

©The Mailbox® · TEC44029 · Feb./Mar. 2007 · Key p. 310

©The Mailbox® · TEC44029 · Feb./Mar. 2007

Because of Winn-Dixie
by Kate DiCamillo

The View From Saturday
by E. L. Konigsburg

STUART LITTLE
by E. B. White

Charlie and the Chocolate Factory
by Roald Dahl

The Chocolate Room

The Cabin Faced West
by Jean Fritz

Caleb's Choice
by G. Clifton Wisler

Coral Reef
by Jane Burton and Barbara Taylor

Storm Warning: Tornadoes and Hurricanes
by Jonathan D. Kahl

Meet Benjamin Franklin
by Patricia A. Pingry

Pitchers: Twenty-Seven of Baseball's Greatest
by George Sullivan

Aesop's Fables
Retold by Brad Sneed

PAUL BUNYAN
Retold by Steven Kellogg

Fantasy

TEC44029

Realistic
Fiction

TEC44029

Realistic
Fiction

TEC44029

Historical
Fiction

TEC44029

Historical
Fiction

TEC44029

Fantasy

TEC44029

Biography

TEC44029

Informational

TEC44029

Informational

TEC44029

Traditional
Literature

TEC44029

Traditional
Literature

TEC44029

Biography

TEC44029

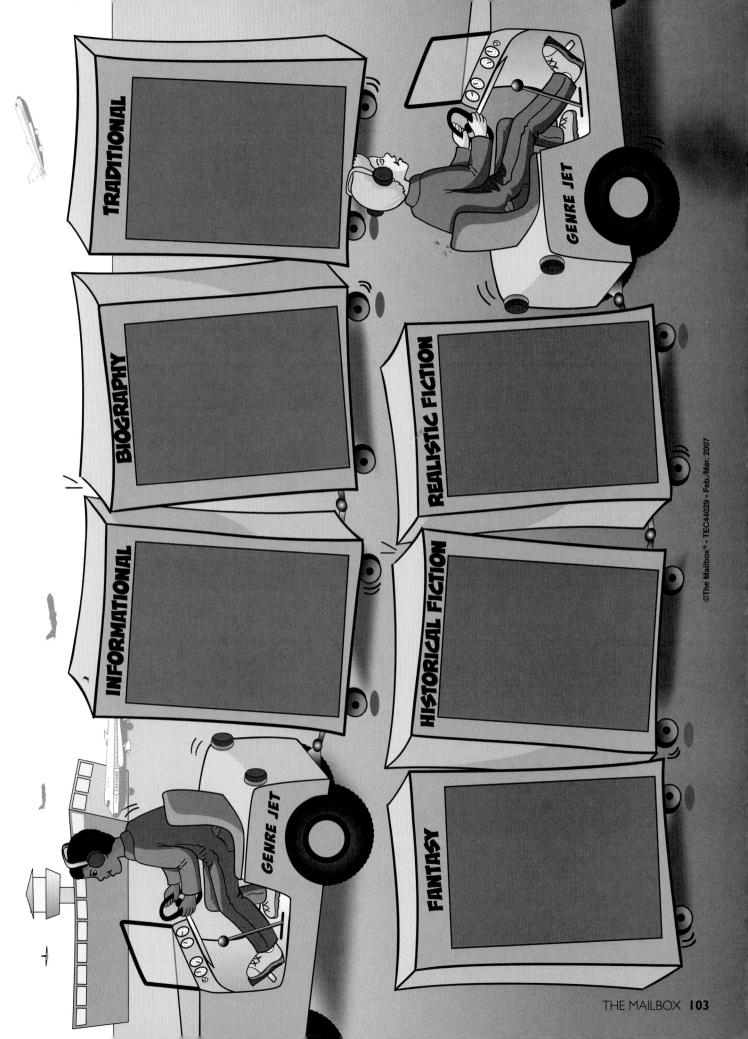

©The Mailbox® • TEC44029 • Feb./Mar. 2007

Clear As a Bell!
Activities to Enhance Reading Comprehension

HANGING BY THE "TALE"
Comparing and contrasting

To help student pairs determine the similarities and differences between stories, use a couple of tall tales and a mobile to spark their interest. Have each duo read two tall tales and then, for each story, cut out a tall construction paper figure that represents the main character. Instruct the pair to write the character's name on each cutout's head and then label the remaining body parts with each story's setting, plot, and theme plus each character's personality traits. Have the partners also write a brief comparison of the two stories on another piece of paper and glue it between the characters. Once students punch holes in their cutouts and tie them to clothes hangers with yarn, the mobiles are ready to share with the class.

Teri Nielsen, Tracey's Elementary
Tracey's Landing, MD

John Henry

Setting
Allegheny Mountains of West Virginia

Character Traits
hard-working
confident
helpful
determined
successful

Plot—A railroad tunnel needs to be cut through a huge rock mountain. John Henry uses his granddaddy's sledgehammers to race a steam drill through the rock.

Theme—Hard work and perseverance earn the respect of others.

Both characters are helpful, hard-working men. Both men left home and became explorers. They both won some type of competition.

Johnny Appleseed

Setting
Massachusetts, Pennsylvania, Ohio, and Indiana

Character Traits
generous
gentle
resourceful
helpful
entertaining
hard-working

Plot—Johnny Appleseed loves apples and wants people who are moving west to have apples along the way and where they settle. He clears land and plants orchards.

Theme—One person can make a difference.

Want your students to read for meaning? This batch of activities can help!

PERUSE THE PAPER
Identifying author's purpose

Divide students into small groups and give each group scissors and a newspaper. Have the groups cut out articles that demonstrate each of the following purposes: to entertain, to inform, and to persuade. After students find the examples, pair the groups to share their findings. Then compile the examples into separate booklets—one for each category—to serve as ready-made samples for future reference. Or challenge each child to rewrite a portion of an article to give it a different purpose. For example, an informative article could be rewritten to be entertaining or persuasive. For another activity on identifying author's purpose, see page 107.

Christina Scannell, San Jose, CA

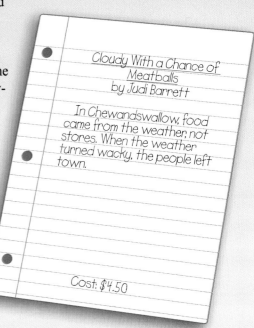

Cloudy With a Chance of Meatballs
by Judi Barrett

In Chewandswallow, food came from the weather, not stores. When the weather turned wacky, the people left town.

Cost: $4.50

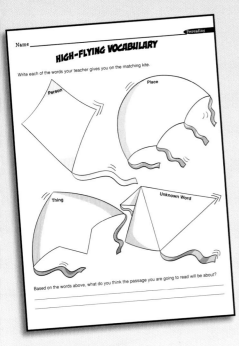

TALE-BARING VOCABULARY
Categorizing words, making predictions

Introduce a story students will be reading by giving them a list of ten to 20 words from the selection and a copy of page 106 to complete as directed. You'll not only find out which vocabulary words they know but also whether those words clue them in to what they'll be reading about! To guide students' discussion after the story has been read, see page 109.

Anastasia Leiphart, Shillington, PA

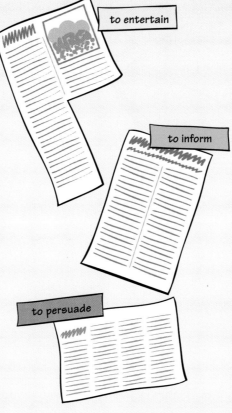

to entertain

to inform

to persuade

LET YOUR WORDS BE FEW
Summarizing text

After reading a portion of text aloud, issue a unique challenge to student pairs about capturing on paper the gist of what was read. Have each duo pretend to have $5.00 to spend on writing a summary of 20 words or less. Explain that each word used will cost $0.25. This will force students to edit and revise their summaries to make them informative and concise. When all partners are finished, have each pair share its summary and cost with the class.

HIGH-FLYING VOCABULARY

Write each of the words your teacher gives you on the matching kite.

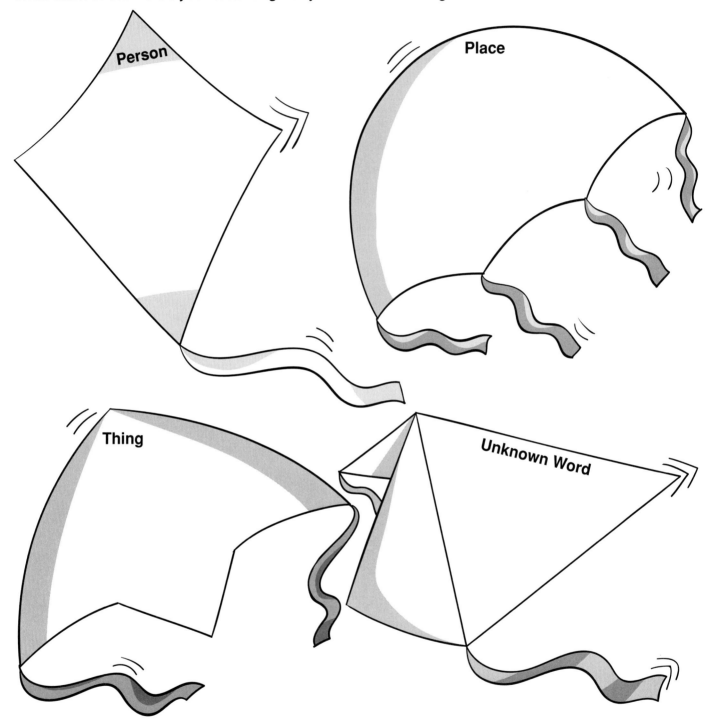

Person

Place

Thing

Unknown Word

Based on the words above, what do you think the passage you are going to read will be about?

_____

_____

Note to the teacher: Use with "Tale-Baring Vocabulary" on page 105.

Entertain, Inform, or Persuade?

Read a selection for each category in a newspaper, magazine, or book.
Record the title and author of each selection.
Then explain how you know the selection belongs in that group.

To Entertain

Title: _____
_____
_____
_____

Author: _____
_____
_____

Reason: _____
_____
_____
_____
_____
_____
_____
_____

To Inform

Title: _____
_____

Author: _____

Reason: _____
_____
_____
_____
_____
_____
_____
_____
_____
_____

To Persuade

Title: _____
_____

Author: _____

Reason: _____
_____
_____
_____
_____
_____
_____
_____
_____

©The Mailbox® • TEC44030 • April/May 2007 • adapted from an idea by Judy Haun, Maryville, TN

Note to the teacher: Use alone or with "Peruse the Paper" on page 105.

Pointing Out the Details

Write the main idea or topic of the selection you are
   reading on the hand at the right.

Write a detail that supports that main idea or topic next
   to each hand below.

Decide which details are the most important. Color the
   hands of those details.

Main Idea or Topic

Detail

Detail

Detail

Detail

Detail

Detail

Detail

Detail

©The Mailbox® • TEC44030 • April/May 2007 • written by Kim Minafo, Raleigh, NC

Literary Response Cube Pattern

Use alone or with "Tale-Baring Vocabulary" on page 105.

Directions:

1. Cut out the cube and fold it along the dotted lines. Then glue the sides together.
2. Take the cube to your small group.
3. Listen as someone in your group talks about a selection that the group has read. Turn your cube to a side that shows your response to what is being said.
4. Take turns sharing your thoughts and ideas with the group.

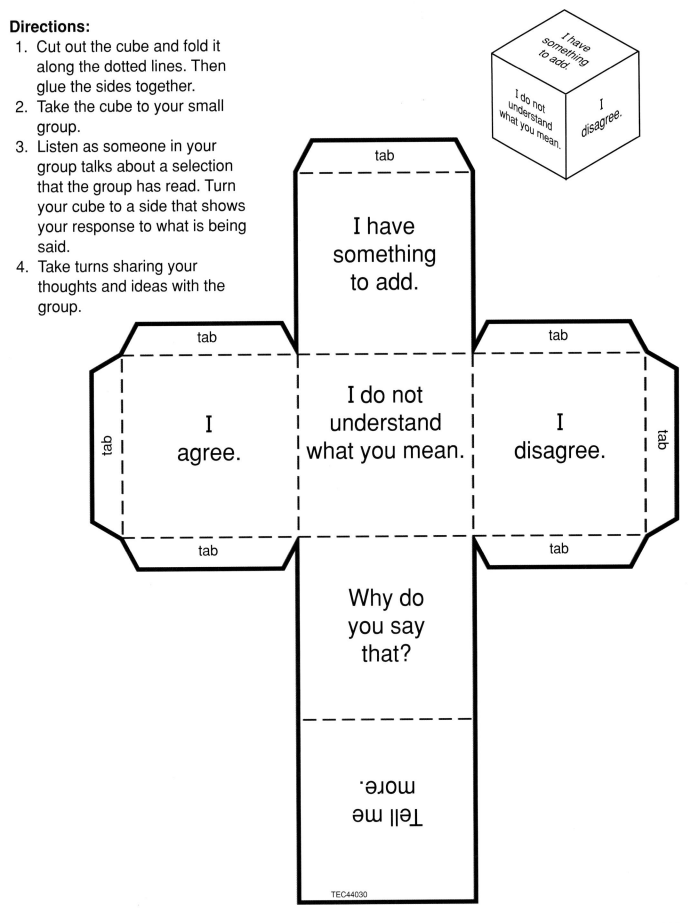

tab

I have something to add.

tab

tab

tab

I agree.

I do not understand what you mean.

I disagree.

tab

tab

tab

Why do you say that?

Tell me more.

TEC44030

Buy Into It!
Identifying and Using Persuasive Tactics

LOW MILEAGE!

SWEET DEAL

JIMMY B

IMPROVED!

New!

Buzzwords

CONVINCING MAIL
Persuasive techniques

For this individual or small-group project, collect a class supply of junk mail ads. Next, review with students the meaning of tactics such as bandwagon, testimonial, exaggeration, and flattery. Also discuss examples of buzzwords. Then post a chart, such as the one shown, that lists point values for different types of junk mail. Challenge students to cut examples from the mail that represent each technique, mount the examples on separate sheets of paper, and then add the correct labels. Did everyone's point total equal or exceed 40?

Karen Slattery, St. Vincent's Elementary, Oakville, Ontario, Canada

Point Chart

Buzzword (new, improved, better, etc.) = 1 point
Envelope labeled "Urgent!" or "Open at Once!" = 2 points
Promise of a free gift = 3 points
Sticker that has to be placed on an order form = 4 points
Postcard that says a prize has been won = 5 points
Envelope that appears to have a check inside = 7 points
Envelope that looks like a telegram = 8 points
Envelope that appears to have a credit card inside = 10 points

Are you in the market for persuasive activities? Check these out. They're priced to go!

with ideas by Heather Kime Markland, Chatham Park Elementary, Springfield, PA

FIRST-CLASS ARGUMENTS
Persuasive letter

Have each student choose a famous or historic person whom he would like to see pictured on a stamp. Next, have the child complete a copy of the graphic organizer on page 112. Have him use the completed organizer to write a persuasive business letter convincing the post office to create a stamp of that person. When he's finished, he can make a colorful drawing of the stamp he'd like to have created and display it on a board next to his completed letter!

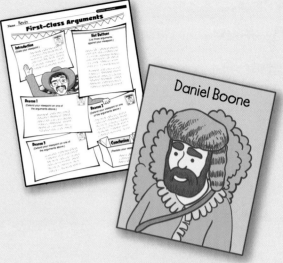

CANDY CREATION
Identifying persuasive techniques, writing a persuasive essay

Provide each small group of students with several different print ads for candy. Discuss the persuasion techniques the candy companies used to try to get people to buy their products. Next, have each group invent an original type of candy and create a colorful advertising poster that includes at least one persuasive tactic. Then have each group member write a persuasive essay arguing why vending machine companies should sell that candy in their machines. If desired, allow students to use the organizer on page 112 to help organize their thoughts. To review persuasive tactics, have each child complete a copy of page 115 as directed.

THE FLIP SIDE
Point of view, writing an argumentative essay

Help students understand that there are usually two sides to every persuasive argument—those who are for something and those who are against it. Laminate a back-to-back copy of the coin cards on page 113. Then cut out the cards and place them in a resealable plastic bag at a center. To use the center, a child draws a coin from the bag, flips the coin in the air, and then writes a persuasive argument to support the topic on the side of the coin that lands faceup. If time permits, he turns the coin over and writes a response to argue the other side of the issue.

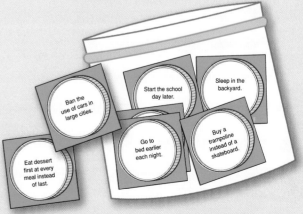

Sue Fleischmann, Sussex, WI

First-Class Arguments

Introduction
(State your viewpoint.)

Hot Buttons
(List three arguments *against* your viewpoint.)

Reason 1
(Defend your viewpoint against one of the arguments above.)

Reason 2
(Defend your viewpoint against one of the arguments above.)

Reason 3
(Defend your viewpoint against one of the arguments above.)

Conclusion
(Restate your viewpoint.)

©The Mailbox® • TEC44030 • April/May 2007

Note to the teacher: Use with "First-Class Arguments" and "Candy Creation" on page 111.

Coin Cards

Use with "The Flip Side" on page 111.

Eat dessert first at every meal instead of last. TEC44030	Sleep in the backyard. TEC44030	Start the school day later. TEC44030
Ban the use of cars in large cities. TEC44030	Watch nothing but scary movies. TEC44030	Watch cartoons in the cafeteria. TEC44030
Form a rock band instead of a rap group. TEC44030	Take all news shows off TV. TEC44030	Buy a trampoline instead of a skateboard. TEC44030
Eat all of the candy you want. TEC44030	Give a friend your last piece of gum. TEC44030	Go to bed earlier each night. TEC44030

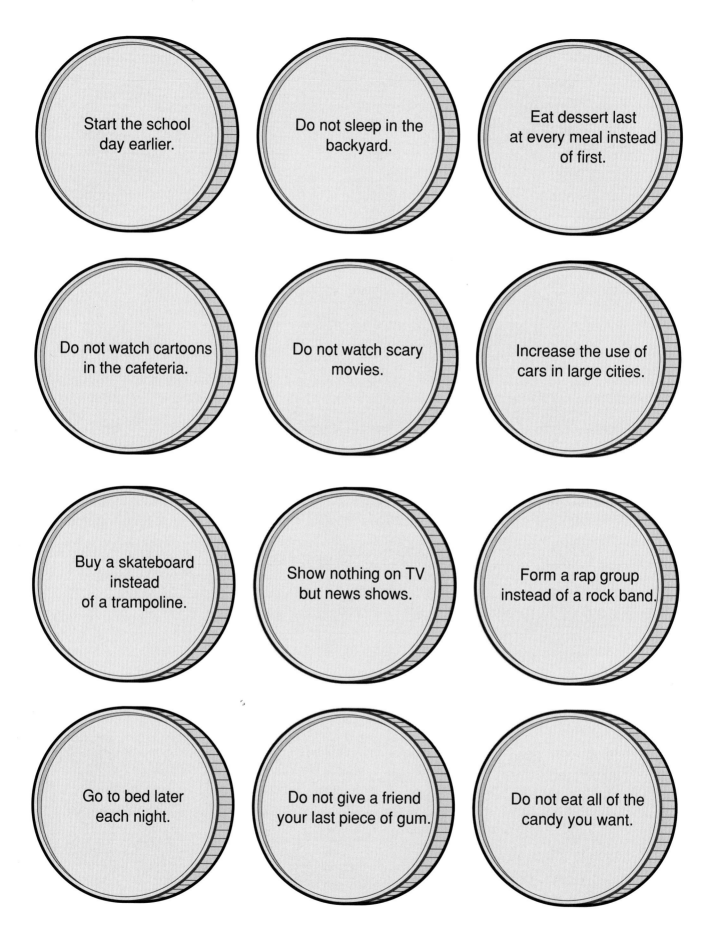

Start the school day earlier.

Do not sleep in the backyard.

Eat dessert last at every meal instead of first.

Do not watch cartoons in the cafeteria.

Do not watch scary movies.

Increase the use of cars in large cities.

Buy a skateboard instead of a trampoline.

Show nothing on TV but news shows.

Form a rap group instead of a rock band.

Go to bed later each night.

Do not give a friend your last piece of gum.

Do not eat all of the candy you want.

Name

Ultimate Ads

Read each slogan. Write the letter of the persuasive technique used.

A. Bandwagon
B. Testimonial
C. Exaggeration
D. Flattery

____ 1.
It's the most refreshing soda ever!

____ 2.
Healthy-Os are the best for you!

____ 3.
I always use Silky Shampoo. Just look at how shiny my hair is!

____ 4.
Act now! Don't be the only person without one!

____ 5.
Look cool in Celebrity Shades!

____ 6.
Play better than Tracy McGrady!

____ 7.
It's THE place to shop and be seen!

____ 8.
Vine swinging ADVENTURE
BEST MOVIE OF THE YEAR!

____ 9.
Buy today! Don't be the only one to miss this smart-shopper deal!

©The Mailbox® • TEC44030 • April/May 2007 • Key p. 60

Note to the teacher: Use alone or with "Candy Creation" on page 111.

On Stage

Perfect Performances by Adjectives and Adverbs

THE PURPLE-HAIRED ORKIE BUILDING THE SANDY STRUCTURE HAS NOT HAD ANY NECTAR ALL DAY.

FOLLOW THE CLUES!
The importance of adjectives

Provide each child with a copy of page 118 and colored pencils. Explain to students that the look-alike Orkies on the page survive by drinking nectar from a rare flower that grows only on their island and that one naughty Orkie drank their entire supply of nectar today. In order to identify him, students must be able to tell one Orkie from the next. Have the class brainstorm and then agree on different ways to color (or add accessories or features to) the creatures to distinguish one from the next. When everyone is finished, secretly select one Orkie for the culprit. Then give students one adjective-rich clue at a time until all other suspects have been eliminated (crossed out on the page). Follow up by discussing how helpful descriptive adjectives are when specifying one particular creature in a group.

Kim Hintze, Show Low Intermediate School, Show Low, AZ

Adjectives and adverbs are sure to take center stage with this grand performance of ideas!

with ideas by Shawna Miller, Wellington Elementary, Flower Mound, TX

SILLY SENTENCE STRIPS
Adverbs

To begin this fun flipbook-making activity, call out a noun-verb pair such as *boy-ran*. Have students brainstorm a list of adverbs that tell how, when, and where the boy ran. Next, provide each child with half of a sentence strip. Have him cut six equal flaps into his strip, leaving about one inch at the top of each section, and then label the flaps with the parts of speech shown. Next, have him think of his own noun-verb pair and add it to his strip. Have him also add an adjective and three appropriate adverbs where directed to provide details. Then staple the completed strips inside a folded sheet of colorful paper to make a book. Students will love flipping through the sections to find all the possible silly combinations!

SILLY ADVERB SENTENCES

| Yesterday | the | boy | ran | quickly | adverb (where) |
| adverb (when) | adjective | noun | verb | adverb how | adverb (where) |

LIGHT UP THE BOARD!
Adjective and adverb game for two

This easy-to-adapt review is perfect for a center! Laminate a copy of the gameboard on page 119 and the cards and answer key on page 120. Then cut the cards apart and store them and the key in a resealable plastic bag along with the gameboard, two game pieces, and a die. Then send one pair of students at a time to the center to play the game by following the directions on the gameboard. To include other parts of speech in the review, just add additional sentence cards!

GOOD-FOR-A-LAUGH STORIES
Adjectives and adverbs

For a quick review, cut 15 index cards in half. Label 15 halves with a number from 1 to 15. Label each of the remaining halves with a letter from *A* to *O*. Then provide each child with at least one card half and a copy of page 121. Direct the students with number cards to write an adjective on the back of the card and the students with letter cards to write an adverb on the back. Next, have students read the passage on page 121 in unison until they come to an answer blank. Then have the child with that answer blank's matching letter or number share the adjective or adverb written on the back of her card. Continue in this manner, reading in unison and having individual students say the words on their cards, until the entire passage has been read. If desired, have students record the words on their papers as they go along. The resulting story will be unique no matter how often the activity is repeated!

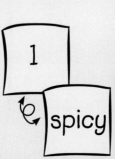

FILL IN THE BLANKS!
Follow your teacher's directions to complete this story.

1 / spicy

A

late

Name _____

Orkie Island

Color each Orkie as directed by your teacher.
Using the clues your teacher gives you, cross out the Orkies that did not drink the nectar to find out which one did.

Note to the teacher: Use with "Follow the Clues!" on page 116.

Light Up the Board!

Directions for two players:

1. Place the game pieces on Start.
2. Player A rolls the die and moves his marker ahead that number of spaces. Then he draws a card from the bag, reads the sentence aloud, and tells whether the underlined word is an adjective or an adverb. Player B checks with the key.
3. If Player A is correct, he puts the card back in the bag and moves his marker ahead the number of spaces written on his space. If Player A is incorrect, he returns the card to the bag and his marker stays where it is.
4. Player B then takes a turn in the same manner.
5. The first player to reach Finish wins.

Game Cards and Answer Key

Use with "Light Up the Board!" on page 117.

A. Kelly and Kristin like to perform <u>funny</u> skits and plays. TEC44031	B. The girls <u>often</u> invite friends and family to watch. TEC44031
C. Kelly can sing <u>well</u>. TEC44031	D. Kristin <u>usually</u> takes the role of narrator. TEC44031
E. <u>Sometimes</u> the girls ask friends to perform with them. TEC44031	F. Jake <u>once</u> played the role of a pirate. TEC44031
G. Jamal likes any <u>exciting</u> part with action. TEC44031	H. <u>Many</u> kids want to be in their plays. TEC44031
I. Kristin hopes their <u>amazing</u> plays will make it to Broadway. TEC44031	J. Kelly thinks they will need <u>more</u> practice. TEC44031
K. Jake and Jamal just laugh <u>uncontrollably</u>. TEC44031	L. The boys really like the <u>crazy</u> skits and plays. TEC44031
M. The audience claps and laughs <u>frequently</u>. TEC44031	N. Some <u>loyal</u> fans even shout, "Bravo!" TEC44031
O. Kelly and Kristin are <u>best</u> friends. TEC44031	P. The girls hope to become <u>famous</u> actresses in Hollywood. TEC44031
Q. Jake wants to be a movie star <u>someday</u>. TEC44031	R. Jamal wants to go to college and become a <u>rich</u> director. TEC44031
S. These kids work <u>very</u> hard. TEC44031	T. Their parents are happy and <u>proud</u>. TEC44031

Answer Key

A. adjective	F. adverb	K. adverb	P. adjective
B. adverb	G. adjective	L. adjective	Q. adverb
C. adverb	H. adjective	M. adverb	R. adjective
D. adverb	I. adjective	N. adjective	S. adverb
E. adverb	J. adjective	O. adjective	T. adjective

TEC44031

FILL IN THE BLANKS!

Follow your teacher's directions to complete this story.

Grant and Greg woke up _____ because it was a _____ day.
A   1

The two brothers _____ put on their _____ clothes and walked
B   2

_____ down the street. They _____ headed to the _____
C   D   3

park. Grant swung _____ on the _____ swings. Greg yelled
E   4

_____ as he slid down the _____ slide. They both _____
F   5   G

climbed into the _____ tree house to take a look at the _____ traffic
6   7

_____ filling the streets _____. Grant announced _____
H   I   J

that he wanted to play on the _____ monkey bars. Greg _____ ran
8   K

to get there first. Both boys _____ swung on the bars and then started playing
L

_____ tag. The _____ field was perfect for running. The _____
9   10   11

sun shone _____ on them as they played. Soon it was time to head home for
M

some _____ lunch. They laughed _____ the whole way home as
12   N

they _____ thought about their morning at the _____ park. "We had
O   13

_____ fun," Grant said. "Yes!" replied Greg, "A _____ morning."
14   15

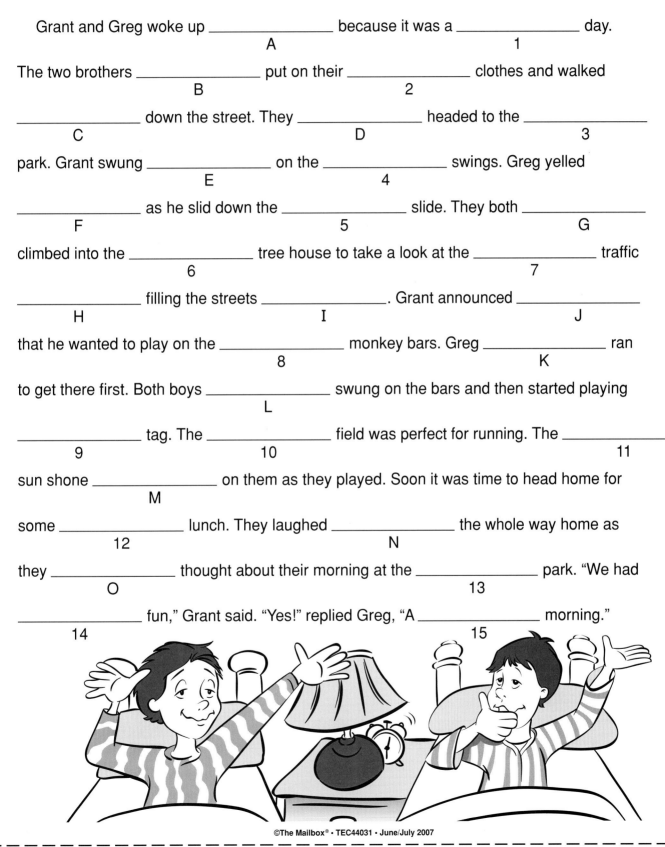

Note to the teacher: Use with "Good-for-a-Laugh Stories" on page 117.

Take Note!

Nifty Note-Taking Activities

WATCH, LISTEN, AND WRITE
Demonstration and practice

Model for students how to take notes by tape-recording two brief segments of an educational TV show or the evening news. As students watch the recording, have them listen for clues about the video's main idea, such as repeated words. Next, replay the segment and demonstrate on the board or on an overhead how to take notes, using fragments, symbols, and abbreviations to eliminate unnecessary words. Then play the second segment and have each child practice the skill by taking his own notes as he watches and listens.

What Sharks Look Like
- about 6" to 40' long
- about 1 oz. to over 15 short tons
- torpedo-shaped body on most species
- pectoral fins
- crescent-shaped tail on faster-swimming species
- mouth on underside of head on most species
- several rows of teeth
- body with small, toothlike scales
- 5 to 7 slits on each side of head for gills
- sensitive eyes
- small pores on head

Hone students' note-taking skills with these top-notch activities that can help them capture important facts!

with ideas by Bonnie Franz, Staten Island, NY

PARAPHRASE, PLEASE!
Mechanics of note taking

For guided practice, give each group of two or three students an identical paragraph duplicated from an appropriate student magazine, a nonfiction book, or an encyclopedia. Instruct students to circle any unfamiliar words, replacing them with more familiar synonyms. Next, have each group underline the paragraph's important ideas and write them as fragments or phrases on index cards. When everyone is finished, invite each group to share its notes with the class. Have students discuss the similarities and differences and then choose the phrases that best represent the paragraph's information.

Water
- is made up of tiny particles called molecules
- is made up of one atom of oxygen and two atoms of hydrogen
- dissolves many substances
- freezes at 32°F and boils at 212°F
- expands when it gets colder than 39°F

Note taking, outlining

Name _____

Noteworthy Outlining

Write the reading selection's topic on each notecard and as the outline's title.
Record the selection's section headings as subtopics on the notecard.
Take notes on each subtopic as you read. When you finish, circle two or three of the most important ideas on each card.
Then write each card's subtopic as a main heading (I–III) in the outline and each circled idea as a detail (A–C).

Topic: Different Kinds of Pets
Subtopic: Fish
- fun to watch
- live in tank or bowl
- good pet for people with allergies
- saltwater fish
- freshwater fish

Topic: Different Kinds of Pets
Subtopic: Dogs
- need to be walked
- need exercise
- less space needed for small dog
- more space needed for large dog

Topic: Different Kinds of Pets
Subtopic: Cats
- don't need to be walked
- can use a litter box
- some have long hair that must be brushed

OUTLINE

Different Kinds of Pets
title

I. Fish
  A. Two types: saltwater and freshwater
  B. Good pet for people with allergies
  C.
II. Dogs
  A. Are different sizes
  B. Need to be walked and exercised
  C.
III. Cats
  A. Can have long or short hair
  B. Don't need to be walked or exercised
  C.

NOTEWORTHY OUTLINING
Organizing written notes

If sorting information is difficult for your students, the graphic organizer on page 124 can help. First, choose a chapter from a nonfiction book or from a social studies or science textbook that students can read along with you. Then display a transparency of page 124 on an overhead projector and discuss the page's directions together. Next, model how to take notes about the chosen selection, using the section headings as subtopics and listing supporting details from each section. Finally, demonstrate how to write a topic outline that contains only words and phrases rather than a more detailed sentence outline. Repeat the activity using a different text selection until students are comfortable with the process. Then give each child a copy of page 124 and have her complete it using a new text selection. If a child's reading selection has more than three sections, give her one or more additional copies of the page as needed.

Noteworthy Outlining

Write the reading selection's topic on each notecard and as the outline's title.

Record the selection's section headings as subtopics on the notecards.

Take notes on each subtopic as you read. When you finish, circle two or three of the most important ideas on each card.

Then write each card's subtopic as a main heading (I–III) in the outline and each circled idea as a detail (A–C).

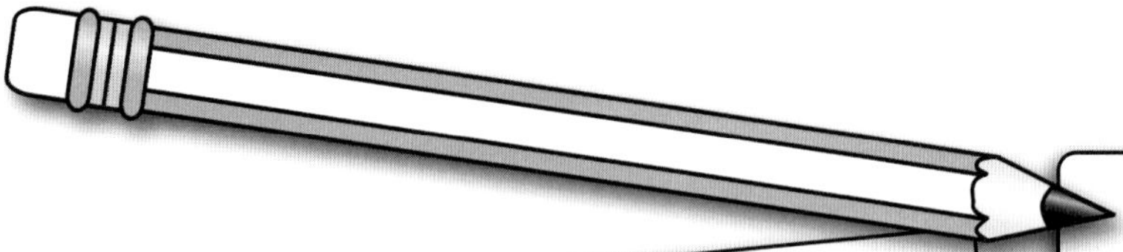

OUTLINE

Topic:
Subtopic:

Topic:
Subtopic:

Topic:
Subtopic:

○ title

I.
   A.
   B.
   C.
II.
   A.
○   B.
   C.
III.
   A.
   B.
   C.

○

Note to the teacher: Use with "Noteworthy Outlining" on page 123.

MATH UNITS

Get in Position!
Winning Place-Value Activities

The crowd cheered for Stacy when the judges announced she won the long jump by 0.2 meters!

EVENTFUL TALES
Place value from thousandths to millions, writing

What can you get when you combine place-value practice and students' imaginations? Terrific ten-page booklets that can be used as review tools! Each student pair folds three sheets of paper in half to make a booklet and staples the pages together along the fold. Next, the partners write about an interesting topic, such as a track meet, an excursion into space, a zoo trip, or a circus visit, making sure each page includes a sentence with a number representing a different place value from thousandths to millions. The order does not matter as long as each place value is used. Then the writers trim the pages into a shape related to their topic and decorate the cover. As students share their completed stories with the class, the listeners can identify the place value featured on each page!

Have a field day with place value using these exciting activities!

with ideas by Jennifer Otter, Oak Ridge, NC

SUBTRACT 600,000.

3,796,212

ENTER THE NUMBER 3,796,212 ON THE CALCULATOR. CHANGE THE HUNDRED THOUSANDS DIGIT TO 1.

DIGIT SWITCH
Adding and subtracting to change a digit's place value

Bring out the calculators for this partner review game! Announce a number for students to enter on their calculators. Then share the change in place value to be made, providing during the game a mix of addition and subtraction opportunities. After a set amount of time, reveal the solution. Award a point to each partner with a correct answer. The partner with more points after ten rounds wins!

RELAY RACE
Place value from ones to millions

This two-player game takes first place when it comes to identifying a number's position! Each student pair cuts apart the game cards on a copy of page 128 and places them face-down next to the gameboard. Then each player writes a four-digit number for Leg 1. Player 1 draws a card from the pile and reads it aloud. Players check to see whether either of the recorded numbers for that leg contains a matching digit for that value. If so, the recorder of that number checks the winner's box. If both numbers contain a matching digit, both players check a box. If neither number contains a matching digit, players take turns drawing cards until there is a match. Partners play Legs 2 through 5 in the same manner. The player with more points after Leg 5 wins!

DIAL A MILLION!
Reading, writing, and ordering whole numbers to millions

Place-value practice is just a phone number away with this small-group activity! Each child writes her seven-digit telephone number (omitting the area code) in standard form on an index card. Group members take turns reading their numbers aloud and then arrange the cards in order from least to greatest. For a greater challenge, students can include their zip codes!

EIGHT MILLION, EIGHT HUNDRED SEVENTY-FOUR THOUSAND.

8,874,000

Susan Peterson, Arcohe School, Herald, CA

Game Cards

Use with "Relay Race" on page 127.

4 tens TEC44026	7 ten thousands TEC44026	7 ones TEC44026	0 tens TEC44026	1 thousand TEC44026	2 thousands TEC44026	2 ten thousands TEC44026	4 thousands TEC44026	5 hundreds TEC44026	3 ten thousands TEC44026	8 thousands TEC44026	6 thousands TEC44026
8 ten thousands TEC44026	3 millions TEC44026	6 hundred thousands TEC44026	9 millions TEC44026	0 ten thousands TEC44026	5 hundred thousands TEC44026	9 hundred thousands TEC44026	2 millions TEC44026	4 hundred thousands TEC44026	7 hundred thousands TEC44026	3 ones TEC44026	7 hundreds TEC44026

Names _____

RELAY RACE

	Player 1	Winner		Player 2	
Leg 1	_____ four-digit number	☐	☐	Leg 1	_____ four-digit number
Leg 2	_____ five-digit number	☐	☐	Leg 2	_____ five-digit number
Leg 3	_____ five-digit number	☐	☐	Leg 3	_____ five-digit number
Leg 4	_____ six-digit number	☐	☐	Leg 4	_____ six-digit number
Leg 5	_____ seven-digit number	☐	☐	Leg 5	_____ seven-digit number

Total Points: _____   **Total Points:** _____

©The Mailbox® • TEC44026 • Aug./Sept. 2006

128 THE MAILBOX **Note to the teacher:** Use with "Relay Race" on page 127. Players will need scissors to complete this page.

Sports- Shoe Sales

Order the sales by style from least to greatest. The first one has been done for you.

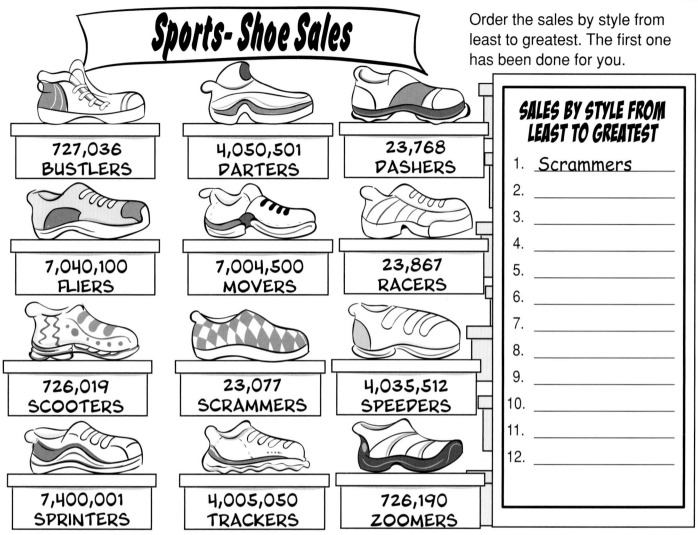

727,036 BUSTLERS

4,050,501 DARTERS

23,768 DASHERS

7,040,100 FLIERS

7,004,500 MOVERS

23,867 RACERS

726,019 SCOOTERS

23,077 SCRAMMERS

4,035,512 SPEEDERS

7,400,001 SPRINTERS

4,005,050 TRACKERS

726,190 ZOOMERS

SALES BY STYLE FROM LEAST TO GREATEST

1. Scrammers
2. _____
3. _____
4. _____
5. _____
6. _____
7. _____
8. _____
9. _____
10. _____
11. _____
12. _____

Write each standard-form number above next to its matching word form below.

13. seven hundred twenty-six thousand, one hundred ninety _____

14. seven million, four thousand, five hundred _____

15. twenty-three thousand, seventy-seven _____

16. four million, thirty-five thousand, five hundred twelve _____

17. twenty-three thousand, eight hundred sixty-seven _____

18. four million, five thousand, fifty _____

19. seven million, forty thousand, one hundred _____

20. seven hundred twenty-six thousand, nineteen _____

21. twenty-three thousand, seven hundred sixty-eight _____

22. four million, fifty thousand, five hundred one _____

23. seven million, four hundred thousand, one _____

24. seven hundred twenty-seven thousand, thirty-six

MATCH 'EM UP!

DIRECTIONS:
Write each product code in standard form. Then use the clues on the boxes to label each product with the correct code.

RUNNING SHOES

__ __ . __ __ __ __

Tens digit is the sum of tenths digit and thousandths digit.

RUNNING SHORTS

__ __ __ . __ __

Hundreds digit is the smallest. Tenths digit is 4.

RUNNING SHIRTS

__ __ . __ __ __

Hundredths digit minus thousandths digit equals ones digit.

HOODIES

__ __ __ . __ __

Product of tens digit and hundredths digit is 10.

RUNNERS' SAFETY VESTS

__ __ . __ __ __

Tenths digit is the same as thousandths digit.

RUNNING SOCKS

__ __ . __ __

Sum of ones digit and tenths digit is 15. Product of tens digit and tenths digit is 40.

RUNNING JACKETS

__ __ __ . __ __ __

Product of tens digit and hundredths digit is 4.

RUNNING PANTS

__ __ . __ __

Tenths digit equals hundredths digit.

PRODUCT CODES

1. fifty-seven and eighty thousandths _____
2. fifty-six and ninety-nine hundredths _____
3. fifty-seven and eight tenths _____
4. one hundred twenty-eight and five hundredths _____
5. one hundred twenty-eight and four tenths _____
6. ninety-two and eight hundred forty-one thousandths _____
7. one hundred twenty-nine and twenty-six thousandths _____
8. fifty-seven and eighty-one thousandths _____

Bonus Box: On the back of this page, list the standard form of the product codes in order from least to greatest.

On the Move

Activities for Practicing Slides, Flips, and Turns

TOTALLY TRANSFORMED
Drawing the results of translations, reflections, and rotations

For some nifty practice with transformations, give each student a copy of page 133. In one square on the directions sheet, he draws a simple symbol, such as a heart, an isosceles triangle, an uppercase letter, or a one-digit number. Then he writes five brief directions about how to transform that symbol. On the answer key, he draws and numbers the symbol's corresponding transformations according to those directions. Once his answer key is verified, he folds the paper in half, tapes the open edges together, and trades papers—directions side up—with a partner. He follows his partner's written directions and then turns the paper over to check his work. To create a self-checking center instead, laminate all the sheets after verifying the answer keys. Then fold the sheets in half, hole-punch them, and put them in a 6" x 9" three-ring binder at a center along with wipe-off markers!

Having students perform transformations correctly and with consistency is just one benefit of using these terrific robotic activities!

with ideas by Melissa Bryan, Valley Forge Middle School, Wayne, PA

CHECK IT OUT!
Using concrete models to demonstrate translations, reflections, and rotations

This two-player game is perfect for practicing slides, flips, and turns. Laminate a copy of page 134 to construction paper for durability; then cut out the gameboard, spinner, and game pieces. Fold each game piece along the center line; then glue the back sides together. Put the cutouts in a resealable plastic bag, along with a pencil and paper clip, and place the bag at a center. To use the center, players align five matching game pieces in squares on opposite sides of the gameboard. Each player takes a turn spinning to determine which transformation to perform with a game piece of her choice. When a spin results in a game piece landing on a square occupied by her opponent, she captures the opponent's game piece. If a player cannot make a move after a particular spin, she loses her turn. The player who moves more game pieces to the opposite side of the gameboard wins!

WHAT WEIRD WRITING!
Performing rotations and reflections

Students will gawk at their names after putting them through these eye-popping transformations! Each child glues white paper to one side of a sheet of construction paper and colorful paper to the other side. He chooses one of the following directions written on the board and writes it at the top of the white sheet: "Rotate 90°/180°/270° clockwise" or "Reflect up/down/right/left." Below the direction, he writes his name in uppercase letters and adds a horizontal or vertical line as shown. On the colorful sheet, he creates an answer key showing how each letter in his name should appear after the directed transformation has been made. The keys are checked; then students trade projects, white side up. Each child performs the written direction on another sheet of paper and then turns his partner's project over to check his work. For an eye-catching display, hang the projects from the ceiling!

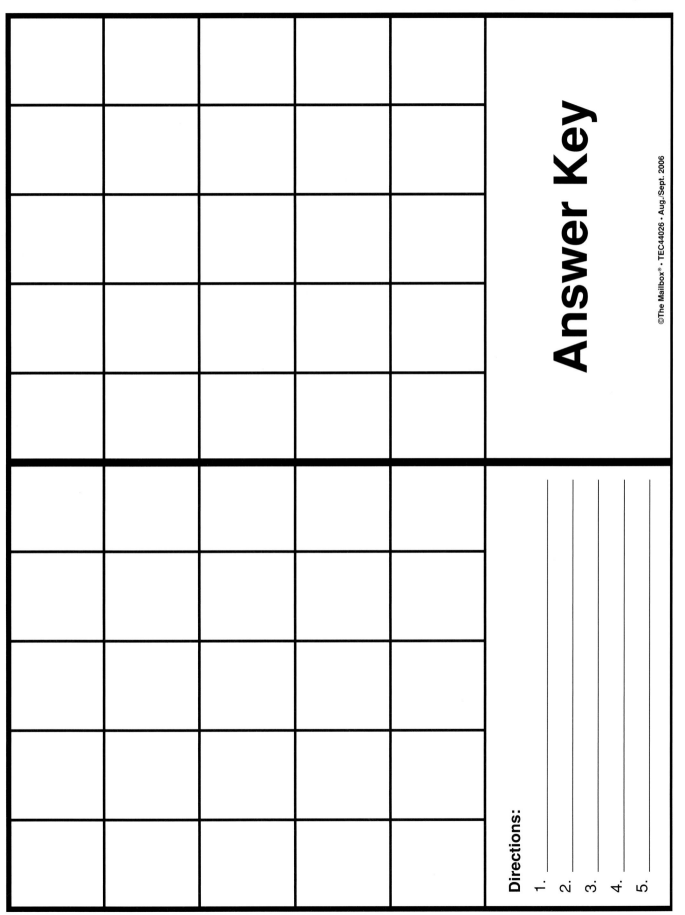

Answer Key

©The Mailbox® • TEC44026 • Aug./Sept. 2006

Directions:
1. _____
2. _____
3. _____
4. _____
5. _____

Gameboard, Spinner, and Game Pieces

Use with "Check It Out!" on page 132.

TEC44026

Confused Robot

Which ones are right?

Read each direction.
Perform the move with each letter, one at a time, in the given word.
Cut out the letters below if you need help.
Circle the correct answer.

1. Rotate 90° clockwise: MOO.

   a. ≲ O O

   b. W O O

   c. ≲ O O

2. Reflect right: TOM.

   a. ⊢ O ≲

   b. T O M

   c. ⊥ O W

3. Reflect down: MAD.

   a. ≲ ∀ ◰

   b. ≲ ∀ ◰

   c. W ∀ D

4. Rotate 180° clockwise: SOAP.

   a. S O ∀ d

   b. ꙅ O A ꟼ

   c. ꙅ O ∀ b

5. Rotate 270° clockwise: REST.

   a. ꓤ ⪫ ꙅ ⊢

   b. ꓩ Ǝ S ⊥

   c. ꓤ ⪫ ꙅ ⊢

6. Reflect left: MIT.

   a. W I ⊥

   b. M I T

   c. ≲ ⊣ ⊢

Bonus Box: Which word(s) did not change after the move?

©The Mailbox® • TEC44026 • Aug./Sept. 2006 • Key p. 310

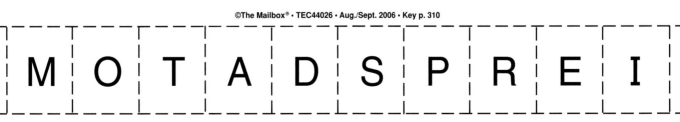

| M | O | T | A | D | S | P | R | E | I |

Note to the teacher: Each student may need scissors to complete this page.

THE MAILBOX 135

Timber-r-r!

Clearing the Way for Adding and Subtracting Multidigit Numbers

LUMBERJACK LOGIC
Problem solving

This intriguing math trick will make adding three-digit numbers as much fun as logrolling! Ask a child to write any three-digit number on the board. Near this number, record your prediction for the sum of three such numbers ([child's number + 1,000] – 1). Next, have the student write a second three-digit number below his first number. Write the third number yourself, using digits that when added to the child's second number equal 999. Finally, ask the student to add all three numbers together and then compare the sum to your prediction. He'll think you're brilliant! Repeat the activity several times, inviting the first person to figure out how the trick works to take your place. Conclude by selecting one child to explain to everyone how the trick works.

Teacher's prediction	1,745
Student's first number	746
Student's second number	891
Teacher's number	+ 108
	1,745

Adding and subtracting a forest of multidigit numbers

won't be a problem if your loggers use these mighty activities to tackle the task!

with ideas by Ann Fisher, Toledo, OH

LOG CHOP
Game for two or three players

Cutting a number's size is just an ax swing away with this small-group activity. Program several copies of the game cards on page 138, writing a different six-digit number on each log card and a different three-, four-, or five-digit number on each ax card. To begin, players shuffle the cards and stack them in two piles. Each player draws a card from each pile and writes a math problem with the cards' numbers, subtracting the number on the ax from the number on the log. Players check their work by adding the two smaller numbers together. The player with the smallest difference earns one point. The first player to win five points becomes the Log Chop champion!

Line up the digits,
Beginning at the right.
Keep the columns in order
And line them up tight.

Borrow from the left.
Carry from the right.
Start with the ones.
That's always right!

253,904
− 16,478
237,426

253,904

16,478

MEMORY LOG
Study aid

If students have trouble remembering specific addition and subtraction facts, they can encounter a logjam when solving problems with multidigit numbers. To prevent such pileups, give each child a copy of the log pattern on page 138 to cut out. Have her label the cutout with her most troublesome facts, writing addition facts on one side and subtraction facts on the other. (Allow her to label a separate memory log with tough-to-learn multiplication and division facts.) Then have her color the cutout. Once she folds it along the center line and glues the sides together, she'll have a handy tool to keep the problem-solving waterways clear!

MEMORY LOG

Addition Facts

6 + 7 = 13

7 + 9 = 16

8 + 5 = 13

6 + 9 = 15

MEMORY LOG

Subtraction Facts

15 − 8 = 7

16 − 7 = 9

13 − 6 = 7

14 − 8 = 6

Game Cards

Use with "Log Chop" on page 137.

TEC44027

TEC44027

Log Pattern

Use with "Memory Log" on page 137.

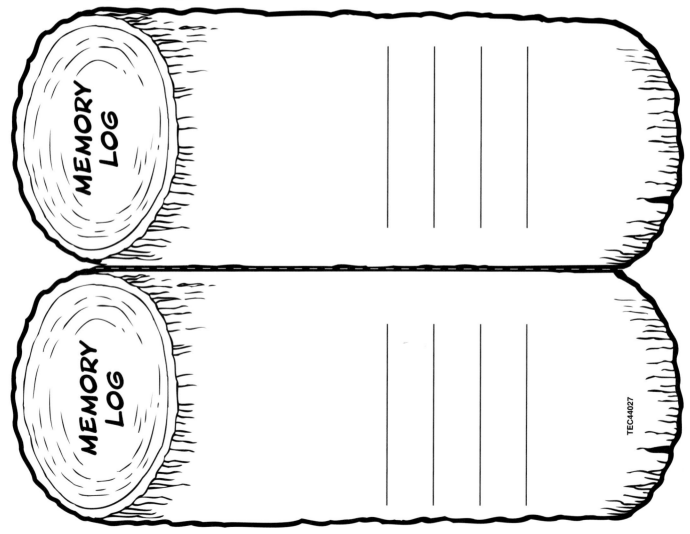

TEC44027

Lumberjack Lingo

Solve each problem by writing a letter from the code in each
 answer blank.
If your answers are correct, the letters will spell a logging word.
The first one has been done for you.

1. C + <u>U</u> + <u>T</u> = 20,739

2. ___ + O + ___ = 57,808

3. S + ___ + ___ = 49,751

4. ___ + R + E + ___ = 798,603

5. C + ___ + O + ___ = 432,784

6. ___ + O + O + ___ = 95,752

7. ___ + ___ = 22,243

8. P + ___ + ___ + E = 634,276

Code

A = 13,601	H = 289,413	P = 97,045
C = 4,082	I = 13,602	R = 38,261
D = 5,903	L = 8,419	S = 30,789
E = 375,062	N = 148,567	T = 10,218
G = 7,145	O = 42,244	U = 6,439

W = 5,361
X = 8,642

Fenced In

An Entire Estate of Perimeter Activities

Elliot's Estate

Pigpen
4 inches

Cornfield
14 inches

Cow Pasture
14 inches

Wheat Field
18 inches

Horse Corral
10 inches

Vegetable
Garden
5 inches

House
9 inches

Barn
8 inches

BUILD YOUR OWN FIEFDOM!
Problem solving

This activity transforms students into landowners who find the perimeter of and decide where to locate structures, fields, pastures, pens, gardens, and corrals on their acres of land. Have each child refer to a copy of the guidelines at the top of page 142 to cut out a colorful rectangle for each farm part listed and then label it with the correct name and perimeter. Then have him arrange the pieces on a sheet of brown construction paper (his land) and glue them in place. Once he names the estate, invite him to share his project with the class. To practice finding the perimeter of other polygons, have pairs of students cut apart a copy of the cards and answer key on page 143, solve the problems, and then use the key to check each other's answers.

Cultivate this rolling expanse of perimeter activities
to reap a harvest of student understanding!

with ideas by John Hughes, Green River, UT,
and Christina Scannell, San Jose, CA

A-HUNTING WE WILL GO
Same perimeter but different shape

Help students see that the distance around some rectangles can be the same even if their shapes are not. Assign each group of four students a different one of the following numbers: 16, 18, 20, 22, 24, 26, 28, or 30. Then have each child draw on a copy of a graph card at the bottom of page 142 a rectangle whose perimeter equals the assigned number but is shaped differently from the other rectangles in his group. Verify each perimeter and pencil it lightly on the back of the drawing. Collect and shuffle the drawings; then place each one in a different room location. Also assign each group a different number than before. Then, at your signal, challenge each four-some to be the first group to collect all four rectangles whose perimeters match the new number. If time permits, repeat the activity to see whether students can scavenge faster the second time around!

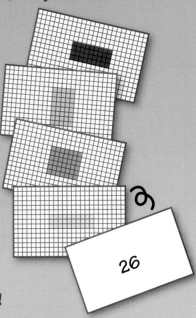

The length is five units.
The width is three units.

CATCH ME IF YOU CAN!
Mental math

Head outside to play a version of Steal the Bacon that has participants calculating perimeter mentally! Divide students into two teams and have the teams line up facing each other about 30 feet apart. Place a whiteboard eraser on the ground midway between the teams. Assign players diagonally across from each other the same number. Then call out a rectangle's dimensions. All players immediately calculate the perimeter. As soon as a player realizes that the perimeter of that rectangle is her assigned number, she races to pick up the eraser and returns to her place in line. If she makes it back without being tagged by her opponent, her team wins a point. If she gets tagged before she reaches her spot in line, neither team scores a point. The first team to earn ten points wins.

THE LINEUP
Ordering numbers

Determining and then arranging the perimeters of polygons from least to greatest is the focus of this small-group activity. First, each child draws a polygon on a copy of a graph card at the bottom of page 142; collect and shuffle the cards. Next, one group of six students comes to the front of the room. Each group member receives one card. At your signal, the other groups time these students to see how long it takes them to calculate the perimeters of the polygons on the cards and then line up so that the displayed cards show the shapes ordered from least to greatest perimeter. The team that lines up correctly in the least amount of time after all groups have had a turn wins.

Measurement Guidelines

Use with "Build Your Own Fiefdom!" on page 140.

Farm Part	Dimensions
House	2 in. x 2.5 in.
Barn	2 in. x 2 in.
Cornfield	3 in. x 4 in.
Wheat Field	4 in. x 5 in.
Horse Corral	2 in. x 3 in.
Pigpen	1 in. x 1 in.
Cow Pasture	2 in. x 5 in.
Vegetable Garden	1 in. x 1.5 in.

TEC44027

Half-Centimeter Graph Cards

Use with "A-Hunting We Will Go" and "The Lineup" on page 141.

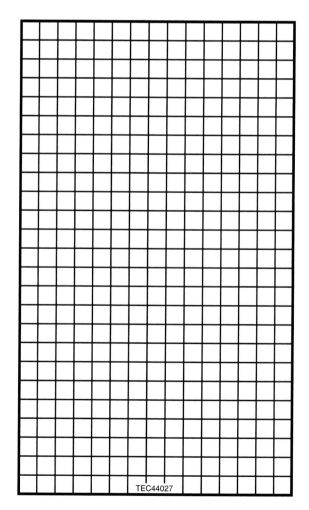

TEC44027

TEC44027

1.

I have four congruent sides.
One side is 5 cm long.
What is my perimeter?

TEC44027

2.

I have three sides.
My longest sides are 7 cm.
My shortest side is 3 cm.
I am an isosceles triangle.
What is my perimeter?

TEC44027

3.

I am a regular octagon.
One of my sides is 4 cm long.
What is my perimeter?

TEC44027

4.

I have three sides.
Each side is _____ long.
My perimeter is 27 cm.

TEC44027

5.

I am a regular hexagon.
Each side is 6 cm long.
My perimeter is _____.

TEC44027

6.

I have four sides.
My length is 7 cm.
My width is _____.
My perimeter is 20 cm.

TEC44027

7.

I have four sides.
My length is _____.
My width is 5 cm.
My perimeter is 30 cm.

TEC44027

8.

I am a regular pentagon.
One side is 3 cm long.
My perimeter is _____.

TEC44027

Answer Key for Perimeter Cards

1. 20 cm
2. 17 cm
3. 32 cm
4. 9 cm
5. 36 cm
6. 3 cm
7. 10 cm
8. 15 cm

TEC44027

PASTURE PROBLEMS

Find the perimeter of each pasture. Then match each cow to the correct pasture by writing the cow's name inside the fence. Circle the cow that doesn't belong.

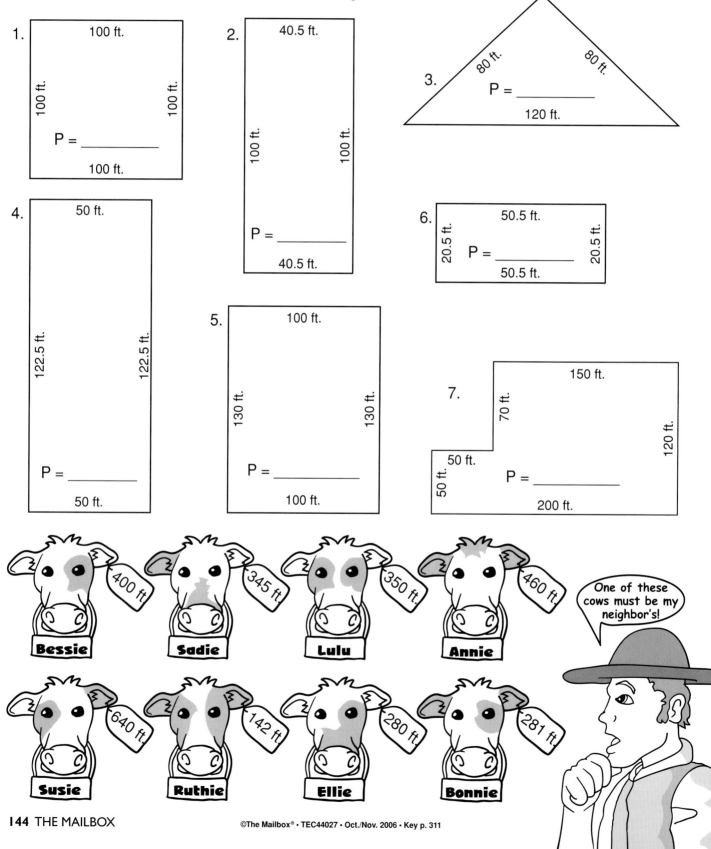

1.
100 ft.
100 ft.
100 ft.
100 ft.
P = _____

2.
40.5 ft.
100 ft.
100 ft.
40.5 ft.
P = _____

3.
80 ft.
80 ft.
120 ft.
P = _____

4.
50 ft.
122.5 ft.
122.5 ft.
50 ft.
P = _____

5.
100 ft.
130 ft.
130 ft.
100 ft.
P = _____

6.
50.5 ft.
20.5 ft.
20.5 ft.
50.5 ft.
P = _____

7.
150 ft.
70 ft.
50 ft.
50 ft.
200 ft.
120 ft.
P = _____

400 ft — Bessie
345 ft. — Sadie
350 ft. — Lulu
460 ft. — Annie
640 ft — Susie
142 ft — Ruthie
280 ft — Ellie
281 ft — Bonnie

One of these cows must be my neighbor's!

Name_____

Forgetful Fred

Use the total distance around each field to find the missing measurement.

I didn't write them down.

1. Perimeter of cornfield: 786 ft.
   Missing measurement = _____

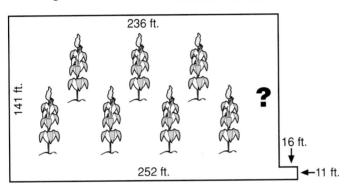

236 ft.

141 ft.

?

16 ft.

252 ft.

←11 ft.

2. Perimeter of wheat field: 982 ft.
   Missing measurement = _____

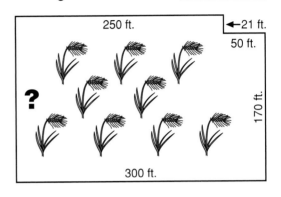

250 ft.

←21 ft.

50 ft.

?

170 ft.

300 ft.

3. Perimeter of pumpkin field: 1,500 ft.
   Missing measurement = _____

40 ft.   350 ft.   40 ft.

50 ft.   50 ft.

?

260 ft.

450 ft.

4. Perimeter of turnip field: 1,016 ft.
   Missing measurement = _____

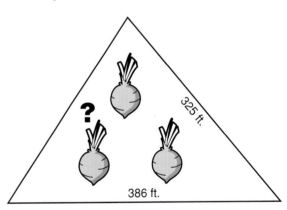

?

325 ft.

386 ft.

5. Perimeter of carrot field: 652 ft.
   Missing measurement = _____

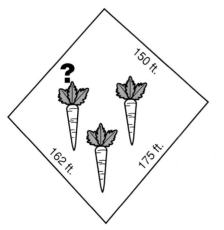

?

150 ft.

162 ft.

175 ft.

6. Perimeter of potato field: 626 ft.
   Missing measurement = _____

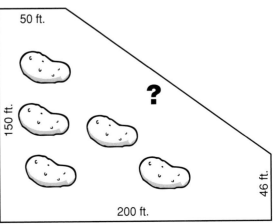

50 ft.

?

150 ft.

46 ft.

200 ft.

Icy Treats
Cool Fraction Activities

1. How many ice cubes can the tray hold?
2. If one ice cube is taken from the tray, what fraction of the cubes is left?
3. If half of the ice cubes in the tray are removed, what fraction of the cubes is left?
4. If three ice cubes are taken from the tray, what fraction of the cubes is left?

CUBE COUNTING
Parts of a whole

For this hands-on activity, provide each small group of students with an inexpensive ice cube tray and several small paper squares. Have the groups place paper squares in the tray to help them answer and discuss questions similar to those shown. Follow up by challenging each group member to draw on graph paper one or more rectangles that each represent the array of a different-size ice cube tray and then answer the same questions. Students will have fractions down cold!

Give students the scoop on fractions with these solid tips and ideas!

with ideas by Ann Fisher, Toledo, OH

To make this activity more challenging, first match the numerical forms of the fractions and then flip to the shaded sides to check the answer!

MAKE IT STICK!
Equivalent fractions

To create this self-checking center, cut five small index cards into equal-size strips. Shade the front of one strip to represent a common fraction; then write the fraction on the back. Program a second strip in the same manner, using a fraction that is equivalent to the first. Repeat the process with the remaining strips, using different fractions. When finished, place the fraction sticks in a baby food jar or plastic cup at a center. To use the center, a student selects a stick and places it shaded side up in front of her. She then draws a second stick and places it shaded side up alongside the first one. If the shaded parts are equivalent, she turns the sticks over to check and records the fractions on paper. If the shaded parts are not equivalent, she pulls another one from the container and continues in this manner until all the sticks are matched.

CHILL OUT!
Review game

Prepare for this challenging competition by labeling a set of 12–15 small cards with common fractions. Program a second set of cards with matching diagrams to use as an answer key. Place each set of cards in a resealable plastic bag at a center along with an ice cube tray and several small paper squares for each player. To play, one student draws a fraction card from the bag and places it faceup for all players to see. Each player then places paper squares in an ice cube tray to represent an equivalent fraction for the one being displayed. Players use the answer key cards to check their work. Each player with a correct answer gets one point. A player earns a bonus point if his correct answer is different from other players' answers. Play continues in this manner with the next player drawing a new fraction card. The player with the most points after all cards have been drawn wins.

Fractions From the Freezer

Complete each step. Then answer the questions.

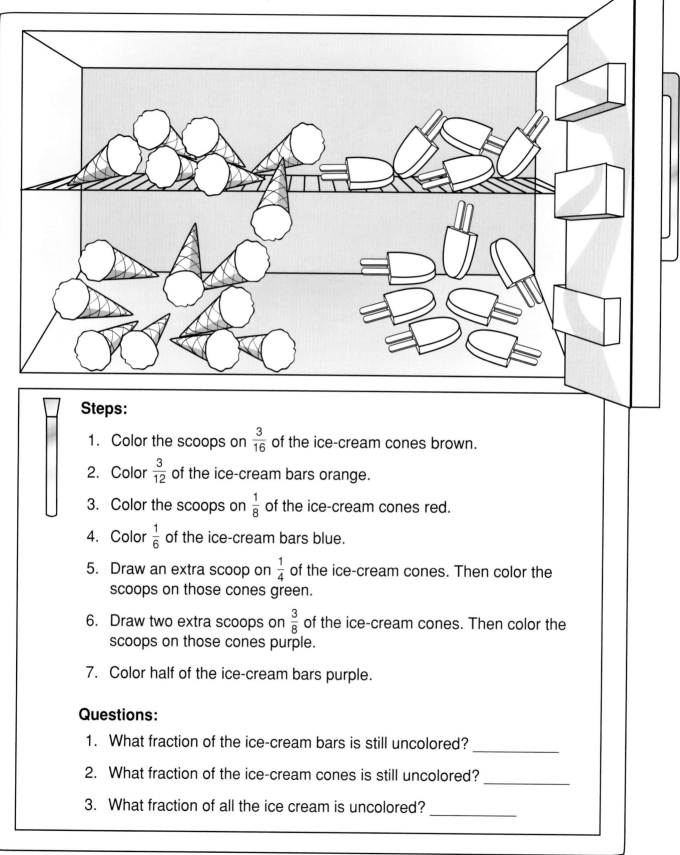

Steps:

1. Color the scoops on $\frac{3}{16}$ of the ice-cream cones brown.

2. Color $\frac{3}{12}$ of the ice-cream bars orange.

3. Color the scoops on $\frac{1}{8}$ of the ice-cream cones red.

4. Color $\frac{1}{6}$ of the ice-cream bars blue.

5. Draw an extra scoop on $\frac{1}{4}$ of the ice-cream cones. Then color the scoops on those cones green.

6. Draw two extra scoops on $\frac{3}{8}$ of the ice-cream cones. Then color the scoops on those cones purple.

7. Color half of the ice-cream bars purple.

Questions:

1. What fraction of the ice-cream bars is still uncolored? _____

2. What fraction of the ice-cream cones is still uncolored? _____

3. What fraction of all the ice cream is uncolored? _____

©The Mailbox® • TEC44028 • Dec./Jan. 2006–7 • Key p. 311

Name _____

COOL TREATS

Color the equivalent fractions by the code.

COLOR CODE

purple = $\frac{1}{2}$

green = $\frac{1}{4}$

blue = $\frac{1}{3}$

brown = $\frac{2}{3}$

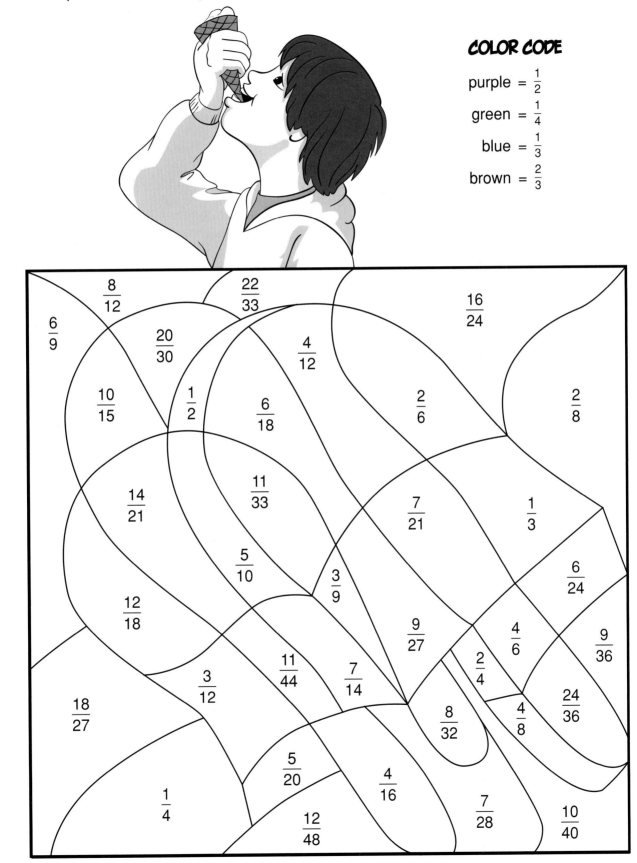

Hit the Slopes!

Adventures With Angles and Triangles

Code
A = acute
R = right
O = obtuse

O

A

R

R

A

STICKS, PICKS, 'N' STRAWS
Interior angles

Allow pairs of students about 15 minutes to design unconventional closed shapes using craft sticks, toothpicks, or plastic straws. As they work, have the partners identify whether each interior angle is acute, right, or obtuse. Then have them glue their favorite design to construction paper, measure the angles with a protractor, and label the vertex of each angle by the code shown above. If desired, have students include the degrees as well. For added fun, poll the partners to see whose shape has the most of each type of angle and have them share those designs with the class!

Explore these awesome angle and triangle
activities. Your students will definitely enjoy each run!

with ideas by Melissa Hauck Bryan, Valley Forge Middle School, Wayne, PA

THE ABCS OF ANGLES
Identifying, reviewing

To create this self-checking class booklet, first make enough copies of page 152 so that each student will have a booklet page. Also cut enough 4" x 6" index cards into six 2" x 2" squares so that each child will have three squares. Next, list the uppercase alphabet on the board. Point out the angles in each letter, one at a time, and have students identify each angle's type. As they do, label each letter's angles using the code on page 150. Afterward, have each student write her first name on unlined paper using large block letters, label the angles in each letter by the code, and tally the number of each angle type. Check her work. Then give her a booklet page. Have her print her name inside the rectangle, record in the corresponding boxes the total number of each angle type, and tape a square over each box as a flap to hide each answer. Once you compile the pages, the book is ready to use!

HUMAN TRIANGLES
Modeling

For this out-of-your-seat review, write "Acute," "Obtuse," and "Right" on separate index cards. Then divide students into four groups. Have one group of students stay at their seats with their heads down and eyes closed. Give each of the other groups a different index card. The students in each group then create that type of triangle by lying on the floor so that each child's body forms one side of a triangle or part of a side. When all three groups are positioned, Group 4 goes to each group and guesses the type of triangle its members have formed. After the guessing ends, Groups 1–3 reveal their cards to Group 4. Collect the cards and repeat the activity until every group has formed each type of triangle and has also been the guessers.

Booklet Pages

Use with "The ABCs of Angles" on page 151.

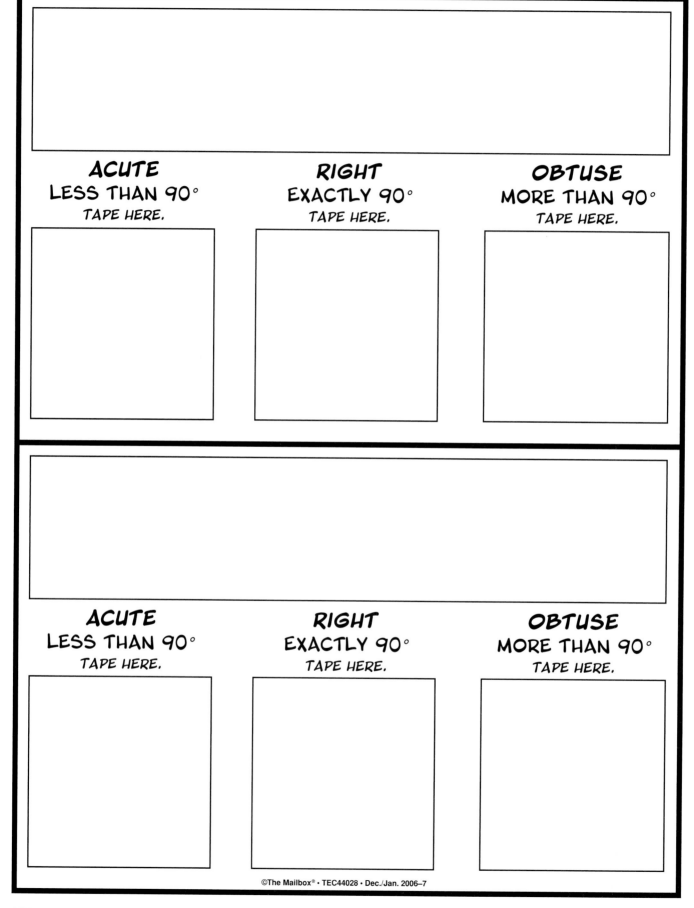

ACUTE
LESS THAN 90°
TAPE HERE.

RIGHT
EXACTLY 90°
TAPE HERE.

OBTUSE
MORE THAN 90°
TAPE HERE.

ACUTE
LESS THAN 90°
TAPE HERE.

RIGHT
EXACTLY 90°
TAPE HERE.

OBTUSE
MORE THAN 90°
TAPE HERE.

Cruisin' On!

Measure each angle with a protractor.
Record each measurement. Then find the sums.

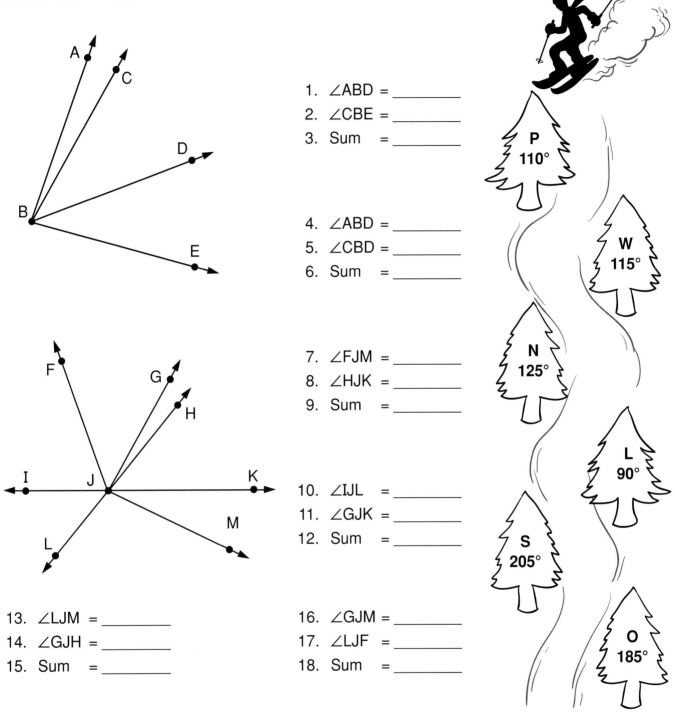

1. ∠ABD = _____
2. ∠CBE = _____
3. Sum   = _____

4. ∠ABD = _____
5. ∠CBD = _____
6. Sum   = _____

7. ∠FJM = _____
8. ∠HJK = _____
9. Sum   = _____

10. ∠IJL = _____
11. ∠GJK = _____
12. Sum   = _____

13. ∠LJM = _____
14. ∠GJH = _____
15. Sum   = _____

16. ∠GJM = _____
17. ∠LJF = _____
18. Sum   = _____

P 110°
W 115°
N 125°
L 90°
S 205°
O 185°

Complete the sentence by writing the letter for each sum on its matching numbered line below.

To control speed, a skier can do a ____ ____ ____ ____ ____ ____ ____ ____ .
205° 125° 185° 115° 110° 90° 185° 115°

Up and Away!

Exploring Fractions, Decimals, and Percents

CROSS-COUNTRY CHALLENGE
Review game

Set sail across the United States to search for percents! Make a copy of the game cards on pages 156 and 159. Laminate the cards and cut them apart. Next, mount a copy of the gameboard on page 157 onto construction paper and laminate it. Store the cards and gameboard in a large resealable bag along with a calculator. Then place the bag at a center with a copy of the rules shown and two different-colored wipe-off markers. To play the game, pairs of students stack the cards facedown between them, read the rules, and then begin!

adapted from an idea by Karen Slattery
St. Vincent's Elementary
Oakville, Ontario, Canada

5% of 100
5

Rules for two players:
1. Player B draws a card and reads it aloud to Player A. Player A solves the problem, using a calculator if necessary. If Player A's answer is correct, he colors a state on the gameboard and then discards the card. If the answer is incorrect, Player A colors nothing and places the card at the bottom of the pile.
2. Player A reads a card aloud to Player B. If Player B's answer is correct, he colors a state on the gameboard using a different color of marker.
3. If the deck runs out of cards before the end of the game, players shuffle the cards in the discard pile to continue.
4. The first player to color a line of states (or, for a shorter game, more states in a line) that connects the East Coast and West Coast wins.

Students' knowledge of fractions, decimals, and percents will rise to new heights with this high-flying collection of activities!

with ideas by Jennifer Otter, Oak Ridge, NC

MYSTERY WORDS
Equivalent fractions and decimals

Have each child secretly select a classroom object. Then have him write four clues, similar to those shown, that could help someone identify that object. Explain that each clue should include a different fraction or decimal. Then have each student trade papers with a partner and try to solve his partner's puzzle. If desired, collect the puzzles and use a different puzzle each day as a warm-up exercise before class begins!

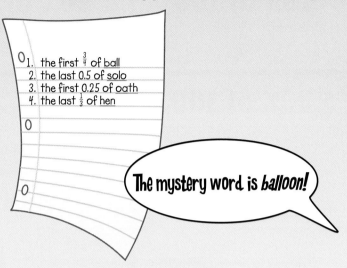

1. the first $\frac{3}{4}$ of ball
2. the last 0.5 of solo
3. the first 0.25 of oath
4. the last $\frac{1}{3}$ of hen

The mystery word is *balloon!*

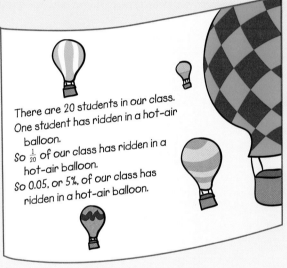

There are 20 students in our class.
One student has ridden in a hot-air balloon.
So $\frac{1}{20}$ of our class has ridden in a hot-air balloon.
So 0.05, or 5%, of our class has ridden in a hot-air balloon.

PICTURING PERCENTS
Representing fractions and decimals as percents

Start by brainstorming with students a list of favorite activities. Next, poll each child and record on the board how many have completed each activity. Then have each student use the directions below to write four true sentences about his class. When he's finished, have him copy the sentences onto unlined paper and add illustrations. Post the completed projects on a display titled "Picturing Percents."

Directions:
Sentence 1: Tell the total number of students.
Sentence 2: Write a statement that describes part of those students.
Sentence 3: Rewrite sentence 2 as a fraction statement.
Sentence 4: Rewrite sentence 3, replacing the fraction with its equivalent decimal and percent.

ROLL 'N' REDUCE
Writing fractions in simplest form

For this simple partner game, provide each pair of students with a die and a calculator. To play the game, Player 1 rolls the die three times. The first digit rolled becomes the numerator of a fraction. The second and third digits rolled become the fraction's two-digit denominator. Player 1 writes the fraction rolled in simplest form. If the fraction is already in simplest form, she must say so. Next, she writes the fraction as a decimal and as a percent. Player 2 uses the calculator to check her answers. If Player 1's answers are correct, she draws a star next to them. If her answers are not correct, she draws nothing and works with her partner to correct her work. Player 2 then takes a turn in the same manner. The player with more stars after ten rounds is the winner.

Four-sixteenths reduces to one-fourth, and that's the same as 25 hundredths and 25 percent!

$\frac{4}{16} = \frac{1}{4} = 0.25 = 25\%$ ☆

Game Cards

Use with "Cross-Country Challenge" on page 154.

10% of 100 10 TEC44029	**20% of 100** 20 TEC44029	**50% of 100** 50 TEC44029
30% of 100 30 TEC44029	**5% of 200** 10 TEC44029	**25% of 100** 25 TEC44029
10% of 80 8 TEC44029	**25% of 80** 20 TEC44029	**50% of 50** 25 TEC44029
100% of 500 500 TEC44029	**50% of 62** 31 TEC44029	**50% of 80** 40 TEC44029
50% of 150 75 TEC44029	**40% of 100** 40 TEC44029	**60% of 100** 60 TEC44029
40% of 200 80 TEC44029	**10% of 50** 5 TEC44029	**80% of 100** 80 TEC44029
75% of 100 75 TEC44029	**75% of 200** 150 TEC44029	**100% of 100** 100 TEC44029
5% of 100 5 TEC44029	$\frac{1}{2}$ = _____ **%** 50% TEC44029	$\frac{1}{4}$ = _____ **%** 25% TEC44029
$\frac{3}{4}$ = _____ **%** 75% TEC44029	$\frac{3}{5}$ = _____ **%** 60% TEC44029	$\frac{9}{10}$ = _____ **%** 90% TEC44029

©The Mailbox® • TEC44029 • Feb./Mar. 2007

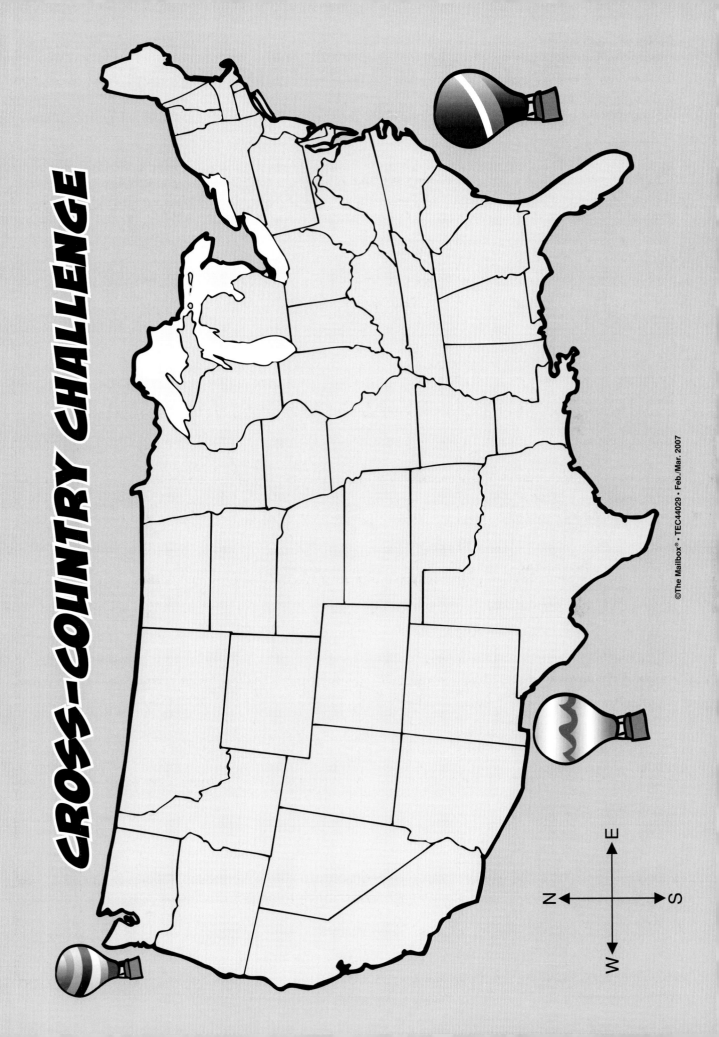

CROSS-COUNTRY CHALLENGE

High-Flying Percents

Convert each fraction to a decimal. Change each decimal to a percent. Then color by the code.

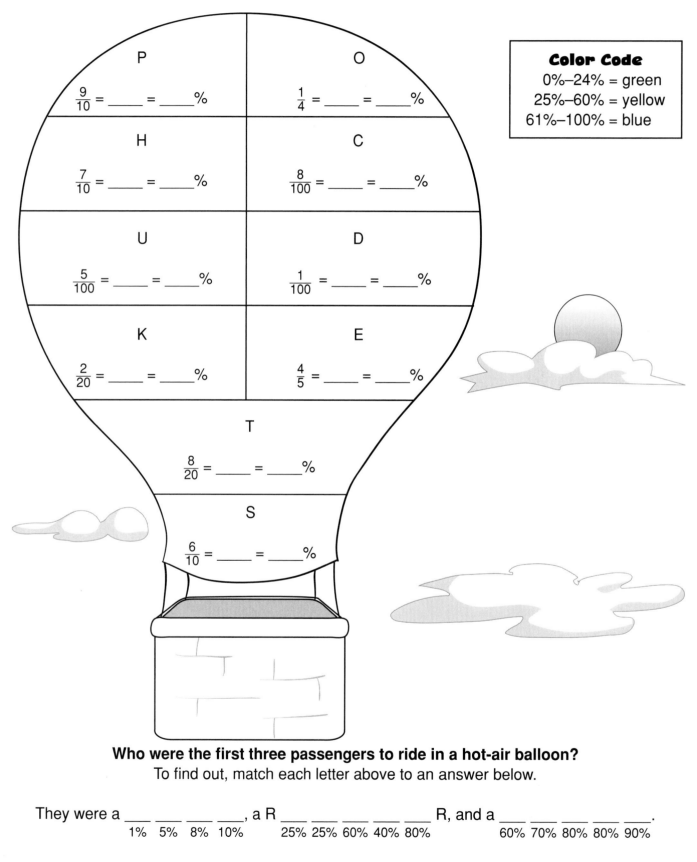

Color Code
0%–24% = green
25%–60% = yellow
61%–100% = blue

P
$\frac{9}{10}$ = _____ = _____%

O
$\frac{1}{4}$ = _____ = _____%

H
$\frac{7}{10}$ = _____ = _____%

C
$\frac{8}{100}$ = _____ = _____%

U
$\frac{5}{100}$ = _____ = _____%

D
$\frac{1}{100}$ = _____ = _____%

K
$\frac{2}{20}$ = _____ = _____%

E
$\frac{4}{5}$ = _____ = _____%

T
$\frac{8}{20}$ = _____ = _____%

S
$\frac{6}{10}$ = _____ = _____%

Who were the first three passengers to ride in a hot-air balloon?
To find out, match each letter above to an answer below.

They were a ___ ___ ___ ___ , a R ___ ___ ___ ___ ___ R, and a ___ ___ ___ ___ ___ .
1% 5% 8% 10%   25% 25% 60% 40% 80%   60% 70% 80% 80% 90%

©The Mailbox® • TEC44029 • Feb./Mar. 2007 • Key p. 311

25% of 80 20 TEC44029	**75% of 40** 30 TEC44029	**75% of 80** 60 TEC44029
75% of 88 66 TEC44029	**25% of 40** 10 TEC44029	**15% of 100** 15 TEC44029
15% of 200 30 TEC44029	**25% of 200** 50 TEC44029	**30% of 300** 90 TEC44029
10% of 300 30 TEC44029	**40% of 300** 120 TEC44029	**10% of 1,000** 100 TEC44029
60% of 320 192 TEC44029	**90% of 300** 270 TEC44029	**50 of 410** 205 TEC44029
25% of 480 120 TEC44029	**25% of 400** 100 TEC44029	**10% of 560** 56 TEC44029
20% of 780 156 TEC44029	**10% of 800** 80 TEC44029	**30% of 900** 270 TEC44029
20% of 900 180 TEC44029	**50% of 900** 450 TEC44029	**100% of 900** 900 TEC44029
50% of 400 200 TEC44029	**50% of 60** 30 TEC44029	**10% of 200** 20 TEC44029

Revved Up!
Finding Mean, Median, Mode, and Range

How many pencils are in your desk right now?

How many days did you play outside last week?

How many minutes per week do you read for fun?

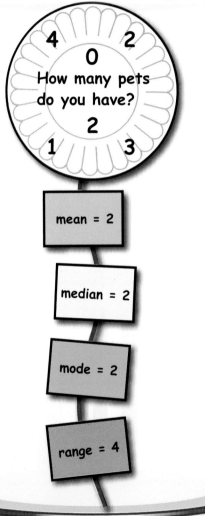

4 2
0
How many pets do you have?
2
1 3

mean = 2

median = 2

mode = 2

range = 4

MOBILE MATTERS
Small-group project

Divide students into groups of four to six students. Give each group four index cards and a paper plate labeled with one of the questions shown. Have each group member write his answer to the question directly on the plate. Then have the group calculate the mean, median, mode, and range of the data and label separate index cards with the corresponding answers. Check students' work. Then have each group tape its cards to a length of yarn and join the yarn to the plate as if adding a tail to a kite. Hang the completed mobiles in the classroom as eye-catching reminders of each type of statistic.

These well-designed data analysis activities can help put your students in the driver's seat!

with ideas by Terry Healy, Marlatt Elementary, Manhattan, KS

IT'S ALL IN THE CARDS!
Review game

Divide students into groups of four; then subdivide each group into two teams of two. Give each group a copy of the rules card on page 162, a calculator, and a deck of cards with the face cards, aces, and twos removed. To play, a player on Team 1 draws a card from the deck and turns it faceup. The players on Team 2 draw a number of cards equal to the number on the displayed card and then perform the action directed by the rules. If the answer is correct, Team 2 earns the same number of points as its answer. If incorrect, no points are awarded. If the required action is to find the mode and there is no mode for the cards drawn, the points earned equal the number on the lowest card drawn. Then the cards are placed at the bottom of the deck and play alternates. The team with more points when time is called wins.

PLAYING CARD	ACTION
Odd-numbered red card	Find the mean. Round it to the nearest whole number.
Even-numbered red card	Find the median
Odd-numbered black card	
Even-numbered black card	

The mean is 6.

"AD" IT UP!
Center

Clip kid-pleasing ads from newspaper and department store flyers. Make sure each ad includes the price. Sort the ads. Then glue the ads for kids' shirts and other tops on one side of a large paper grocery bag. On each of the other three sides, glue ads for kids' pants, shoes, or accessories. Put a class supply of the reproducible at the bottom of page 162 in the bag along with a calculator, and place the bag at a center. To use the center, a child chooses five items from each category and completes the page as directed.

Virginia Zeletzki, Banyan Creek Elementary
Delray Beach, FL

Rules Card

Use with "It's All in the Cards!" on page 161.

PLAYING CARD	ACTION
Odd-numbered red card	Find the mean. Round it to the nearest whole number.
Even-numbered red card	Find the median.
Odd-numbered black card	Find the mode.
Even-numbered black card	Find the range.

TEC44029

Name_____

All Decked Out

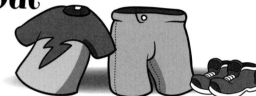

Choose five items from each group.
Record each item's price in the correct column.
Use the data in the chart to answer the questions.
Round each answer to the nearest dollar.

	Tops	Bottoms	Shoes	Accessories
Item 1				
Item 2				
Item 3				
Item 4				
Item 5				

1. What is the mean price of the shoes? _____

2. Is the price range greater for tops or for bottoms? _____

3. What is the mode for the accessories? _____

4. What is the median price of the tops? _____

5. What is the mode of the bottoms? _____

6. Which has the higher mean price: the shoes or the accessories? _____

©The Mailbox® • TEC44029 • Feb./Mar. 2007

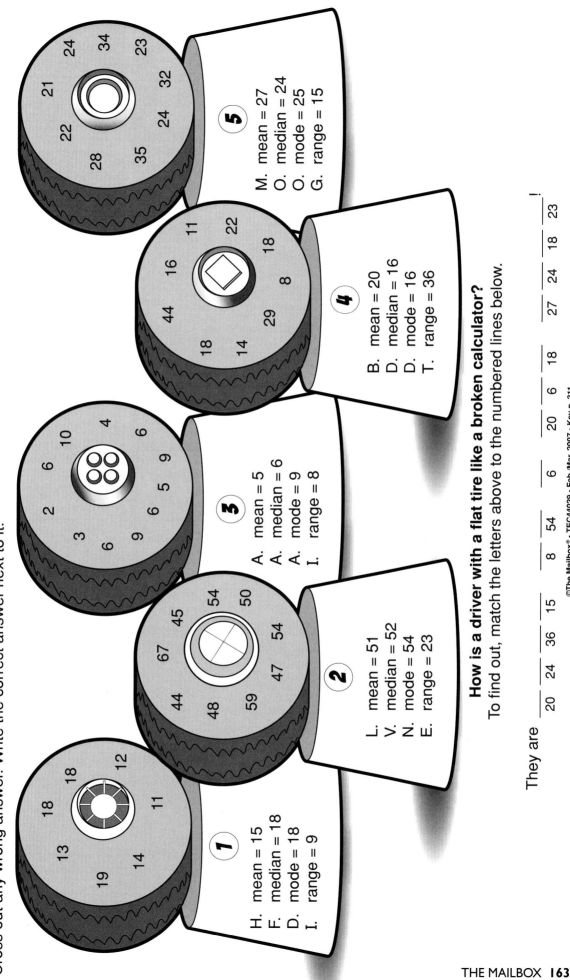

Name _____

WHERE THE RUBBER MEETS THE ROAD

Find the mean, median, mode, and range for each set of numbers.
Cross out any wrong answer. Write the correct answer next to it.

1
H. mean = 15
F. median = 18
D. mode = 18
I. range = 9

2
L. mean = 51
V. median = 52
N. mode = 54
E. range = 23

3
A. mean = 5
A. median = 6
A. mode = 9
I. range = 8

4
B. mean = 20
D. median = 16
D. mode = 16
T. range = 36

5
M. mean = 27
O. median = 24
O. mode = 25
G. range = 15

How is a driver with a flat tire like a broken calculator?
To find out, match the letters above to the numbered lines below.

They are $\overline{20}$ $\overline{24}$ $\overline{36}$ $\overline{15}$ $\overline{8}$ $\overline{54}$ $\overline{6}$ $\overline{6}$ $\overline{20}$ $\overline{6}$ $\overline{18}$ $\overline{27}$ $\overline{24}$ $\overline{18}$ $\overline{23}$!

Order Up!

Multiplying Decimals and Fractions

Score Card

Player: Mike

Round 1: $\dfrac{1}{2}$ x $\dfrac{3}{5}$ = $\dfrac{3}{10}$ Points: 1

Round 2: ____ x ____ = ____   Points: ____

Round 3: ____ x ____ = ____   Points: ____

Round 4: ____ x ____ = ____   Points: ____

Round 5: ____ x ____ = ____   Points: ____

Round 6: ____ x ____ = ____   Points: ____

Round 7: ____ x ____ = ____   Points: ____

Round 8: ____ x ____ = ____   Points: ____

Round 9: ____ x ____ = ____   Points: ____

Round 10: ____ x ____ = ____   Points: ____

Total Score _____

Points

product less than $\frac{1}{2}$ = 1 point

t greater than or equal to $\frac{1}{2}$ = 2 points

$\dfrac{3}{5}$

$\dfrac{1}{2}$

JUST A SLICE
Multiplying fractions

To prepare this fun center game, laminate a copy of the cards on page 167 and cut them out. Place the cards in a resealable plastic bag along with copies of the score card on page 166. To play, a pair of students shuffles the cards and stacks them facedown in a pile. Player A draws two cards. He multiplies the two fractions on the cards and records his answer on his score card. Player B checks Player A's answer. If the answer is correct, Player A awards himself the number of points as shown at the bottom of his score card and then puts his two cards in a discard pile. Player B then takes a turn in the same manner. The player with more points at the end of ten rounds wins.

Multiplication is the special of the day with this smorgasbord of fraction and decimal activities!

with ideas by John Hughes, Book Cliff Elementary, Green River, UT

PASS THE ROLLS!
Multiplying decimals to the hundredths

Set up this small-group game by providing each group of four with a die and each player with a copy of the game card on page 166. To begin, Player A rolls the die. Each group member writes the number rolled in one of the boxes for Round 1. Player B then takes a turn in the same manner. Play continues until each box for the first round has been filled. Each group member then solves the problem he has created. The student with the greatest product wins the round. The game ends when five rounds have been completed.

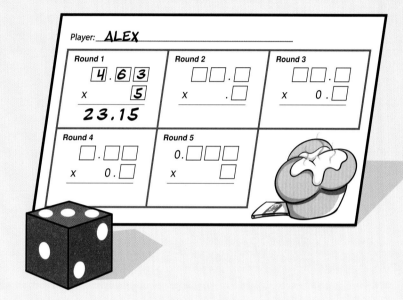

MULTIPLICATION MATCHUP
Multiplying fractions

For this review, each student cuts ten index cards in half. She programs each of ten card halves with a fraction multiplication problem. Then she programs each of the remaining card halves with a matching answer. (For an added challenge, have the student include several extra answer cards that do not match any of the problems.) She places the cards in a resealable plastic bag and then trades bags with another student. Challenge her to match each problem to its answer in as little time as possible. Once she solves all of the problems in that set, she trades cards with another child and repeats the process. Encourage students to solve the problems on each subsequent set of cards in less time than they spent on the set before.

adapted from an idea by Gail Peckumn, Jefferson, IA

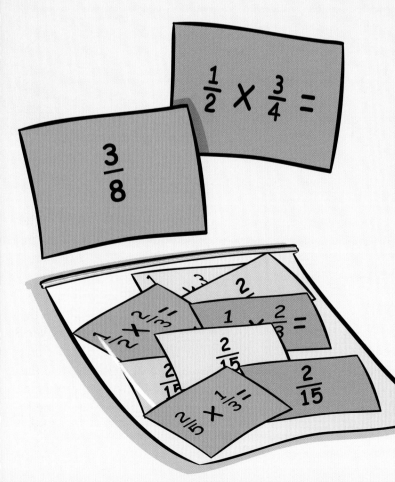

Score Card

Use with "Just a Slice" on page 164.

Score Card

Player: _____

Round 1: _____ x _____ = _____ Points: _____

Round 2: _____ x _____ = _____ Points: _____

Round 3: _____ x _____ = _____ Points: _____

Round 4: _____ x _____ = _____ Points: _____

Round 5: _____ x _____ = _____ Points: _____

Round 6: _____ x _____ = _____ Points: _____

Round 7: _____ x _____ = _____ Points: _____

Round 8: _____ x _____ = _____ Points: _____

Round 9: _____ x _____ = _____ Points: _____

Round 10: _____ x _____ = _____ Points: _____

Total Score _____

Points

product less than $\frac{1}{2}$ = 1 point

product greater than or equal to $\frac{1}{2}$ = 2 points

TEC44030

Game Card

Use with "Pass the Rolls!" on page 165.

Player: _____

Round 1

□ . □ □

x   □

Round 2

□ □ . □

x   . □

Round 3

□ □ . □

x   0 . □

Round 4

□ . □ □

x   0 . □

Round 5

0 . □ □ □

x   □

TEC44030

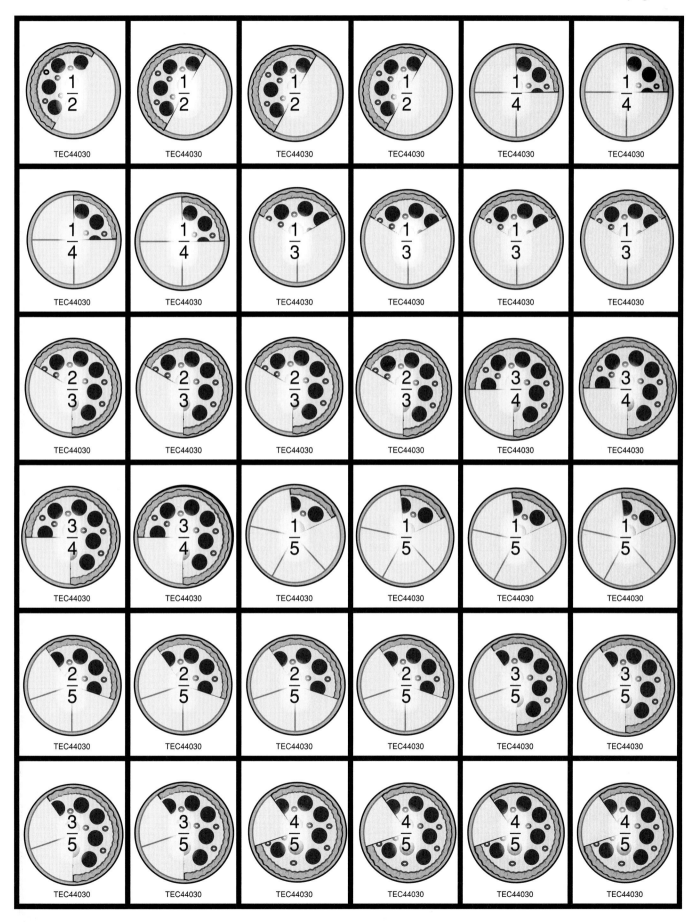

Name_____

Right This Way!

Multiply. Then round each product to the nearest hundredth.
Find the sum of the rounded products. If the sum equals Trisha's tips, your answers are correct.

Table 1

6.9
x 0.4
_____

Table 2

2.68
x 1.9
_____

Table 3

6.75
x 2.4
_____

Table 4

4.7
x 1.3
_____

Table 5

0.93
x 8
_____

I MADE $37.60 IN TIPS!

Hungry for Humor

Multiply. Match each answer to a letter below. Some letters will not be used.

1. $\frac{1}{2} \times \frac{1}{5} =$

2. $\frac{1}{3} \times \frac{2}{3} =$

3. $\frac{1}{4} \times \frac{3}{5} =$

4. $\frac{2}{3} \times \frac{2}{3} =$

5. $\frac{3}{4} \times \frac{1}{4} =$

6. $\frac{5}{6} \times \frac{1}{3} =$

7. $\frac{2}{7} \times \frac{2}{3} =$

8. $\frac{2}{3} \times \frac{2}{5} =$

9. $\frac{3}{4} \times \frac{1}{2} =$

10. $\frac{7}{5} \times \frac{1}{2} =$

How do you fix a broken pizza?
To answer the question, match each letter from
above to a numbered line below.

$\overline{}$ $\overline{}$ $\overline{}$ $\overline{}$ $\overline{}$ $\overline{}$ $\overline{}$ $\overline{}$ $\overline{}$ $\overline{}$ $\overline{}$ $\overline{}$ $\overline{}$ $\overline{}$ $\overline{}$!
 7   1   10   6   10   8   4   2   10   8   5   2   9   10   3

$A = \frac{2}{9}$	$B = \frac{1}{2}$	$C = \frac{1}{3}$	$D = \frac{5}{16}$	$E = \frac{3}{20}$	$F = \frac{1}{4}$	$G = \frac{1}{5}$	$H = \frac{5}{18}$	$I = \frac{1}{10}$
$J = \frac{2}{5}$	$K = \frac{3}{4}$	$L = \frac{2}{3}$	$M = \frac{4}{9}$	$N = \frac{2}{7}$	$O = \frac{4}{15}$	$P = \frac{3}{16}$	$Q = \frac{5}{9}$	$R = \frac{9}{20}$
	$S = \frac{3}{8}$	$T = \frac{7}{10}$	$U = \frac{4}{7}$	$V = \frac{8}{9}$	$W = \frac{4}{21}$	$X = \frac{2}{21}$	$Y = \frac{3}{10}$	$Z = \frac{5}{14}$

Off and Running

Getting Out of the Gate With Variables

PHOTO-FINISH EXPRESSIONS
Evaluating

Give each child three sticky notes and a sheet of unlined paper. Have him label the paper with a simple algebraic expression, write a sentence explaining its meaning, and then illustrate the sentence. Next, have him arrange his sticky notes along the bottom of the page and label each one with a different value for the variable. Instruct him to evaluate his expression for each value and record the answer under the corresponding sticky note. When he's finished, have him trade papers with a classmate and evaluate his partner's expression for the values recorded on her sticky notes. When everyone is finished, bind the papers into a book for independent practice at a center!

Expression: n + 4

Sentence: Andy's horse had won some races, but now it has won four more.

Evaluate the expression using these values:

n = 3   n = 1   n = 20
                              24

Hitting a stride with variables can be easier for your students with help from these thoroughbred activities!

with ideas by Melissa Bryan, West Chester, PA

REVEAL THE DEAL!
Representing, translating, and solving equations with variables

Once students understand the use of word and number forms of algebraic expressions and equations (see the chart), give each student pair a paper cup and 15 index cards. Have the partners write "n" on the bottom of their cup. Have them also write "+," "–," and "=" on three separate cards and label their remaining cards from 1 to 12. Then have one child turn her back while her partner selects cards, secretly arranges them to form an equation, and covers one number with the cup. When she's finished, she asks her partner to look at the equation, translate its meaning, and solve it. To check her partner's answer, she lifts the cup. If the answer is correct, the partners switch roles. If not, she helps her partner solve the equation correctly and then they switch roles. For practice with multiplication, division, decimals, or fractions, just add more cards!

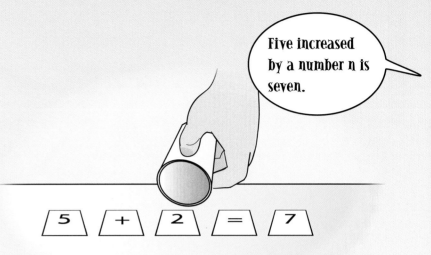

Five increased by a number n is seven.

Expression		Equation	
Word Form	**Number Form**	**Word Form**	**Number Form**
Six more than a number *n*	*n* + 6	Six more than a number *n* is fifty-eight.	*n* + 6 = 58
A number *x* increased by four	*x* + 4	A number *x* increased by four is seven.	*x* + 4 = 7
Seven fewer than a number *y*	*y* – 7	Seven fewer than a number *y* is ten.	*y* – 7 = 10
A number *z* decreased by 13	*z* – 13	A number *z* decreased by 13 is 49.	*z* – 13 = 49
Eighteen less than a number *r*	*r* – 18	Eighteen less than a number *r* is 9.	*r* – 18 = 9
Nine greater than a number *w*	*w* + 9	Nine greater than a number *w* is 72.	*w* + 9 = 72

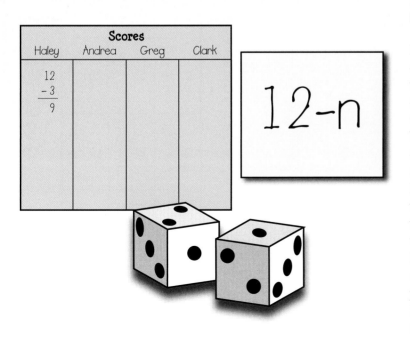

Scores

Haley	Andrea	Greg	Clark
12 – 3 / 9			

$12 - n$

HEADING DOWN THE HOME STRETCH
Review game

Divide students into groups of three or four. Give each group two dice and a sheet of paper on which to keep score. Give each group member four index cards cut in half. Have her use a letter and the digits 0–12 to label each card half with a different algebraic expression (see the example). Then instruct each group of students to combine their cards, shuffle them, and stack them facedown in a pile. Have Player 1 turn over the top card and roll the dice to determine the value of the variable. If she evaluates the expression correctly, her score equals the value of the variable and she sets the card aside. If not or if the answer is a negative number, she earns no points. If she answered incorrectly, another player can then answer correctly and earn the points. Players take turns in this manner, reshuffling the cards as needed. The player with the most points when time is up wins.

Which horses have six legs?

Horsing Around With Variables

Name _____

Write an algebraic expression for each word expression. Then shade the matching box below.

1. n more than five _____
2. eight less than n _____
3. n increased by two _____
4. five less than n _____
5. six decreased by n _____
6. n decreased by four _____
7. one more than n _____
8. nine less than n _____
9. sixteen less than n _____
10. n less than twelve _____

11. fifteen increased by n _____
12. n more than zero _____
13. seven less than n _____
14. ten more than n _____
15. zero less than n _____
16. two decreased by n _____
17. n more than thirteen _____
18. one increased by n _____
19. eleven decreased by n _____
20. n less than fourteen _____

21. n more than six _____

To answer the question above, write the letters in order in the unshaded boxes in the blanks below.

Those that are being

___ ___ ___ ___ ___ ___ ___ ___ ___ .

T	I	H	N	E	D	R	O	G
$13+n$	$n-7$	$n-16$	$6-n$	$5+n$	$1+n$	$n-2$	$12-n$	$n-4$
E	I	N	C	D	D	I	L	H
$n-8$	$14+n$	$n-0$	$15+n$	$n+8$	$13-n$	$n+10$	$11-n$	$n+1$
U	S	E	C	A	E	V	L	N
$n+2$	$14-n$	$2-n$	$0+n$	$n-9$	$n+4$	$n-5$	$6+n$	$16-n$

©The Mailbox® • TEC44030 • April/May 2007 • Key p. 312

Passing Time at the Track

Write the value of each variable.
The first one has been done for you.

6 n + 2 = 8	n − 3 = 1	8 − n = 3	15 − n = 8	n + 2 = 2
11 − n = 10	n − 3 = 6	n + 1 = 13	19 − n = 17	n − 7 = 7
n + 10 = 20	n + 12 = 15	23 − n = 6	n − 9 = 7	n − 11 = 9
21 − n = 10	n − 3 = 12	n + 2 = 20	n + 8 = 16	1 + n = 20

What's the difference between an old penny and a shiny new quarter?

To create a picture that answers the question, cut out the boxes. Glue each box to its matching space in the grid. One box will not be used.

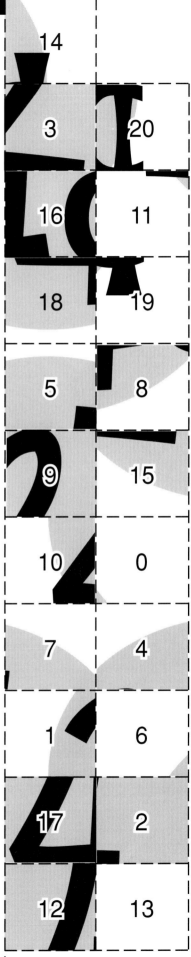

14

3   20

16   11

18   19

5   8

9   15

10   0

7   4

1   6

17   2

12   13

Heroic Measures
Superpowerful Time and Temperature Activities

JUNE

S	M	T	W	T	F	S
					1	2
3						

YEAR-ROUND PROBLEM SOLVING
Days, weeks, and months

To help students solve word problems involving calendar skills, use masking tape to create on the floor a blank calendar grid with squares large enough for a student to stand in. Also label individual sheets of paper with the months, the days of the week, and the numbers 1–31. Laminate the labels, if desired. Next, position the appropriate labels in the grid to represent the current month. Then read aloud one problem at a time and have a different student volunteer act out each solution by walking from one grid box to the next. For problems that span more than one month's time, form additional grids on the floor.

Patricia Buitrago, Three Oaks Elementary, Fort Myers, FL

These extraordinary time and temperature activities can transform your students into measurement superheroes!

JUST A MINUTE!
Estimating and finding elapsed time

Give pairs of students practice with understanding real-time equivalents by providing each child with a copy of page 176 and access to a clock with a second hand. Have each child read the tasks listed in the chart, record an estimated answer for each one, and then perform the tasks (counting out loud or holding up fingers to keep track of repetitions) without looking at the clock as his partner records the start and stop times and calculates the actual answers. When everyone is finished, ask the participants whose estimates were off by five seconds or less in at least five different tasks to stand. Declare these students Just-a-Minute Superheroes!

Terri Myers, Ringgold, GA

CHANGE THE SCALE!
Converting temperatures

Write on the board the directions shown and then provide each student with a calculator and an index card. Have the student fold a sheet of notebook paper into thirds and then label each section as shown. Next, each child writes his name and a two-digit Celsius or Fahrenheit temperature on the index card. He then copies the temperature into the correct column of his paper and converts it using the correct formula. After all students complete the first problem, have them pass their cards to the left. Each student records on his chart both the name of the child and the temperature listed on the new card and then makes the conversion. Students continue making conversions in this manner until each child has made a conversion using all of his classmates' cards. Finally, each child shares his original temperature and its conversion with the class so students can check their answers. For more practice, have each student complete a copy of page 177 as directed.

To change from Fahrenheit to Celsius:
1. Subtract 32 from the given temperature.
2. Multiply the difference by 5.
3. Divide the product by 9.

To change Celsius to Fahrenheit:
1. Multiply the given temperature by 9.
2. Divide the product by 5.
3. Add 32 to the quotient.

Just a Minute!

TASK	ESTIMATED ANSWER	START TIME	STOP TIME	ACTUAL ANSWER	HOW FAR OFF WAS YOUR ESTIMATE?
1. How many seconds will it take you to do 25 jumping jacks?					
2. How many seconds will it take you to hop up and down on one foot 50 times?					
3. How many seconds will it take you to count to 100?					
4. How many seconds will it take you to say your teacher's name 20 times?					
5. How many seconds will it take you to say "Peter Piper picked a peck of pickled peppers" ten times?					
6. How many seconds will it take you to say your school's name 30 times?					
7. How many seconds will it take you to write your first name 25 times?					
8. How many seconds altogether will it take you to complete the first seven tasks? Add to get your answer.					

©The Mailbox® • TEC44031 • June/July 2007

Name _____

Brrrr!

Follow the steps to change each Celsius temperature to Fahrenheit.
Then cross off the matching answer on the ice below.

TO CHANGE CELSIUS TO FAHRENHEIT:

1. Multiply the given temperature by 9.
2. Divide the product by 5.
3. Add 32 to the quotient.

A. 30°C = _____ °F

B. 35°C = _____ °F

C. 0°C = _____ °F

D. 10°C = _____ °F

E. 15°C = _____ °F

F. 25°C = _____ °F

G. 20°C = _____ °F

H. 5°C = _____ °F

WHAT COUNTRY MAKES YOU SHIVER?

To solve the riddle, write the letters that are not crossed off in order on the lines below.

___ ___ ___ ___

K	C	P	T	H	S	I	D	J	M	L	O	E
41°F	35°F	95°F	86°F	55°F	68°F	42°F	77°F	50°F	32°F	25°F	59°F	60°F

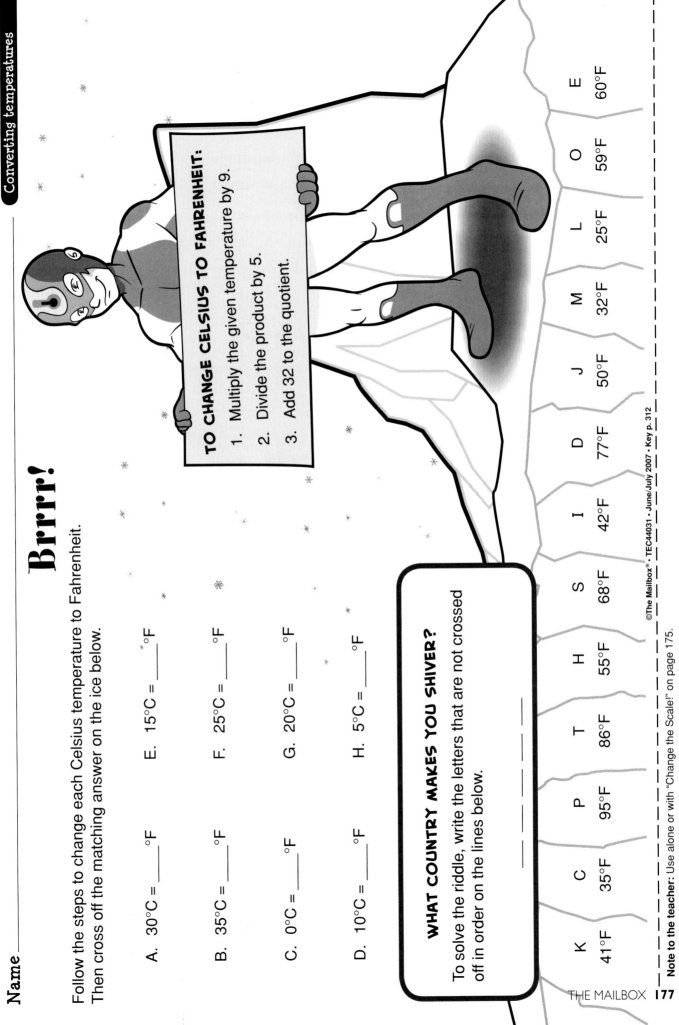

Note to the teacher: Use alone or with "Change the Scale!" on page 175.

Opposite Numbers

Exploring the World of Integers

Temperature Teaser

My lowest temperature is 20 degrees colder than ‾30°F. I am not a western state. Which state am I?

_____
_____

Written by Nick and Jennifer

Temperature Teaser

My highest temperature is warmer than Nevada's but cooler than California's. Which state am I?

_____
_____

Written by Scott and Kate

Vermont

Arizona

Record Temperatures Through 2003 in Degrees Fahrenheit

State	Low	High
Alaska	‾80	100
Arizona	‾40	128
California	‾45	134
Delaware	‾17	110
Florida	‾2	109
Hawaii	12	100
Idaho	‾60	118
Louisiana	‾16	114
Maine	‾48	105
Massachusetts	‾35	107
Montana	‾70	117
Nevada	‾50	125
New Mexico	‾50	122
North Carolina	‾34	110
Oklahoma	‾27	120
Oregon	‾54	119
South Carolina	‾19	111
Tennessee	‾32	113
Texas	‾23	120
Utah	‾69	117
Vermont	‾50	105
Virginia	‾30	110
Washington	‾48	118
Wisconsin	‾55	114
Wyoming	‾66	115

TEMPERATURE TEASERS
Problem solving

Give each pair of students two copies of the thermometer pattern on page 180 and a copy of a chart like the one shown. Have the partners cut out each thermometer, fold and tape it as shown, and then secretly choose two states from the chart, selecting a record high temperature for one state and a record low temperature for the other. Using the examples, challenge each duo to write two riddles whose answers are the chosen states. After checking students' problems, have the student pairs copy a different riddle on the front of each cutout, write the answer on the back, and color the thermometer with the matching temperature. Allow the partners to share the riddles with the class so the listeners can try to identify the state featured in each teaser.

Explore integers with these interactive activities that can help students make sense of both halves of our number system!

with ideas by Jennifer Otter, Oak Ridge, NC

TRAVELING THE NUMBER LINE
Comparing integers

For this game, create a number line with pockets by taping two overlapping rows of sentence strips end to end and labeling them as shown. Also program a set of index cards with numbers from ⁻10 to ⁺10. Then display the number line in front of the class, shuffle the cards, and divide students into four teams. Have Player 1 from Team 1 draw two cards, place them in the correct positions on the number line, and then tell which integer is larger (or smaller). If he is correct, award his team five points (two points for placing the numbers correctly and three for comparing them correctly), remove the cards from the number line, and repeat the process with Player 1 from Team 2. If incorrect, give Player 1 from Team 2 a chance to earn the points. Then continue play with Player 1 from Team 3. Continue until all players have had a turn. Declare the team with the most points the winner. To vary the game, extend the number line to ⁻100 and ⁺100 and add additional integer cards.

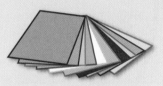

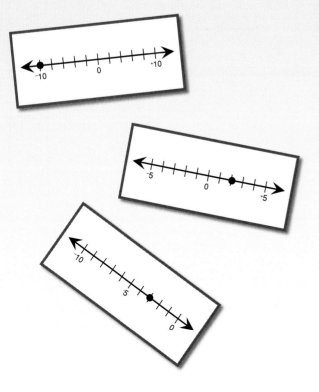

SORT AND REPORT
Ordering integers

Give each child a copy of the number line cards on page 181. Direct students to plot a point on each number line, cut the cards apart, and trade them with a classmate. Have students identify the integers plotted on the cards, arrange the cards in order from least to greatest, and report the order to the giver. Continue in this manner until the cards have been traded and ordered several times. Then have each child combine cards with a new partner and work as a team to see which duo can order all 24 cards the fastest!

Thermometer Pattern

Use with "Temperature Teasers" on page 178.

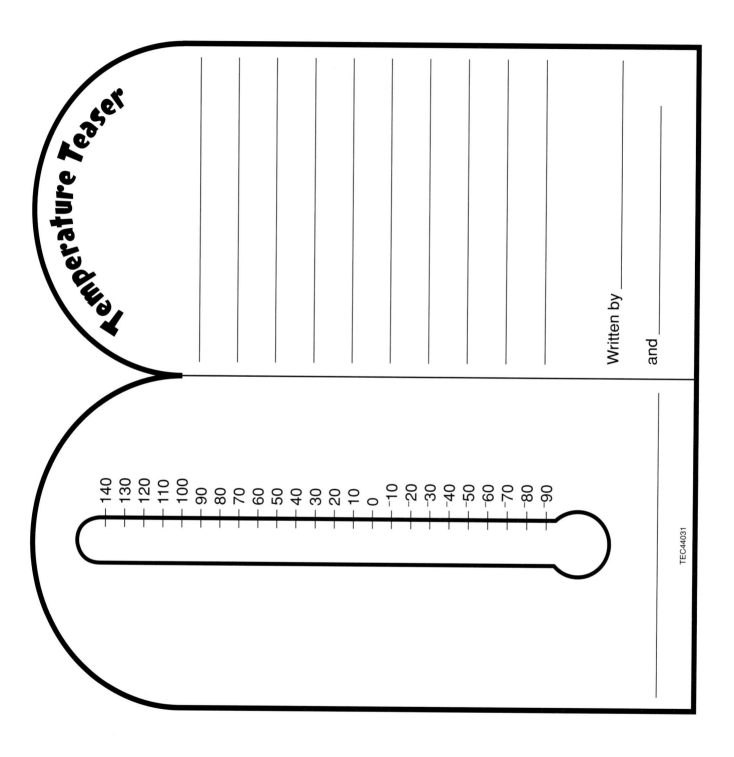

Temperature Teaser

Written by _____

and _____

140
130
120
110
100
90
80
70
60
50
40
30
20
10
0
-10
-20
-30
-40
-50
-60
-70
-80
-90

TEC44031

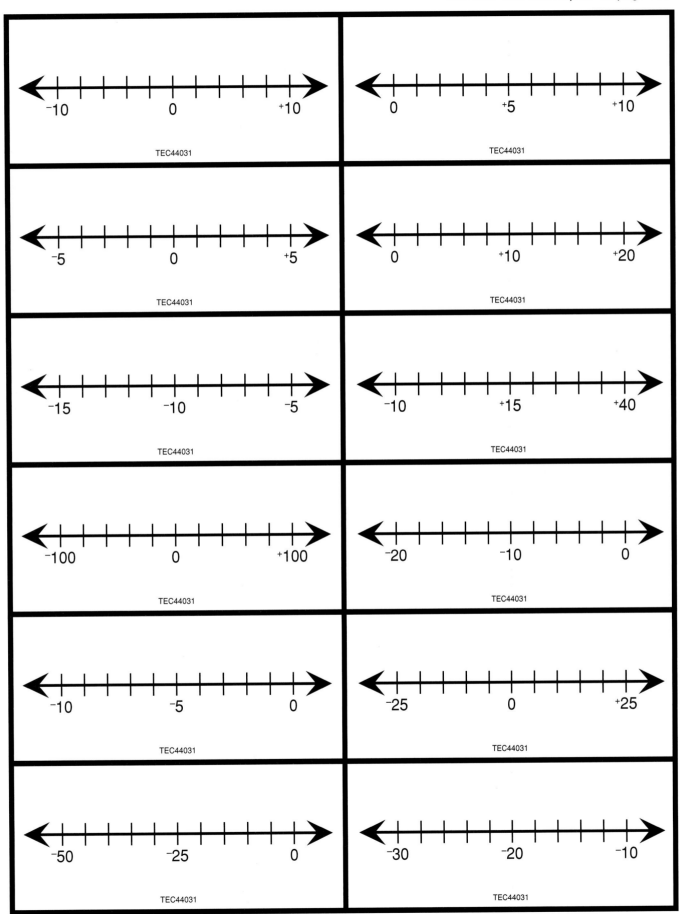

Name

All Packed?

Cut out the boxes below.

Glue each box in the correct order above a number line.

When you are finished, unscramble the letters for each number line to spell three items this family took on a road trip.

Hint: Fill in the missing numbers below each number line. Be careful! Each line has a different scale.

ITEM _____

1. ─10 ─── 0 ─── +10

2. ─15 ─── 0 ─── +45

3. ─20 ─── 0 ─── +10

A	M	A	E	R	O	C	G	U	A	M	E	G	D	A	P	A	L	G	R
+25	+2	−18	+15	−2	+3	−8	−5	+40	−6	+7	−12	+35	−1	+6	+9	−9	+5	−10	−4

©The Mailbox® • TEC44031 • June/July 2007 • Key p. 312

SCIENCE UNITS

Look Inside!
Examining the Digestive System

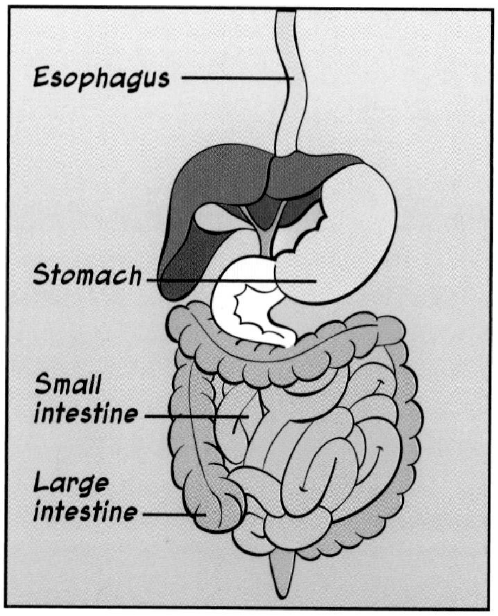

Esophagus

Stomach

Small intestine

Large intestine

Esophagus, about 25 cm
Stomach, about 25 cm
Small intestine, about 480 cm
Large intestine, about 150 cm

HOW LONG?
Esophagus, stomach, large and small intestines

To give students an understanding of the approximate lengths of the digestive system's main parts, place at a center four different colors of yarn, a ruler, a meterstick, and masking tape. To use the center, small groups of students measure and cut pieces of yarn according to the chart shown. The group then ties the yarn pieces together, modeling the length of the human digestive tract, and labels each section with masking tape. Next, group members stretch the yarn out on the floor, take turns lying next to it, and then discuss how a digestive tract that long fits inside their bodies.

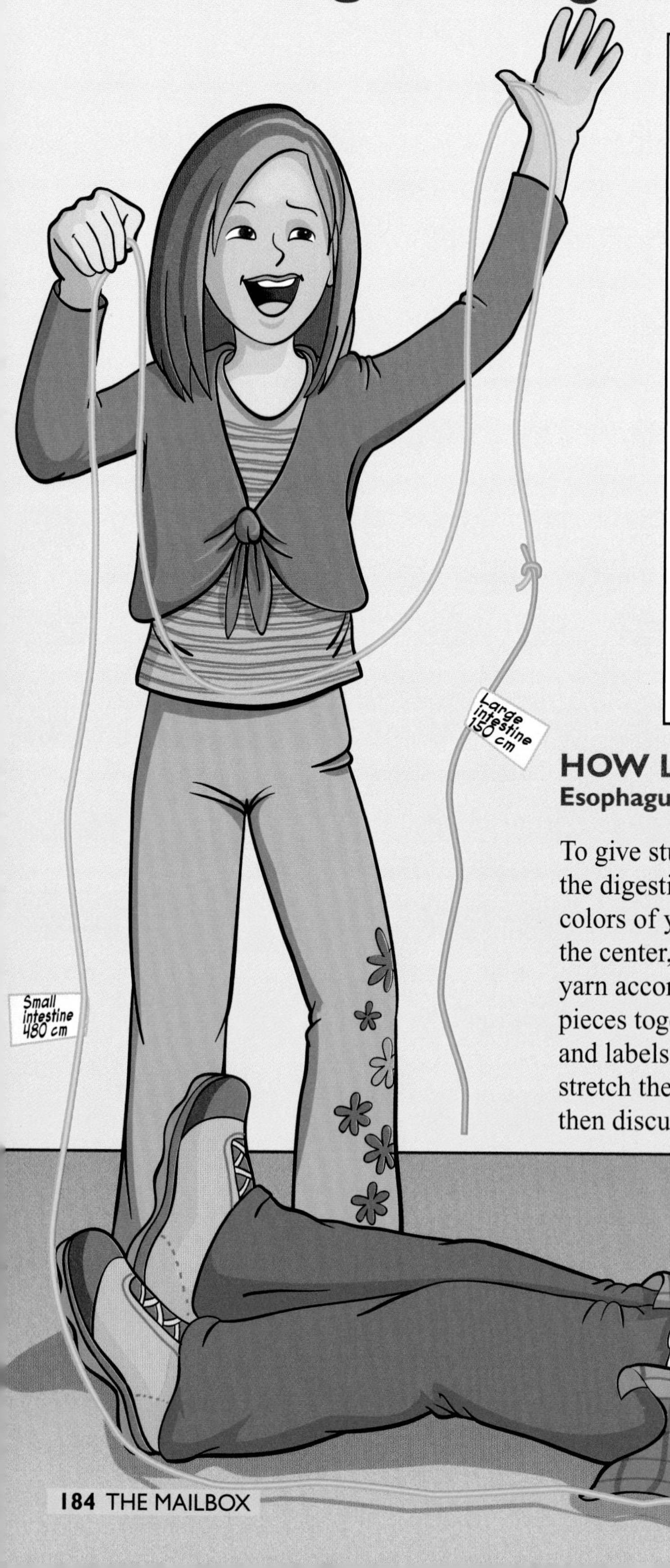

Large intestine 150 cm

Small intestine 480 cm

Esophagus 25 cm

Stomach 25 cm

Give the digestive system a thorough checkup with these absorbing activities!

with ideas by Christina Scerbo, North Arlington Middle School, North Arlington, NJ

CHEW ON THIS!
Mechanical and chemical digestion

Students can review the similarities and differences between mechanical and chemical digestion with this easy organizer. Make several copies and one transparency of the graphic organizer on page 186. Give each small group of students five minutes to complete as much of a copy of the organizer as possible. When time is up, have groups call out their responses for you to record on the overhead. To make a game of it, award points for each correct answer and then declare the group with the most points the winner.

CHEW ON THIS!

Mechanical Digestion
- Teeth cut the food into bite-size pieces.
- The stomach churns the food.
- Muscles in the esophagus push the food down to the stomach.

Both
- are needed to digest food
- begin in the mouth
- use saliva

Chemical Digestion
- Saliva helps to break down starches.
- Enzymes break complex molecules into smaller ones.
- Bile breaks down fatty foods in the small intestine.

The Mac-and-Cheese Journey

One day, a lady carrying a crying baby picked me up off the shelf. We waited in the checkout line forever before I was finally dropped in a plastic bag with some boxes of cereal and taken home. A little while later, the same lady ripped the top off my box and poured me into boiling water.

Esophagus

Stomach

Small Intestine

Large Intestine

DIGESTION DIARY
Descriptive writing

Assessing students' understanding of the digestive system becomes an adventure with this writing activity! Each student selects a food to be the main character of the story. As he writes, he tells where the food was bought and how it was prepared. Then he describes the journey the food takes as it travels through each part of the digestive system after being eaten. To extend the activity, each student can sketch and attach to the story a diagram showing the path the food took through the digestive system.

Juli Engel, Santa Teresa, NM

Name

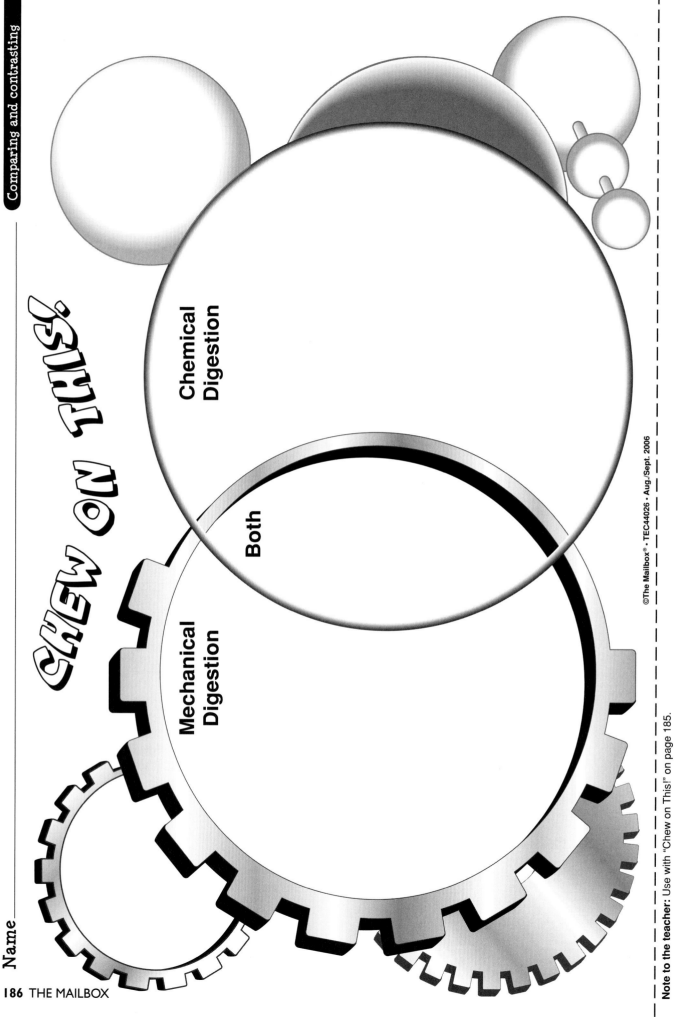

Chew on This!

Chemical Digestion

Both

Mechanical Digestion

Note to the teacher: Use with "Chew on This!" on page 185.

Perform the experiment. Then answer the questions.

Materials:
1 c. vinegar   sugar cube   timer
2 resealable plastic bags $\frac{1}{2}$ tsp. sugar

Steps:
1. Pour one-half cup of vinegar in one plastic bag.
2. Add the sugar cube to the bag and seal it. Gently shake the bag until the cube is completely dissolved.
3. On the chart, record the time it took for the sugar cube to dissolve.
4. Pour the rest of the vinegar in the second plastic bag. Add the half teaspoon of sugar to the bag and seal it. Gently shake the bag until the sugar grains are completely dissolved.
5. Record the time it took the sugar grains to dissolve.

Item	Time
sugar cube	
$\frac{1}{2}$ tsp. sugar	

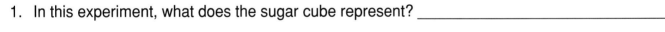

1. In this experiment, what does the sugar cube represent? _____

2. What does the half teaspoon of sugar represent? _____

3. What does the vinegar represent? _____

4. What does the plastic bag represent? _____

5. What does the shaking of the bag represent? _____

6. Which form of sugar took the least amount of time to dissolve? Why? _____

_____

_____

On the Go

Hands-On Activities for Exploring Motion

Newton's First Law of Motion
An object at rest will remain at rest and an object moving in a straight line will continue in a straight line unless acted upon by an outside force.

WHY DID IT SLOSH?
Newton's first law of motion

Head outside for a relay race that has participants observing the movements of a ball being carried in a bowl of water! Mark off a distance of about 15 feet. Have players on each half of two teams line up facing each other at opposite ends of the playground. Put a Ping-Pong ball in each of two plastic bowls of water; then place one bowl on the ground in front of each team. At your signal, the first player on each team picks up a bowl and runs toward a teammate at the opposite end of the course. During the race, each runner, in turn, notes how and when the ball and water move. The first team to finish the race without losing the ball wins. Then have students discuss their observations. *(The water and ball do not move until the runner picks up the bowl. The runner's movements cause the water and ball to move around in the bowl, often causing the water to spill. The biggest sloshes occur when the runner changes speed or direction.)*

Snatch up this sensational batch of motion activities.
They're easy to do and too good to miss!

with ideas by JoAnn Brandenburg, Hatcher Elementary, Ashland, KY

DOES MASS MATTER?
Newton's second law of motion

This simple experiment clearly shows that it takes more force to move an object with greater mass than one with less mass. Give each group of students a miniature toy truck, three feet of yarn, a three-ounce cup with two holes punched near the rim on opposite sides, 20 pennies, 20 small paper clips, and a copy of the recording sheet on page 190. Students tie each end of the yarn through a different cup hole and then loop the yarn around the truck's front bumper or axle. Once they place three pennies in the truck bed, the experimenters position the truck on a smooth, flat desk or table so that the cup dangles over the edge. Next, they predict how many paper clips must be put into the cup to make the truck roll forward without stopping. After students conduct the experiment and record their findings, they repeat the activity two more times, using a different number of pennies each time, and then summarize their conclusions as directed.

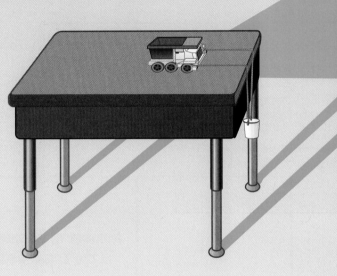

MAKE IT TWIRL!
Newton's third law of motion

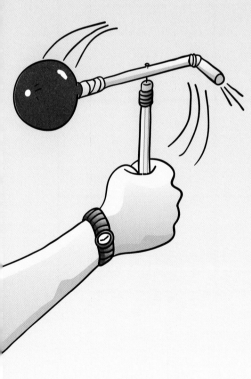

To help young physicists understand that for every action, there is an equal and opposite reaction, have them conduct this "spinner-ific" experiment!

Materials: flexible straw, ruler, straight pin, marker, round balloon, masking tape, pencil with eraser

Steps:
1. Mark the center of the straw. Then stretch the balloon to make it easier to inflate.
2. Insert the straight end of the straw into the balloon's mouth. Wrap masking tape tightly around the end of the balloon so no air will escape. Bend the flexible part of the straw to form a right angle.
3. Push the straight pin through the center mark on the straw and into the top of the pencil eraser. Spin the straw a few times to make sure it stays on the pencil.
4. Blow through the flexible end of the straw to inflate the balloon fully. Then release the straw and watch the balloon spin.

(The air pressure in the inflated balloon produces an exhaust that travels from the open end of the straw. The exhaust pushes against the stationary air in the room to create a force called thrust. The thrust causes the balloon to spin.)

Move That Truck!

Predict how many paper clips must be put into the cup
   to make the truck roll forward without stopping.
Test to find out if you are correct.
Use a different number of pennies for tests 2 and 3.

Newton's Second Law of Motion
It takes more force to move an object with greater mass than one with less mass.

Test	Number of Pennies in the Truck Bed	Predicted Number of Paper Clips Needed to Move the Truck	Actual Number of Paper Clips Needed to Move the Truck
1	3		
2			
3			

Conclusions: What did you learn from these tests about Newton's second law of motion? _____

_____

_____

©The Mailbox® • TEC44027 • Oct./Nov. 2006

190 THE MAILBOX   Note to the teacher: Use with "Does Mass Matter?" on page 189.

What Newton Knew

Law 1: An object at rest will remain at rest and an object moving in a straight line will continue moving in a straight line unless acted upon by an outside force.

Color the box that matches each example to the law of motion it represents. If you are correct, you will find out what Sir Isaac Newton saw fall from a tree that caused him to start thinking about the force of gravity.

Law 2: The change in motion of an object depends on its mass and the force acting upon it.

Law 3: For every action, there is an equal and opposite reaction.

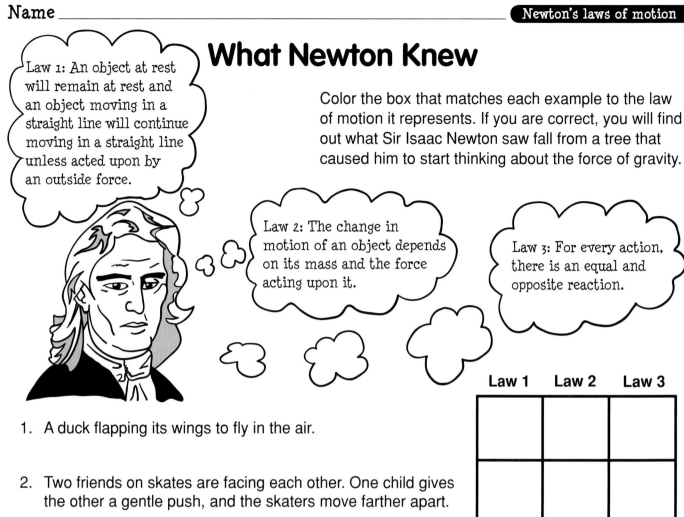

Law 1	Law 2	Law 3

1. A duck flapping its wings to fly in the air.

2. Two friends on skates are facing each other. One child gives the other a gentle push, and the skaters move farther apart.

3. One box of apples is on a platform next to a stack of five boxes of apples. The stack of five boxes is harder to push than the single box.

4. A coin is on a playing card. The card is on top of a mug. The card is quickly pulled away from the mug, and the coin drops into the mug.

5. One coin is flicked toward a stack of coins on a table. It hits the coin at the bottom of the stack, causing the bottom coin to fly out from under the stack.

6. A passenger in a car is thrown forward when the car stops quickly.

7. A bulldozer pushes a wrecked car into a junkyard.

8. A child dribbles a basketball on a sidewalk.

On Safari

An Expedition for Tracking Properties of Matter

Item	Flat Raft (no sides)	Flat Barge (with sides)	Canoe
dried beans	24	50	43
pennies	9	30	24
grapes	5	16	11

RAFT, BARGE, OR CANOE?
Buoyancy

For this experiment, give each group of three students three 3" x 6" pieces of aluminum foil, 50 dried beans, and a rectangular pan of water. Child A floats one piece of foil in the pan. Child B folds up half-inch sides of a second foil piece, creases its corners to make a barge, and then floats it in the pan. Child C folds up one-inch sides of the third foil piece, creases the ends to form a canoe, and then floats it in the pan. The threesome predicts how many beans each boat might hold before it sinks, records the prediction in a chart, and tests the prediction. Each child then writes a paragraph based on the results, explaining which boat he would use and why. *(Each boat's mass increases as beans are added. When the combined mass of the beans and boat exceeds the buoyant force of the water pushing upward against it, the boat sinks. The barge holds more items because it has the greatest volume.)* As an extension, the groups can repeat the test using pennies or grapes instead of beans.

Properties of matter will be the type of game students are after on this scientific excursion!

with ideas by Dr. Barbara B. Leonard, Winston-Salem, NC

TAKE A TREK!
Center

To create this game for four, make a copy of the recording sheet on page 196 for each child. Next, fill a shoebox with the items on the key on page 196. Then mount on construction paper a copy of the gameboard on page 194 and the game pieces and answer key on page 196 and laminate them for durability. Cut the game pieces apart; then put them at a center in a resealable bag with a die, the gameboard, and the answer key along with the shoebox and copies of the recording sheet. To play, have four players at a time follow the gameboard's directions.

POWDERY PROPERTIES
Experiment

To prepare, gather the materials listed on page 195. For each group of four students, put one teaspoon of the following items in separate foil cupcake liners: all-purpose flour, granulated sugar, salt, and baking soda. Also, fill a different plastic bag with one of the following mystery mixtures (one teaspoon of each substance) for each group: Mixture 1—flour and salt; Mixture 2—baking soda and flour; Mixture 3—sugar, salt, and flour (for a group that needs a challenge); and Mixture 4—salt and baking soda. Then give each group a copy of page 195 and have students complete the page as directed. To conduct the heat test, place the liners from one group of students at a time on the hot plate at low heat. Have each group observe what happens to the substances and record the results. If students analyze the substances correctly, they'll have no problem at all identifying the contents of the mystery bags!

LIQUID LAYERS
Density

To conduct this small-group experiment or teacher demonstration, follow the steps below. Then have each child answer these questions: Where is the water? *(It's the middle layer.)* Where are the oils? *(They're the top two layers.)* Which liquid is the densest? *(The corn syrup is heaviest; it is at the bottom.)* Which is the least dense? *(The mineral oil is lightest; it is at the top.)*

Materials: ¼ c. light corn syrup mixed with a few drops of red food coloring, ¼ c. glycerin (found at a pharmacy in the skin-products area), ¼ c. water mixed with 1–2 drops of blue food coloring, ¼ c. vegetable oil, ¼ c. mineral oil (found at a pharmacy), straight-sided clear plastic cup

Steps:
1. Pour the red corn syrup into the center of the cup, avoiding contact with the cup's sides.
2. Slowly pour the glycerin down the side of the cup. Observe the two layers.
3. Slowly pour the blue water down the side of the cup. Observe the three layers.
4. Slowly pour the vegetable oil down the side of the cup. Observe the four layers.
5. Slowly pour the mineral oil down the side of the cup. Observe the five layers.
6. Draw and label the five layers.

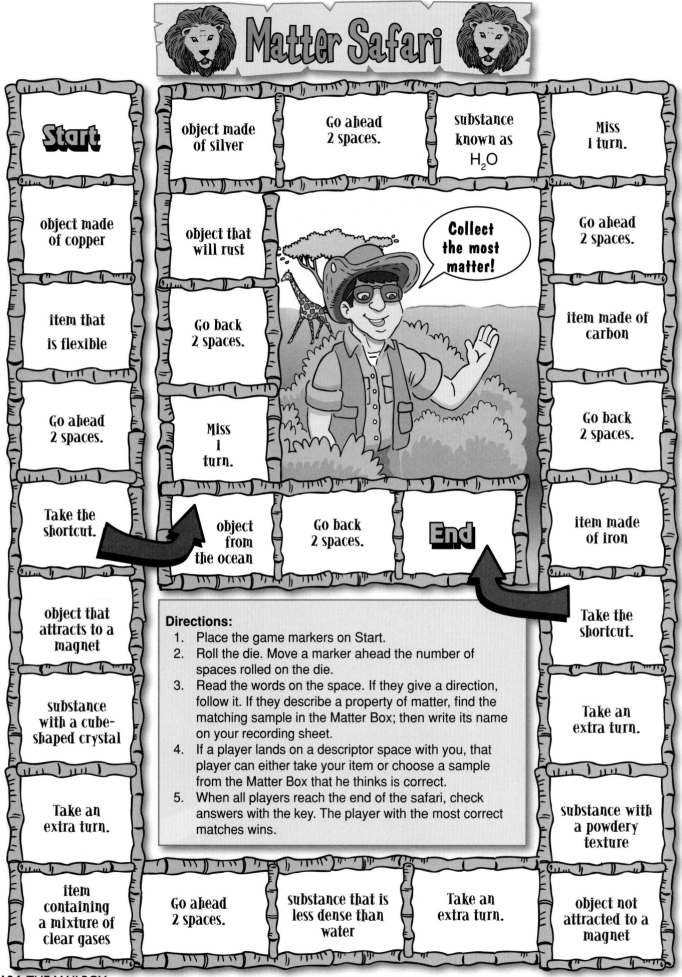

Matter Safari

Start

object made of silver

Go ahead 2 spaces.

substance known as H_2O

Miss 1 turn.

object made of copper

object that will rust

Go ahead 2 spaces.

item that is flexible

Go back 2 spaces.

item made of carbon

Go ahead 2 spaces.

Miss 1 turn.

Go back 2 spaces.

Take the shortcut.

object from the ocean

Go back 2 spaces.

End

item made of iron

object that attracts to a magnet

Take the shortcut.

substance with a cube-shaped crystal

Take an extra turn.

Take an extra turn.

substance with a powdery texture

item containing a mixture of clear gases

Go ahead 2 spaces.

substance that is less dense than water

Take an extra turn.

object not attracted to a magnet

Collect the most matter!

Directions:
1. Place the game markers on Start.
2. Roll the die. Move a marker ahead the number of spaces rolled on the die.
3. Read the words on the space. If they give a direction, follow it. If they describe a property of matter, find the matching sample in the Matter Box; then write its name on your recording sheet.
4. If a player lands on a descriptor space with you, that player can either take your item or choose a sample from the Matter Box that he thinks is correct.
5. When all players reach the end of the safari, check answers with the key. The player with the most correct matches wins.

 ©The Mailbox® • TEC44028 • Dec./Jan. 2006–7

Name _____

Putting Powders to the Test!

Follow the steps to find out what makes four common substances different from each other.

Materials for each group of four students: 4 white powders as listed in the chart below in separate foil cupcake liners labeled A–D, 5 toothpicks, magnifying lens, eyedropper, 1 tbsp. water in small cup, 1 tbsp. vinegar in small cup, mystery bag, empty foil cupcake liner

Materials for teacher: tincture of iodine, eyedropper, hot plate

Steps:

1. Have each group member choose a different substance to test.
2. Use the toothpick to divide the substance into four sections.
3. Use the magnifying lens to observe the color, shape, and texture of the substance. Record your observations in the chart. Put one or two drops of water on one section. Stir with the toothpick. Record what happens.
4. Put one drop of vinegar on the substance in another section. Record what happens.
5. Watch your teacher put one drop of iodine on the substance in the third section. Record what happens.
6. Watch your teacher heat each substance. Record what happens.
7. Circle the observation that makes each substance different.

Substance	Color	Shape	Texture	Water Test	Vinegar Test	Iodine Test	Heat Test
A. flour							
B. sugar							
C. salt							
D. baking soda							

Now clean the eyedropper. Use the extra toothpick and cupcake liner to repeat the tests on the contents of the bag. Record your observations.

Bag Number	Color	Shape	Texture	Water Test	Vinegar Test	Iodine Test	Heat Test

Based on your observations, what substances are in the mystery bag? _____

Game Markers, Recording Sheet, and Answer Key

Use with "Take a Trek!" on page 193.

Player 1 — TEC44028

Player 2 — TEC44028

Player 3 — TEC44028

Player 4 — TEC44028

Name of Player:

Gameboard Descriptor	Matter-Box Item
object made of copper	
item that is flexible	
object that attracts to a magnet	
substance with a cube-shaped crystal	
item containing a mixture of clear gases	
substance that is less dense than water	
object not attracted to a magnet	
substance with a powdery texture	
item made of iron	
item made of carbon	
substance known as H_2O	
object made of silver	
object that will rust	
object from the ocean	

TEC44028

GASES
LIQUIDS
SOLIDS
LIQUIDS
GASES

Answer Key for "Matter Safari"

Gameboard Descriptor	Matter-Box Item
object made of copper	penny
item that is flexible	4-inch square of aluminum foil
object that attracts to a magnet	steel can
substance with a cube-shaped crystal	grains of salt in a sealed plastic bag
item containing a mixture of clear gases	sealed plastic bag filled with air
substance that is less dense than water	vegetable oil in a sealed plastic bag
object not attracted to a magnet	aluminum soda can
substance with a powdery texture	flour in a sealed plastic bag
item made of iron	iron nail
item made of carbon	piece of charcoal
substance known as H_2O	water in a sealed plastic bag
object made of silver	jewelry
object that will rust	steel wool pad
object from the ocean	seashell

TEC44028

Eye on the Sky

Studying Weather and Climates

Color	What the Color Represents
blue	forms of precipitation
brown	water soaking into the ground or collecting as runoff in a body of water
yellow	heat from the sun causing water to evaporate
white	water condensing into clouds that hold water molecules until they are heavy enough to fall to the earth

WATER CYCLE BRACELET
Study aid

To help students remember the steps of the water cycle, give each child a ½" x 9" strip of white poster board and a piece of clear tape. Size the strip to fit his wrist and then tape the ends together. Have him divide the band into four equal parts and then use permanent markers to color the first three parts blue, brown, and yellow (in that order), leaving the fourth part white. Explain that the bracelet's circular shape represents the continuous nature of the water cycle. Then use the information listed in the chart to explain what each color represents. Each time students wear the bracelets, they'll be reminded of these important steps.

adapted from an idea by Amy Berry
Holmes Elementary, Spring Lake, MI

Understanding weather and different kinds of climates will be easier for students if these activities are in the forecast!

with ideas by Dr. Barbara Leonard, Winston-Salem, NC

SOLAR-POWERED CLIMATES
Teacher demonstration, measurement

Gather a globe, two thermometers, and a gooseneck lamp with a 60-watt bulb. Tape one thermometer at the equator and the other at the North Pole. Turn the globe so that North America is tilted toward the lamp and the lamp's bulb is aimed at the Tropic of Cancer. Have a child record the thermometers' temperatures on the board. Ask students which seasons are being represented *(summer for the Northern Hemisphere and winter for the Southern Hemisphere)*. Next, aim the lamp directly at the equator. After students predict the new temperature readings, have a child record them. Students will see that the temperature at the equator rose slightly while the temperature at the North Pole stayed about the same. Use the globe and lamp to represent different seasons in each hemisphere. As you do, discuss how energy from the sun affects the earth due to its tilt and the distance the sunlight travels. Then have each child draw, measure, and label a diagram, such as the one shown, to illustrate why the equator is warmer than the middle latitudes or the North Pole.

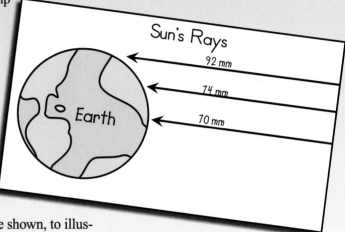

CLIMATE MATCH
Game for two to four players

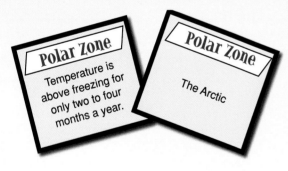

Mount a copy of the game cards on page 200 onto construction paper and laminate the page for durability. Then cut the cards apart and place them in a bag at a center. To play, each player is dealt four shuffled cards. The remaining cards are stacked facedown in a pile, with the top card turned faceup next to the pile. Player 1 tries to match a card from her hand to the displayed card. If she has a match, she reads her card aloud and places it atop the displayed card. (A "Crazy Climate" card can be used to make any match.) If she cannot make a match, she draws a card from the pile and Player 2 takes a turn. The first player to get rid of all her cards wins. If the pile runs out before there's a winner, the player holding fewer cards wins.

GROWTH-RING DETECTIVES
Climate

Transform students into dendrochronologists, or people who study climate using tree growth rings, by giving each child a copy of page 199 to complete as directed. Explain that the core samples on the page show the annual growth rings of four different trees and that such rings can help determine what the climate might have been like during the trees' growth. To follow up, have students either graph the growth of one of the trees or write a paragraph comparing the climates of two of the trees.

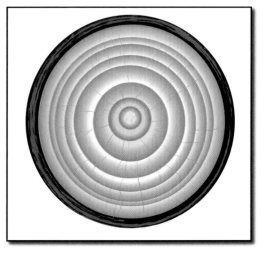

Getting at the Core of Climate

Use the diagram to help you describe what the tree rings tell about the climate during the trees' growth.

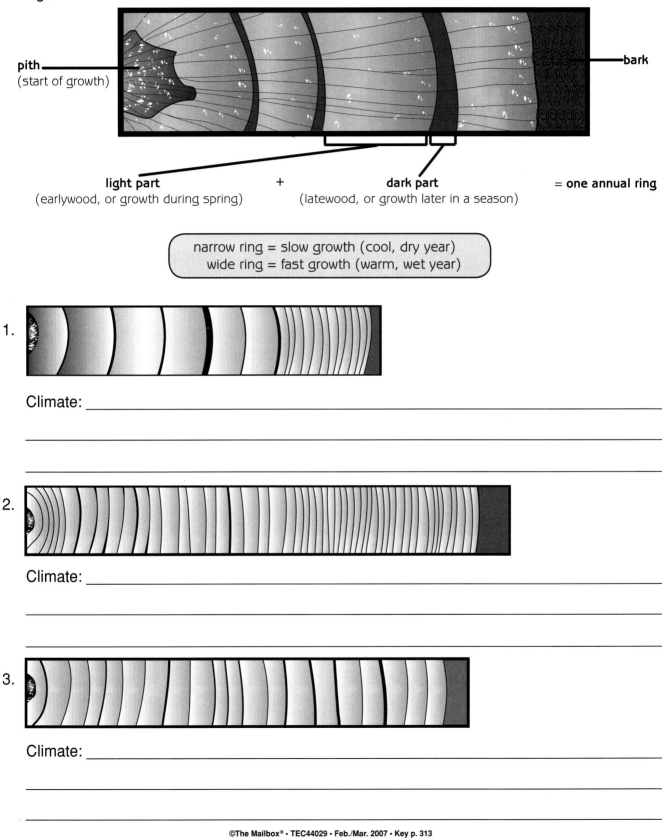

pith
(start of growth)

bark

light part   +   dark part   = one annual ring
(earlywood, or growth during spring)   (latewood, or growth later in a season)

narrow ring = slow growth (cool, dry year)
wide ring = fast growth (warm, wet year)

1.

Climate: _____

_____

_____

2.

Climate: _____

_____

_____

3.

Climate: _____

_____

_____

Note to the teacher: Use with "Growth-Ring Detectives" on page 198.

Game Cards

Use with "Climate Match" on page 198.

Polar Zone	Polar Zone	Polar Zone	Polar Zone
Little precipitation, only about ten inches of snow and ice TEC44029	Little or no sunshine in winter TEC44029	Temperature is above freezing for only two to four months a year. TEC44029	The Arctic TEC44029

Tropical Zone	Tropical Zone	Tropical Zone	Tropical Zone
Precipitation is often more than 100 inches per year. TEC44029	Sunlight seldom reaches the rain forest floor. TEC44029	Average year-round temperature is 80°F. TEC44029	South American rain forest TEC44029

Desert Zone	Desert Zone	Desert Zone	Desert Zone
Precipitation of less than ten inches per year TEC44029	Ninety percent of the sun's rays reach the ground. TEC44029	Extreme temperatures range from 100°F during the day to 20°F at night TEC44029	Mojave Desert TEC44029

Temperate Zone	Temperate Zone	Temperate Zone	Temperate Zone
Precipitation ranges from 20 to 60 inches per year. TEC44029	The earth's tilt creates four seasons. TEC44029	Warm, humid summers and cold, snowy winters TEC44029	Deciduous forest TEC44029

Mountain Zone	Mountain Zone	Mountain Zone	Mountain Zone
Precipitation ranges from moderate to heavy. TEC44029	Land shape greatly affects climate. TEC44029	Cold winters and cool summers TEC44029	Rocky Mountains TEC44029

Crazy Climate	Crazy Climate	Crazy Climate	Crazy Climate
TEC44029	TEC44029	TEC44029	TEC44029

Waste Not!
Conservation Activities for Kids

My group made a birdfeeder!

G.E.E.K. SQUAD

FROM GARBAGE TO GOLD
Inventing uses for discarded items

Discuss with students how quickly trash can accumulate around the classroom or at home. If possible, read aloud Olivia Newton-John's *A Pig Tale,* the story of Ziggy the pig and his dad. Ziggy gets teased for living in a house full of trash, but his dad ends up making something useful from it. Have students discuss where trash comes from, consequences related to trash buildup *(odor, unwanted animals, fire hazards),* and useful ways to reduce trash *(give things away, have a yard sale, recycle).* Next, ask small groups of students to collect four classroom items destined for the trash. Then, using only scissors, tape, and glue, and working within a time limit, have each group fashion its items into something useful to share with the class. Expect weird inventions!

Explore conservation with activities that can make preserving and caring for the earth's resources a natural thing for students to do.

with ideas by Juli Engel, Tyler, TX

HOW ARE WE DOING?
Assessing and making changes

To evaluate the status of your class's current efforts at conserving natural resources, have each child complete a copy of the rating sheet at the top of page 203. Did most students give the class the same grade? If not, what were the reasons for the different grades? Which topics need improvement? Select a topic and make it a class project by inviting students to join the G.E.E.K. (Grooming Environmentally Enlightened Kids) Squad. To extend the activity, send groups of three students out to other classes to determine their status and identify areas of improvement. One child can ask the questions, one can count raised hands, and one can record and report the results.

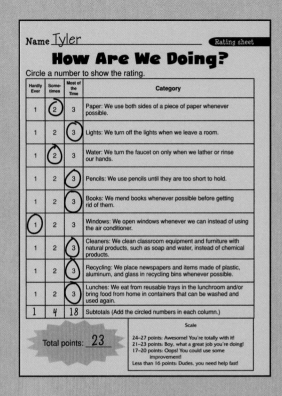

Name Tyler   Rating sheet

How Are We Doing?

Circle a number to show the rating.

Hardly Ever	Some-times	Most of the Time	Category
1	②︎	3	Paper: We use both sides of a piece of paper whenever possible.
1	2	③︎	Lights: We turn off the lights when we leave a room.
1	②︎	3	Water: We turn the faucet on only when we lather or rinse our hands.
1	2	③︎	Pencils: We use pencils until they are too short to hold.
1	2	③︎	Books: We mend books whenever possible before getting rid of them.
①︎	2	3	Windows: We open windows whenever we can instead of using the air conditioner.
1	2	③︎	Cleaners: We clean classroom equipment and furniture with natural products, such as soap and water, instead of chemical products.
1	2	③︎	Recycling: We place newspapers and items made of plastic, aluminum, and glass in recycling bins whenever possible.
1	2	③︎	Lunches: We eat from reusable trays in the lunchroom and/or bring food from home in containers that can be washed and used again.
1	4	18	Subtotals (Add the circled numbers in each column.)

Scale

Total points: 23

24–27 points: Awesome! You're totally with it!
21–23 points: Boy, what a great job you're doing!
17–20 points: Oops! You could use some improvement!
Less than 16 points: Dudes, you need help fast!

REPLACEABLE OR IRREPLACEABLE?
Reviewing renewable and nonrenewable resources

Begin by giving each child a copy of the organizer at the bottom of page 203. Review the terms written on the organizer and have students record on their sheets a meaning for each one. Explain to students that they will have a certain amount of time to look in their science books for examples of the two main types of resources and list them on the page. Then give the signal to start. When time is up, ask students to share their answers. Award one to five points for each correct example, depending on its uniqueness. The player with the most points wins. To play again, have each child list specific examples of a nonrenewable resource, such as minerals, on the back of his sheet.

Name Jeff   Graphic organizer

NATURAL RESOURCES

Renewable
Something that can be replaced as it is used

Examples

Nonrenewable
Something that cannot be replaced once it is used up

Examples

Name _____

How Are We Doing?

Circle a number to show the rating.

Category	Hardly Ever	Some- times	Most of the Time
Paper: We use both sides of a piece of paper whenever possible.	1	2	3
Lights: We turn off the lights when we leave a room.	1	2	3
Water: We turn the faucet on only when we lather or rinse our hands.	1	2	3
Pencils: We use pencils until they are too short to hold.	1	2	3
Books: We mend books whenever possible before getting rid of them.	1	2	3
Windows: We open windows whenever we can instead of using the air conditioner.	1	2	3
Cleaners: We clean classroom equipment and furniture with natural products, such as soap and water, instead of chemical products.	1	2	3
Recycling: We place newspapers and items made of plastic, aluminum, and glass in recycling bins whenever possible.	1	2	3
Lunches: We eat from reusable trays in the lunchroom and/or bring food from home in containers that can be washed and used again.	1	2	3
Subtotals (Add the circled numbers in each column.)			

Total points: _____

Scale

24–27 points: Awesome! You're totally with it!
21–23 points: Boy, what a great job you're doing!
17–20 points: Oops! You could use some improvement!
Less than 16 points: Dudes, you need help fast!

©The Mailbox® • TEC44030 • April/May 2007

Note to the teacher: Use with "How Are We Doing?" on page 202.

Name _____

NATURAL RESOURCES

Renewable

_____
_____
_____

Examples

_____
_____
_____
_____
_____

Nonrenewable

_____
_____
_____

Examples

_____
_____
_____
_____
_____

©The Mailbox® • TEC44030 • April/May 2007

Note to the teacher: Use with "Replaceable or Irreplaceable?" on page 202.

A Natural Link

Investigating the Interdependence of Plants and Animals

FOUR-FLAP FOOD CHAIN

To review producers and primary, secondary, and tertiary consumers, first display a table like the one shown and discuss its examples. Afterward, provide each child with a copy of the four-flap square pattern on page 206. Instruct the student to cut out the pattern, fold the flaps so that they meet in the middle, and label each inside flap with the corresponding definition. Next, have her research a favorite animal's food chain and then illustrate in the center of the square an organism belonging to each category in that chain. Before she shares her completed project with the class, require her to add arrows to her illustration showing the food chain's directional flow and to record on the back of the square how the organisms in the illustrated chain depend on each other.

Producers		Primary Consumers		Secondary Consumers		Tertiary Consumers
algae	→	fish	→	squid	→	orca
grass	→	zebra	→	hyena	→	lion
grass	→	grasshopper	→	rat	→	hawk
flowering plant	→	insect	→	bird	→	fox

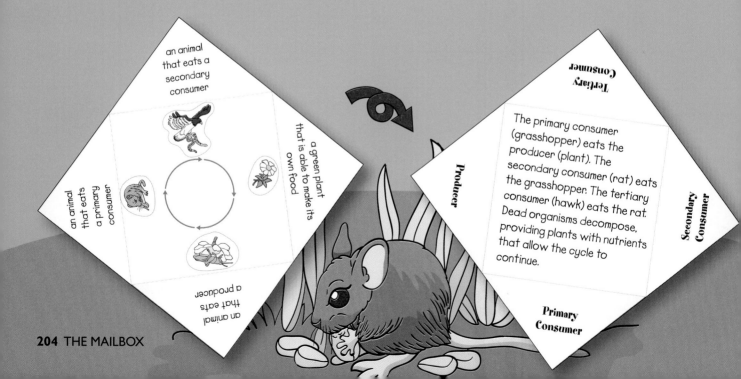

an animal that eats a secondary consumer

a green plant that is able to make its own food

an animal that eats a primary consumer

an animal that eats a producer

Tertiary Consumer

The primary consumer (grasshopper) eats the producer (plant). The secondary consumer (rat) eats the grasshopper. The tertiary consumer (hawk) eats the rat. Dead organisms decompose, providing plants with nutrients that allow the cycle to continue.

Producer

Secondary Consumer

Primary Consumer

Plant and animal interdependence can be more fun for students to investigate when they use these awesome activities!

with ideas by Shawna Miller, Wellington Elementary, Flower Mound, TX

WHAT A WEB!

To help students understand food webs, mount a copy of the cards on page 207 on construction paper and laminate them for durability. Cut the cards apart and give each child any card except the sun. Have the student briefly research living things that belong in that plant or animal's food chain.

When everyone is finished, have students sit with you on the floor in a large circle, holding their cards face out, as you hold one end of a ball of string in one hand and the sun card in the other. Roll the ball of string to any child holding a plant card and explain that the sun provides that plant with energy and light. Have the student holding that card then hold onto the string and roll the ball to another child in the circle. When the ball of string reaches the selected student, the roller explains the connection between his plant and the animal or plant on the card held by the recipient. Continue in this manner until all students are part of the web (a child can be selected more than once). To conclude, discuss the interdependence of all the things in the web and what might happen if one organism became extinct or was threatened by fire or pollution.

PASS THE POLLEN!

This cool experiment allows students to experience firsthand the process of pollination. First, discuss ways in which plants help animals, such as by providing food. For example, a squirrel munching nuts from trees and a hummingbird sucking nectar from flowers are both getting food from plants. Next, tell students that they will be investigating how animals help plants reproduce by moving pollen from one plant to another. Provide each pair of students with a copy of page 208 and the materials listed on the page. Guide the partners to complete the experiment's steps as directed. When everyone is finished, have students discuss factors that may affect pollination and brainstorm other ways that animals and plants assist one another.

Four-Flap Square Pattern

Use with "Four-Flap Food Chain" on page 204.

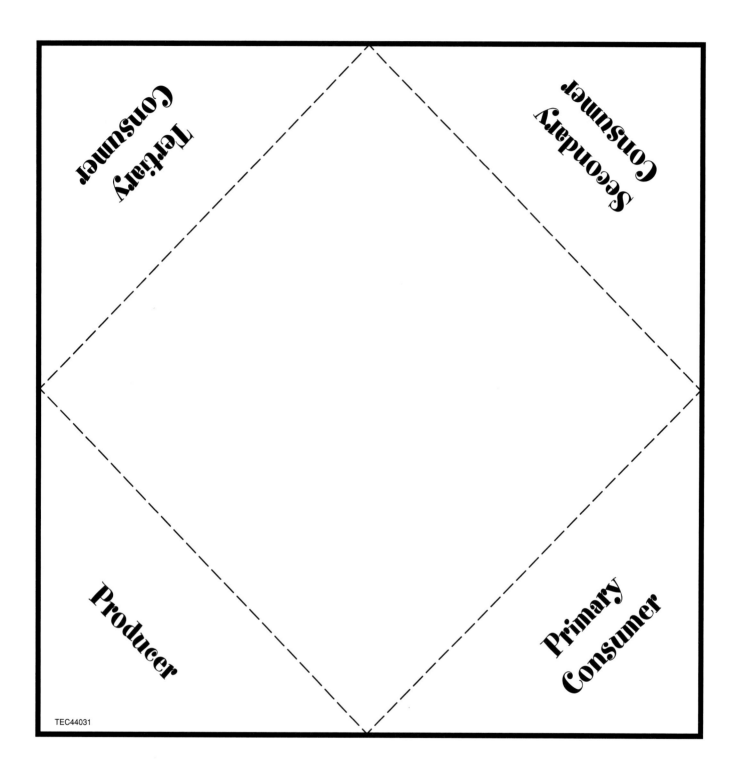

TEC44031

sun TEC44031	**grass** TEC44031	**tree** TEC44031	**flower** TEC44031	**blackberry bush** TEC44031
worm TEC44031	**ant** TEC44031	**butterfly** TEC44031	**grasshopper** TEC44031	**beetle** TEC44031
ladybug TEC44031	**lizard** TEC44031	**rat** TEC44031	**bird** TEC44031	**snake** TEC44031
squirrel TEC44031	**raccoon** TEC44031	**hawk** TEC44031	**fox** TEC44031	**deer** TEC44031
cougar TEC44031	**elk** TEC44031	**bear** TEC44031	**moose** TEC44031	**lion** TEC44031
turtle TEC44031	**cow** TEC44031	**rabbit** TEC44031	**fish** TEC44031	**alligator** TEC44031

Pass the Pollen!

Conduct these tests to find out how a bee can help pollinate a plant.

Materials for each pair of students: 3 coffee filters or cupcake liners, 3 cotton balls, about $\frac{1}{4}$ tsp. each of 3 different-colored flavors of powdered drink mix, 2 cotton swabs

Steps:

1. Place a cotton ball in the middle of each coffee filter or cupcake liner.

2. Sprinkle a different flavor of powdered drink mix over each cotton ball.

3. To conduct Test 1, gently rub the tip of a cotton swab in a circular motion on the first powdered cotton ball. Record your observations in the chart.

4. Repeat Step 3, using the same end of the same cotton swab on each remaining powdered cotton ball. Record your observations in the chart after each rubbing.

5. To conduct Test 2, repeat Steps 3 and 4 using the second cotton swab. Record your observations in the chart.

	After First Rub	After Second Rub	After Third Rub
Test 1			
Test 2			

Questions:

1. In this experiment, what do the cotton balls represent? _____

   What does the powdered drink mix represent? _____ What do the cotton swabs represent? _____

2. Based on your observations, how can a bee help pollinate a plant? _____

3. What other factors could affect pollination? _____

Note to the teacher: Use with "Pass the Pollen!" on page 205.

SOCIAL STUDIES UNITS

Can You Dig It?

Understanding Maps

Facts About Manhattan, Kansas

1. Manhattan is located on the Big Blue River.
2. Manhattan Municipal Airport is southwest of the city.
3. Tuttle Creek Lake is northwest of Manhattan.
4. Manhattan is in Riley County.
5. Manhattan is about 60 miles from Topeka, Kansas.

Inferences About Manhattan, Kansas

1. Families can go fishing because Manhattan is near a lake and a river.
2. People can attend college sporting events because Kansas State University is in Manhattan.
3. A school class can take a field trip to the state capital because it is only 60 miles away.

FLEET-FOOTED INFORMATION
Using and interpreting map data

Partners will put their best foot forward with this road map activity. Each student pair cuts out two footprints from construction paper. Then the duo chooses any town on the map and writes on the left footprint five facts about the town that can be gleaned from the map. On the right footprint, the pair records three inferences that can be made about the town using the map's information. Pairs then share their projects with the class.

Dig deep into map skills with these groundbreaking activities!

with ideas by Terry Healy, Marlatt Elementary, Manhattan, KS

PALEONTOLOGIST'S CHALLENGE
Using coordinates

This center game has pairs of students using a map grid to find absolute location. Program one side of several index cards with the name of a different city, geographic feature, or tourist attraction found on a road map. On the other side of the card, write that place's corresponding coordinates. Then place the cards and a road map at a center. To use the center, players take turns drawing cards, locating the places on the map, and then turning the cards over to check the location. For each correct find, the student earns a letter in the word *excavation*. The first player to spell the word wins!

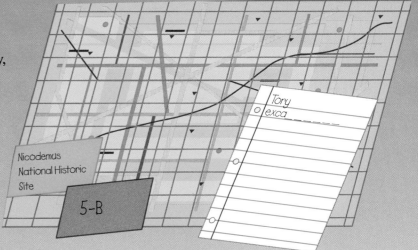

CITY SEARCH
Finding and comparing data on a map

Sharpen students' map skills with this partner activity. Give each twosome a copy of a chart such as the one shown. Then have the partners use a U.S. atlas or the maps in their social studies text to find two cities for each category. To make a game of it, declare the first student pair to complete the chart accurately the winner!

	City 1	City 2
Located along a river		
Located by the Atlantic Ocean		
Located on the Pacific coast		
Located near one of the Great Lakes		
Located on the border with Mexico		
Located on an island		
State capital located in the mountains		
State capital located in the desert		
Located on Interstate Highway 40		
Has a population of more than 250 people per square mile		

TAKE THE TRAIN!
Cardinal and intermediate directions

Download a subway map for this easy-to-set-up center! Laminate the map and place it at a center along with a wipe-off marker and a question such as the one shown. To use the center, a child reads the prompt and traces that route on the map. Next, he records on paper the subway line(s) to take and each stop along the way, using cardinal and intermediate directions. Then he wipes the map clean for the next user. Replace the question frequently to keep interest high!

Beth Hook, Longmont, CO

What is the shortest route from Pentagon City to Chinatown?

GLOBAL PLATES
Latitude and longitude

Understanding the difference between the horizontal and vertical lines on a globe will be clearer for students with this hands-on project. Each child needs a paper plate, two colors of yarn (about eight feet of each color), a ruler, a marker, two 1½" x 2" pieces of construction paper, and glue. On the plate's back, she marks and labels the prime meridian and the equator. Then she labels the construction paper pieces "North Pole" and "South Pole" and glues them in place. Next, she draws three lines of latitude north and south of the equator and chooses a color of yarn to glue on the lines. Then she marks three equidistant points on each side of the prime meridian along the equator. Using the other color of yarn, she connects the North Pole and South Pole through each of those points, curving the yarn as needed, and glues it in place to form the longitude lines. Display the completed projects on a board titled "A Rendezvous of Latitude and Longitude."

Debbie Berris, Poinciana Day School, West Palm Beach, FL

North Pole

Latitude Line

Longitude Line

Prime Meridian

Equator

South Pole

Finding Fossils

Use the latitude and longitude coordinates on the footprints below to plot on the map where each fossil was found. Label each point with the boldfaced letter(s) on the footprint. The first one has been done for you.

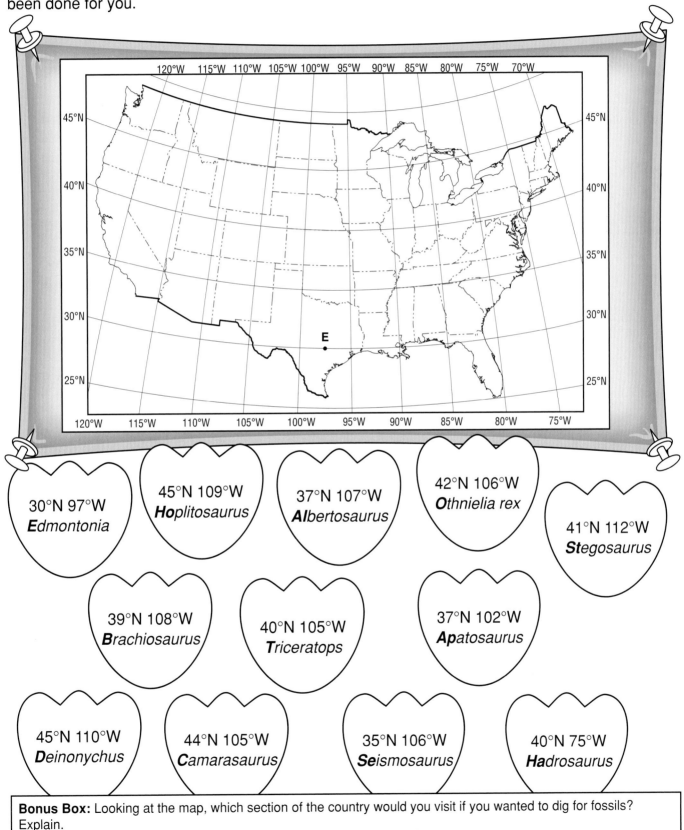

30°N 97°W
Edmontonia

45°N 109°W
Hoplitosaurus

37°N 107°W
Albertosaurus

42°N 106°W
Othnielia rex

41°N 112°W
Stegosaurus

39°N 108°W
Brachiosaurus

40°N 105°W
Triceratops

37°N 102°W
Apatosaurus

45°N 110°W
Deinonychus

44°N 105°W
Camarasaurus

35°N 106°W
Seismosaurus

40°N 75°W
Hadrosaurus

Bonus Box: Looking at the map, which section of the country would you visit if you wanted to dig for fossils? Explain.

Name _____

Prehistoric Park

Use the map to answer the questions below.

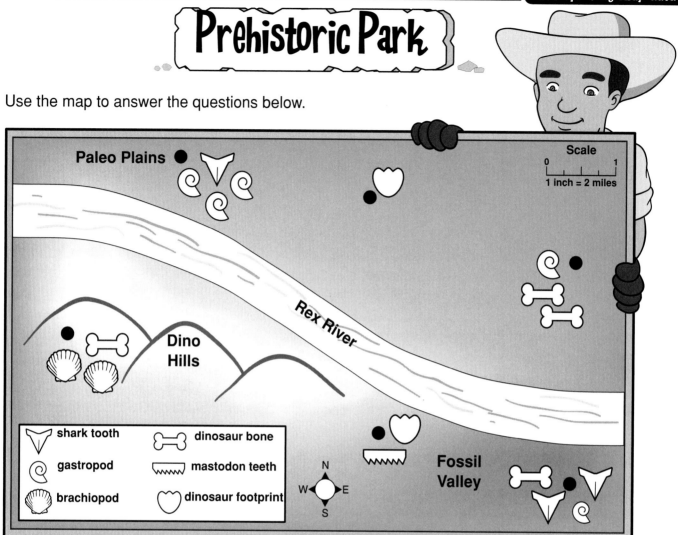

Paleo Plains

Scale
0 _____ 1
1 inch = 2 miles

Rex River

Dino
Hills

shark tooth   dinosaur bone

gastropod   mastodon teeth

brachiopod   dinosaur footprint

N
W◀●▶E
S

Fossil
Valley

1. What is the most common type of fossil in the park? _____

2. In what direction are you going if you hike from Paleo Plains to Fossil Valley? _____

3. Are you more likely to find a brachiopod in the plains or in the hills? Explain. _____

    _____

4. Where are you most likely to find a mastodon tooth? _____

5. In how many places can you find dinosaur bones? _____

6. About how far apart are the two dinosaur footprints? _____

7. Where can you find a shark's tooth? _____

8. On the back of this page, make a bar graph showing the number and type of fossils that can
    be found in the park.

©The Mailbox® • TEC44026 • Aug./Sept. 2006 • Key p. 313

Pieced Together

Studying the Cultural Makeup of Your State and Country

CLUE-CARD SHUFFLE
Identifying different cultures

Use this small-group activity to give students a respectful appreciation of the kaleidoscope of customs and traditions observed by people not only within your own state but throughout the United States as well. Divide the class into six small groups and provide each group with one card from a copy of page 217. The group members then use the clues illustrated on the card to figure out which of the following major cultures is being represented: Australian, Chinese, German, Mexican, Native American, or Russian. The groups trade cards and repeat the process until each group has seen all six cards. When the groups are finished, reveal the correct answers and have students share the clues that were the most helpful.

Answer Key
1. Chinese
2. German
3. Russian
4. Native American
5. Australian
6. Mexican

Dig into this cache of cultural activities to pique students' interest in learning more about their state and country!

with ideas by S. E. H. Riddle, Dorchester, MA

A MELTING POT STATE OF MIND
Identifying cultural characteristics

This picture-perfect activity is sure to clue students in to different ways of life! Mount on colorful paper numbered magazine or newspaper pictures of people or places that represent several major cultures within the United States. Place the pictures at a center along with a list such as the one shown. Have small groups of students inspect each picture and record the clues they find about which culture is being depicted. Then have each group member choose one picture and use his recorded information to write a paragraph explaining which culture he thinks that picture represents and why.

Major Cultures of the United States

African

Asian

European

Hispanic

Native American

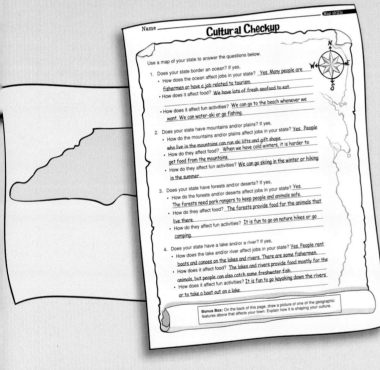

MY STATE, MY CULTURE
Connecting geography and culture

Get down to the nitty-gritty of how a state's culture can be influenced by its landforms and features with this mapping activity. Have pairs of students use a map of your state to complete one copy of page 218 as directed. Follow up by having each child research to answer the same questions about another state of her choice. Then display students' findings next to copies of the appropriate state maps.

AS TIME GOES BY
Comparing cultures

Having students conduct family interviews can help them better understand past and present state cultures. Provide each child with a chart like the one shown. In the "Now" column, have the student list his favorite items. In the "Then" column, have him list the responses of an older relative or a family friend who lives in the same state. Next, give each child a copy of the pyramid pattern on page 219. Have him follow the directions on the page to compare and contrast the culture(s) of his state. Then invite him to share his completed project with the class.

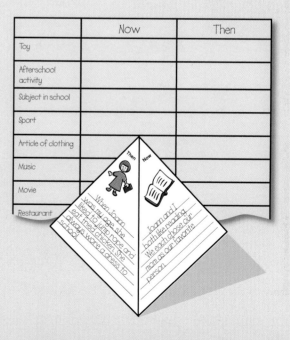

	Now	Then
Toy		
Afterschool activity		
Subject in school		
Sport		
Article of clothing		
Music		
Movie		
Restaurant		

1.

2.

3.

4.

5.

6.

TEC44027

Cultural Checkup

Use a map of your state to answer the questions below.

1. Does your state border an ocean? If yes,
   - How does the ocean affect jobs in your state? _____
   _____
   - How does it affect food? _____
   _____
   - How does it affect fun activities? _____
   _____

2. Does your state have mountains and/or plains? If yes,
   - How do the mountains and/or plains affect jobs in your state? _____
   _____
   - How do they affect food? _____
   _____
   - How do they affect fun activities? _____
   _____

3. Does your state have forests and/or deserts? If yes,
   - How do the forests and/or deserts affect jobs in your state? _____
   _____
   - How do they affect food? _____
   _____
   - How do they affect fun activities? _____
   _____

4. Does your state have a lake and/or a river? If yes,
   - How does the lake and/or river affect jobs in your state? _____
   _____
   - How does it affect food? _____
   _____
   - How does it affect fun activities? _____

Bonus Box: On the back of this page, draw a picture of one of the geographic features above that affects your town. Explain how it is shaping your culture.

©The Mailbox® • TEC44027 • Oct./Nov. 2006

Note to the teacher: Use with "My State, My Culture" on page 216.

Pyramid Pattern

Use with "As Time Goes By" on page 216.

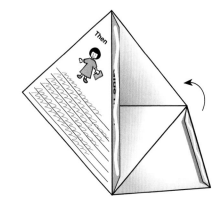

Directions:

1. Complete each section of the pyramid using information from the interview you conducted.
2. Draw a small picture for each section in the space provided.
3. Cut out the pyramid and fold it along the bold lines. Then glue the sides together as shown.

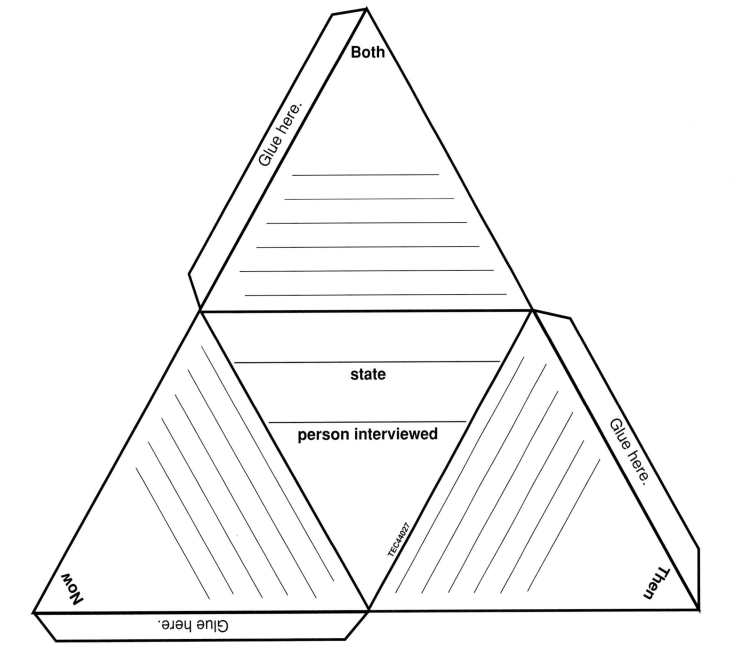

Both

Glue here.

state

person interviewed

Glue here.

Now

Then

Glue here.

TEC44027

Nation Divided
Studying the Civil War

HANGING IN THE BALANCE
Visual aid

Demonstrate that it was important to the balance of power in Congress for there to be an equal number of free and slave states represented in the years before the Civil War. Grab a clothes hanger, index cards, and paper clips. Label one index card "Free States" and another "Slave States." Tape the cards at opposite ends of the hanger; then display the hanger at the front of the room. Next, have seven students each label an index card with one of the following states and attach two interlocking paper clips to the top: Ohio, Vermont, Pennsylvania, North Carolina, Arkansas, Georgia, and Delaware. Then read the names of those states aloud, having the child with each card clip it to the previous one on the correct side of the hanger. It won't take long for students to see that the hanger tilts. Follow up with a discussion about the territories that wanted to become states and the problems that an imbalance of numbers would produce.

Delve into divisive issues that surrounded the Civil War with this batch of hands-on activities.

with ideas by Suzette Westhoff, Fredericksburg, VA

A CHAIN OF EVENTS
Understanding causes and effects

To help students chronicle events that led to the Civil War, give each child a copy of the cards on page 222. Have him use his textbook or other sources to match each event to the correct effect. Instruct him to glue the cards together vertically with the event at the top. Then have him glue the events together horizontally in chronological order and attach the title card at the beginning. When he folds the cards, they form a booklet that becomes a portable study aid!

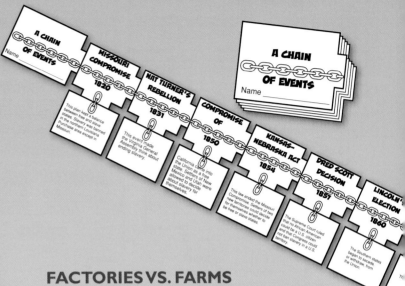

FACTORIES VS. FARMS
Comparing and contrasting

Follow up a lesson on the regional differences between the North and the South by having students make center cards about how these regions were alike or different in terms of slavery, population, and economy. Give each pair of students three index cards. Have the partners label one card with a fact about the North, the second card with a fact about the South, and the third card with a fact that describes both regions; then have them label the backs of the cards accordingly. After checking the cards, create a sorting mat. Place the cards and mat at a center. To use the center, a child sorts the cards on the mat, turns the cards over to check her answers, and then writes a paragraph telling which fact she thinks was the main cause of the Civil War and why.

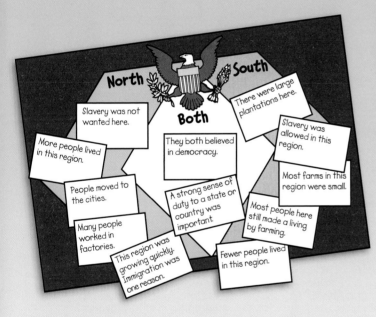

STEP INTO THE SETTING
Readers' theater

Help students understand the various viewpoints of the post–Civil War era and improve reading fluency to boot by giving each child a copy of pages 223 and 224. Divide the class into groups of six students. Allow each student to choose a role and practice her lines. Then have each group read the play together!

Civil War Cards

Use with "A Chain of Events" on page 221.

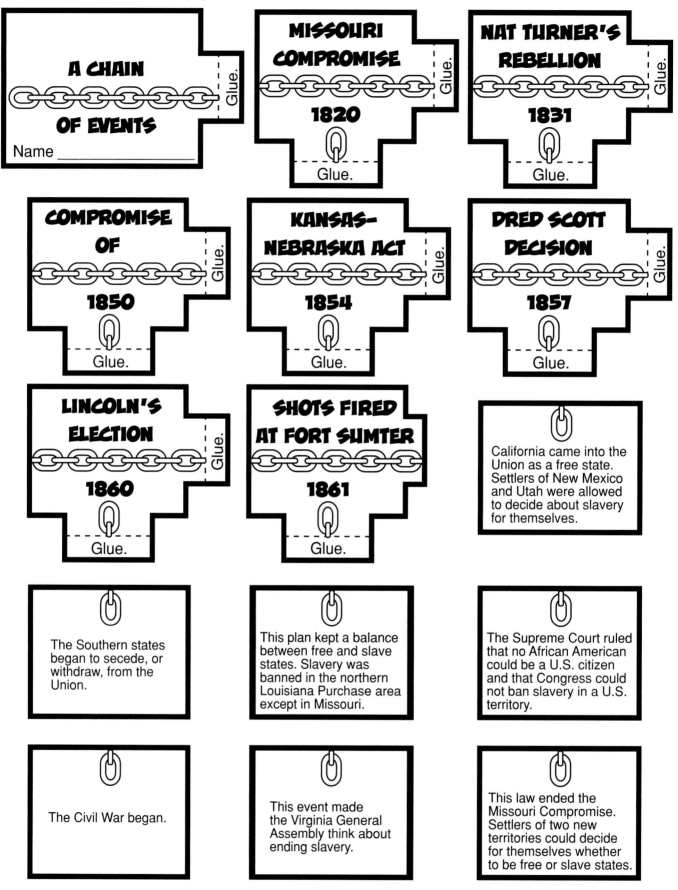

A CHAIN OF EVENTS

Name _____

MISSOURI COMPROMISE
1820
Glue.
Glue.

NAT TURNER'S REBELLION
1831
Glue.
Glue.

COMPROMISE OF 1850
Glue.
Glue.

KANSAS-NEBRASKA ACT
1854
Glue.
Glue.

DRED SCOTT DECISION
1857
Glue.
Glue.

LINCOLN'S ELECTION
1860
Glue.
Glue.

SHOTS FIRED AT FORT SUMTER
1861
Glue.
Glue.

California came into the Union as a free state. Settlers of New Mexico and Utah were allowed to decide about slavery for themselves.

The Southern states began to secede, or withdraw, from the Union.

This plan kept a balance between free and slave states. Slavery was banned in the northern Louisiana Purchase area except in Missouri.

The Supreme Court ruled that no African American could be a U.S. citizen and that Congress could not ban slavery in a U.S. territory.

The Civil War began.

This event made the Virginia General Assembly think about ending slavery.

This law ended the Missouri Compromise. Settlers of two new territories could decide for themselves whether to be free or slave states.

©The Mailbox® • TEC44028 • Dec./Jan. 2006–7 • Key p. 313

The Need to Rebuild

A Readers' Theater About Reconstruction Following the Civil War

ROLES: Narrator, Chris, Sami, Abraham Lincoln, Andrew Johnson, and Thaddeus Stevens

Narrator: Chris and Sami are working at Sami's house on a project about Reconstruction. As usual, Chris is whining.

Chris: *(frustrated)* I don't know anything about Reconstruction after the Civil War. What does [teacher's name] mean by "Write one positive and one negative point for each man's plan?" What plans? I'm confused!

Sami: Settle down. Maybe my new virtual encyclopedia can help. It's awesome! I can look up a topic, press my finger to the page, and a figure appears as a talking hologram with the information. Let's try it!

Chris: Okay! Let's start with Abe Lincoln's plan.

(Sami pretends to touch a computer screen. Abraham Lincoln appears.)

Abraham Lincoln: After our victory at Antietam in September 1862, the Union army was making progress. I saw the need for a plan to unite the country and bring the South back into the Union. In my plan, Southerners who promised to be loyal to the United States would be pardoned. A state could rejoin the Union if ten percent of its voters took the oath. Then it would form a new government that banned slavery.

Some members of Congress did not like my plan and wrote the Wade-Davis Bill. It required half the white males in a state to take an oath before the state could return. It also said that African Americans must be given the right to vote. I felt this bill was too strict, so I carried out a pocket veto.

Five days after the war ended, I was killed. Then Vice President Andrew Johnson had to deal with the problems of mending the broken country.

Note to the teacher: Use pages 223 and 224 with "Step Into the Setting" on page 221.

THE MAILBOX **223**

Chris: *(excitedly)* Wow! Can we find out what happened next?

Sami: *(smiling)* Sure! Find Andrew Johnson and his plan. Then touch the page.

(Chris touches the computer screen. Lincoln disappears and Andrew Johnson appears.)

Andrew Johnson: After President Lincoln's death, the country was shocked and unsure of the future. My Reconstruction plan put an end to slavery. It also pardoned all Southerners who vowed to be loyal to the United States, except the main Confederate leaders and wealthy Confederate supporters. In December 1865, the 13th Amendment to the Constitution became law. Slavery ended, and Southern states began to follow my plan.

Chris: So the nation's problems were solved, huh? I bet the American people were glad that things were returning to normal.

Sami: *(shaking her head)* Wait a minute! Some people felt that the Southern states should be punished for leaving the United States. Maybe you should hear what Thaddeus Stevens had to say.

(Sami touches the screen again. Andrew Johnson disappears and Thaddeus Stevens appears.)

Thaddeus Stevens: As a leader of the Radical Republicans, I thought that we should protect the rights of African Americans. President Johnson's plan was too easy on the former Confederacy. I felt that Congress needed to be in charge of Reconstruction.

Chris: *(puzzled)* Mr. Stevens made some good points, too. That's why I'm having so much trouble with this project.

Sami: I think [teacher's name] wants us to put ourselves in the shoes of President Lincoln, President Johnson, and the Radical Republicans. Then we'll understand how hard it was to create a good plan.

Chris: You're right. Let's start by making a chart.

Note to the teacher: Use pages 223 and 224 with "Step Into the Setting" on page 221.

Entrepreneurs
An Economics Project

STEP 1: GETTING STARTED
Supply and demand, brainstorming

Gather various art materials, including items from past art projects. List the materials on paper along with the available number of each item and a price based on quantity. For example, construction paper could be $0.05 per sheet and wiggle eyes could be $0.50 per pair. Next, divide students into groups of four. Give each group a copy of the list, a "bank loan" of $10.00 to start a business, and a packet consisting of one copy of each of the half-page reproducibles on pages 227 and 228. Then have group members complete the packet's first page as directed to form a company and decide what product they can make from the materials.

Basic economic principles will be easy for students to understand with this step-by-step project. They'll experience firsthand what it's like to create a company and manufacture a product!

with ideas by Kristina Cassidy, Medina, OH

STEP 2: PLANNING
Budgeting expenses, marketing

Once a group completes page 1 of its packet, have its members complete pages 2 and 3 as directed. During this phase of the project, group members determine their product's total manufacturing cost, predict the number of products to make, and set the product's selling price. They'll also decide how to market their product and how much to spend on advertising. Require students to submit a sketch for each flyer, poster, or sign and a script for each commercial.

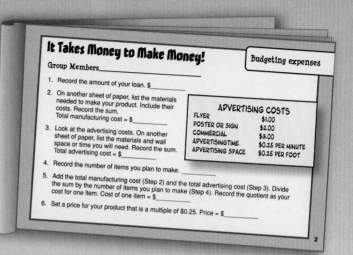

It Takes Money to Make Money! — Budgeting expenses

Group Members_____

1. Record the amount of your loan. $_____
2. On another sheet of paper, list the materials needed to make your product. Include their costs. Record the sum.
   Total manufacturing cost = $_____
3. Look at the advertising costs. On another sheet of paper, list the materials and wall space or time you will need. Record the sum.
   Total advertising cost = $_____
4. Record the number of items you plan to make. _____
5. Add the total manufacturing cost (Step 2) and the total advertising cost (Step 3). Divide the sum by the number of items you plan to make (Step 4). Record the quotient as your cost for one item. Cost of one item = $_____
6. Set a price for your product that is a multiple of $0.25. Price = $_____

ADVERTISING COSTS

FLYER	$1.00
POSTER OR SIGN	$2.00
COMMERCIAL	$3.00
ADVERTISING TIME	$0.25 PER MINUTE
ADVERTISING SPACE	$0.25 PER FOOT

2

STEP 3: MANUFACTURING
Division of labor, assembly line production

Before a group begins this phase, make sure that packet pages 1–3 have been completed. Then allow the group to "purchase" its production and advertising materials and decide who will be responsible for assembling each part of the product and for making the flyers, posters, signs, or commercials. Provide scissors, glue, and markers at no cost.

Work Schedule

Shift	Worker
10:15–10:20	Demarcus
10:20–10:25	Scott
10:25–10:30	Sofia
10:30–10:35	Caroline

$0.25 $0.25 $0.25

Decision making   Evaluating

How Did We Do?

Group Members_____

1. Record the total amount that was spent creating the product. $_____
   Include advertising costs. $_____
2. Record the total amount of money that was made selling the product. $_____
3. Find the difference between the amount that was spent and the amount that was made.
   Difference = $_____
4. Subtract $10.00 to pay back the bank loan. _____
5. Did you make a profit (make more than you spent)? _____
6. If your group could make another product, what would you do differently? Explain.
_____

4

STEP 4: BUYING AND SELLING
Managing a shop, making purchases

When all of the groups are ready, assign each one a space in which to set up shop; arrange products; and display signs, posters, or flyers. Allow time for any commercials to be performed. Next, have each group member sign a work schedule, agreeing to work a five-minute shift in his group's shop. Then "pay" each child a $5.00 salary in play money (one copy of page 229) for working in the shop. Once students have cut their coins apart and the workers for the first shift are in place, the shopping can begin!

STEP 5: EVALUATING
Calculating profits and losses

Conclude the project by having each group complete the last page of its packet to determine whether its venture was profitable. Allow time for the groups to present their findings and share what they might do differently in the future.

Put Your Thinking Caps On!

Group Members _____

List five products that could be made using the materials on the list you received.

1. _____
2. _____
3. _____
4. _____
5. _____

Circle the product you decide to make.

Explain why this product will sell better than other products like it.

_____
_____
_____

Decide on a name for your company and your product.

The company's name will be _____.

The product's name will be _____.

1

Note to the teacher: Use with "Step 1: Getting Started" on page 225.

It Takes Money to Make Money!

Group Members _____

1. Record the amount of your loan. $_____

2. On another sheet of paper, list the materials needed to make your product. Include their costs. Record the sum.
   Total manufacturing cost = $_____

3. Look at the advertising costs. On another sheet of paper, list the materials and wall space or time you will need. Record the sum.
   Total advertising cost = $_____

ADVERTISING COSTS	
FLYER	$1.00
POSTER OR SIGN	$2.00
COMMERCIAL	$3.00
ADVERTISING TIME	$0.25 PER MINUTE
ADVERTISING SPACE	$0.25 PER FOOT

4. Record the number of items you plan to make. _____

5. Add the total manufacturing cost (Step 2) and the total advertising cost (Step 3). Divide the sum by the number of items you plan to make (Step 4). Record the quotient as your cost for one item. Cost of one item = $_____

6. Set a price for your product that is a multiple of $0.25. Price = $_____

2

Note to the teacher: Use with "Step 2: Planning" on page 226.

Pitching Our Product

Group Members _____

1. List the type(s) of advertising your group will do.

   _____
   _____
   _____
   _____
   _____

2. Give two reasons for your choice.

   _____
   _____
   _____
   _____
   _____

3. Record in the chart who will complete each task.

Group Member	Task

3

©The Mailbox® • TEC44029 • Feb./Mar. 2007

Note to the teacher: Use with "Step 2: Planning" on page 226.

How Did We Do?

Group Members _____

1. Record the total amount that was spent creating the product. Include advertising costs. $_____

2. Record the total amount of money that was made selling the product. $_____

3. Find the difference between the amount that was spent and the amount that was made. Difference = $_____

4. Subtract $10.00 to pay back the bank loan.

5. Did you make a profit (make more than you spent)? _____

6. If your group could make another product, what would you do differently? Explain.

   _____
   _____
   _____

4

©The Mailbox® • TEC44029 • Feb./Mar. 2007

Note to the teacher: Use with "Step 5: Evaluating" on page 226.

A Good Balance

Studying Government

Who Does What?

Legislative — It is the branch that makes laws to raise taxes.

Executive — The president heads this branch of government.

Judicial — This branch decides whether the country's laws are fair.

The Three Branches of Government

This branch carries out the laws of the country.

WHO DOES WHAT?
Comparing the branches of government

This ready-to-go center helps students understand the duties of the executive, legislative, and judicial arms of our federal government. Mount a copy of the sorting mat on page 232 on construction paper and laminate it for durability. Also laminate and cut out the cards and answer key on page 233 and place them at a center in a resealable plastic bag along with the sorting mat. When students visit the center, they place each card on a section of the mat and then use the key to check their work. If you wish, add cards labeled with the names of the president, the congresspeople from your state, and the chief justice!

William Heck, Fairlawn, OH
Julie Kaiser, Pine View Elementary, New Albany, IN
Cindy Otto, James E. Freer Elementary, Barnhart, MO
Jennifer Reynolds, Lyme Consolidated School, Lyme, CT

Explore the three branches of government with these creative ideas!

MAKING LAWS
Simulation

Use role-playing to help students understand how a bill becomes a law. Divide the class (Congress) into two houses (Senate and House of Representatives). Next, subdivide each house into three committees. Give each committee a different card copied from page 234. Have the committee discuss the issue on its card and propose a solution (write a bill) that a committee member can present to its house for discussion and then a vote. If a bill receives a majority vote, it is passed to the other house for more discussion and a vote. If a bill fails to receive a majority vote, have students discuss why *(the law might have benefited only a small group of people)*. If a bill passes both houses, assume the role of president and either sign the bill or veto it. Explain that a signed bill becomes law and that a vetoed bill can still become law if two-thirds of each house vote for it. Then guide students to understand how a similar process works at the local or state level as well!

Kristina Cassidy, Medina, OH

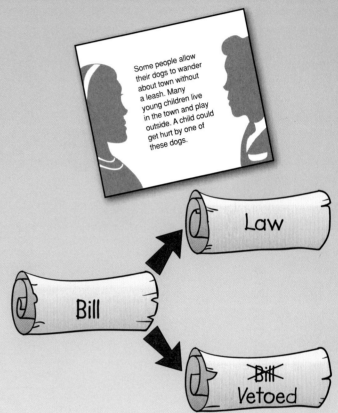

IN THE CENTER OF IT ALL
Making self-to-world connections

To help students realize just how many different levels of government can impact their lives, have each child draw a circle in the center of a paper plate and label it with her name. Have her add a larger concentric circle and label it "Home." Have her continue adding and labeling additional concentric circles until there is one for each group to which she has a connection (see the example). Next, have her record the title of the person(s) in charge at each level and what she is expected to obey, including the laws of another country if she visits it. When students are finished, discuss the relationship between obeying rules at home and school and abiding by the laws of our community, state, and nation.

Diane Coffman, Deland, FL

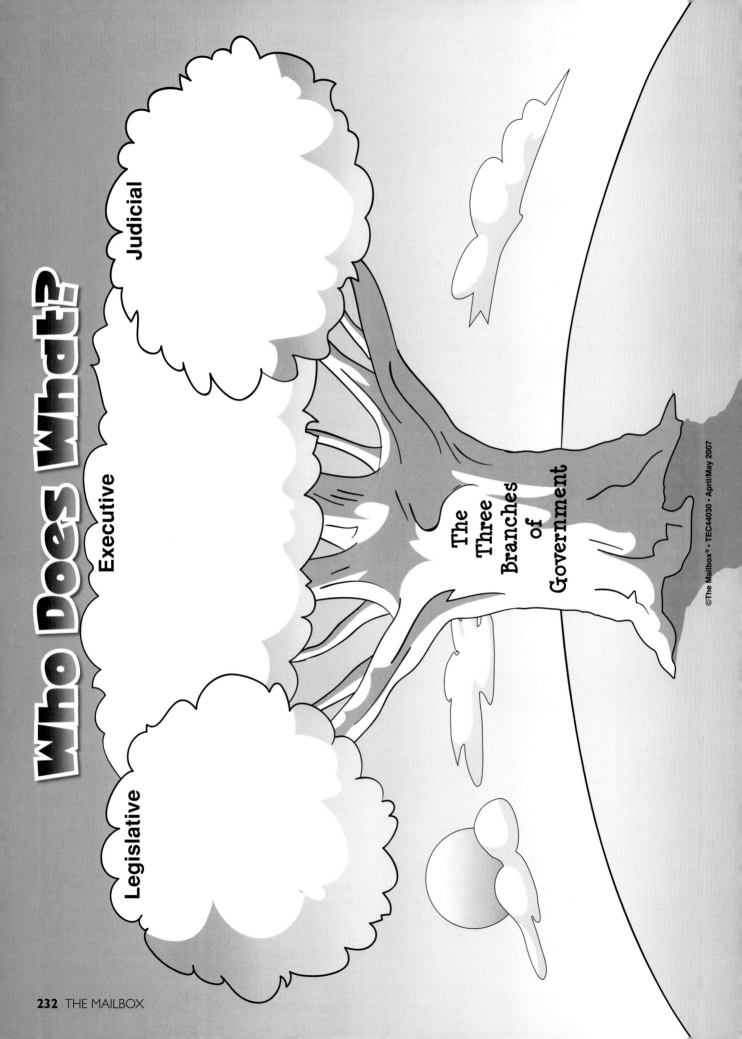

Who Does What?

Judicial

Executive

Legislative

The Three Branches of Government

The president heads this branch of government. TEC44030	This branch decides whether the country's laws are fair. TEC44030	It is the branch that makes laws to raise taxes. TEC44030	This branch is in charge of raising an army and a navy. TEC44030
It is the branch that decides cases about the Constitution or the country's laws. TEC44030	The head of this branch is the commander in chief of our armed forces. TEC44030	This branch decides cases between citizens of different states. TEC44030	This branch controls trade with other countries. TEC44030
The nine members of this branch are named by the president but voted on by the Senate. TEC44030	It is the branch in charge of making the country's laws. TEC44030	The members of this branch can serve for life. TEC44030	This branch decides cases about treaties with other countries. TEC44030
This branch consists of two houses: the Senate and the House of Representatives. TEC44030	This branch represents the country in talks with other nations. TEC44030	This branch is in charge of the day-to-day affairs of the government. TEC44030	The person who heads this branch can be elected to serve only two four-year terms. TEC44030
It is the branch in charge of having money printed and coined. TEC44030	This branch carries out the laws of the country. TEC44030	The head of this branch can veto a bill passed by Congress. TEC44030	It is the branch that has the power to declare war. TEC44030

Answer Key

Executive Branch	Legislative Branch	Judicial Branch
• The president heads this branch of government. • The head of this branch is the commander in chief of our armed forces. • This branch represents the country in talks with other nations. • This branch is in charge of the day-to-day affairs of the government. • The person who heads this branch can be elected to serve only two four-year terms. • This branch carries out the laws of the country. • The head of this branch can veto a bill passed by Congress.	• It is the branch that makes laws to raise taxes. • This branch is in charge of raising an army and a navy. • This branch controls trade with other countries. • It is the branch in charge of making the country's laws. • This branch consists of two houses: the Senate and the House of Representatives. • It is the branch in charge of having money printed and coined. • It is the branch that has the power to declare war. TEC44030	• This branch decides whether the country's laws are fair. • It is the branch that decides cases about the Constitution or the country's laws. • This branch decides cases between citizens of different states. • The nine members of this branch are named by the president but voted on by the Senate. • The members of this branch can serve for life. • This branch decides cases about treaties with other countries.

Discussion Cards

Use with "Making Laws" on page 231.

Some people allow their dogs to wander about town without a leash. Many young children live in the town and play outside. A child could get hurt by one of these dogs.

TEC44030

The residents on First Street have outdoor parties almost every weekend from spring until fall. Many of the parties last until after midnight. Sometimes the music is loud and cars block the street.

TEC44030

Some people in town have begun to burn sticks and leaves in their yards. A few of their neighbors have trouble breathing due to the smoke. Sometimes soot covers many homes and cars.

TEC44030

At the downtown park, groups of teenagers have been gathering in the afternoons after school. These teenagers chase the younger kids from the park and do not allow them to play there.

TEC44030

The speed limit in the town's neighborhoods is 25 miles per hour. Many drivers ignore the speed limit signs. Children ride bikes and play in the neighborhoods.

TEC44030

Door-to-door salespeople have begun to try to sell products in town. Some people do not want any goods sold this way.

TEC44030

Oh, My Stars!

Studying the Famous People of My State and Country

How Remarkable!

Name of important person:

Thomas Jefferson

Contributions made by this person:

Writer of the Declaration of Independence

Founder of the University of Virginia

Two-term president of the United States

Designer of Monticello

Use the contributions listed above to complete the poem below.

Twinkle, twinkle, shining star,
How remarkable you are!

Author of the declaration,

Two-term president of our nation

Twinkle, twinkle, shining star,
How you've made us what we are!

Name _____

REMARKABLE LIVES
Research, poetry

Recognize the positive contributions of famous people with this fun guessing activity. Provide each student with a copy of page 237. Have the child secretly select a famous person the class has studied and then list in the space provided on the page several ways that person has made our lives, culture, or world better. Next, have her complete the song lyrics on the page using some of the contributions she listed. Finally, have the student read her poem aloud (or sing it to the tune of "Twinkle, Twinkle, Little Star") and then give her classmates three tries to guess the person's identity correctly.

The great accomplishments of famous people from the past or the present will shine a little brighter with these stellar activities!

with ideas by Teri Nielsen, Chesapeake Beach, MD

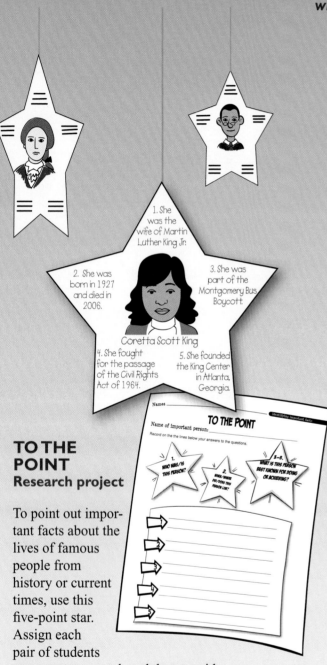

1. She was the wife of Martin Luther King Jr.

2. She was born in 1927 and died in 2006.

3. She was part of the Montgomery Bus Boycott.

Coretta Scott King

4. She fought for the passage of the Civil Rights Act of 1964.

5. She founded the King Center in Atlanta, Georgia.

TO THE POINT
Research project

To point out important facts about the lives of famous people from history or current times, use this five-point star. Assign each pair of students a person to research and then provide each twosome with a copy of page 238. Have the duo work together to find information to complete the page. Once the page is completed, have the partners cut out a large paper star, record an answer neatly in each point, and then draw a picture of the person in the center. Hang completed stars around the room so that the ceiling resembles the night sky or display them on a bulletin board titled "Oh, My Stars!"

THAT STAR QUALITY
Character traits

Select four or five historic figures that students have studied. Work as a class to identify different traits of each figure that could have led to his or her success. Next, discuss what these persons must have been like as kids with these same qualities and what each figure's strongest trait was. Then record each figure's name and strongest trait on a star-shaped cutout and post each star in a different area of the room. Give students three minutes to walk around the room, reading the qualities written on the stars. Each student chooses and stands near the star that best describes him. Ask each student to explain why he chose that quality. Repeat a second time, this time having each child stand near the next-closest trait that describes him.

Paul Revere
brave

Name _____

How Remarkable!

Name of important person:

_____

Contributions made by this person:

_____

_____

_____

_____

_____

_____

_____

Use the contributions listed above to complete the poem below.

Twinkle, twinkle, shining star,

How remarkable you are!

_____

_____

Twinkle, twinkle, shining star,

How you've made us what we are!

©The Mailbox® • TEC44031 • June/July 2007

TO THE POINT

Name of important person: _____

Record on the lines below your answers to the questions.

1.
WHO WAS/IS
THIS PERSON?

2.
WHEN/WHERE
DID/DOES THIS
PERSON LIVE?

3–5.
WHAT IS THIS PERSON
BEST KNOWN FOR DOING
OR ACHIEVING?

1 _____
_____

2 _____
_____

3 _____
_____

4 _____
_____

5 _____
_____

Note to the teacher: Use with "To the Point" on page 236.

Math Mailbag

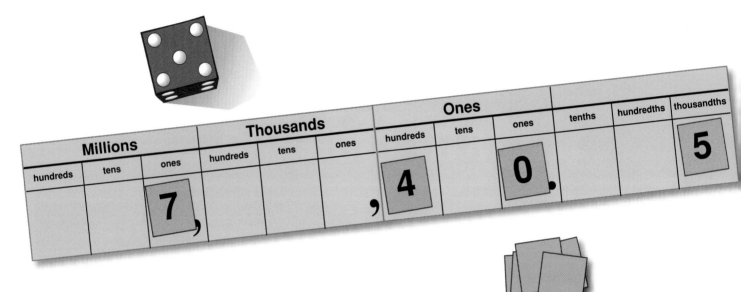

Millions			Thousands			Ones					
hundreds	tens	ones	hundreds	tens	ones	hundreds	tens	ones	tenths	hundredths	thousandths
		7 ,			,	4		0 .			5

It's in the Cards!

Place value

This small-group game reinforces place value from thousandths to hundred millions. Each student cuts apart a copy of the cards and strip on page 242. He glues the strip together and stacks the cards upside down. Player 1 rolls a die to determine the game's objective. If an even number is rolled, each player tries to create the largest possible number. If an odd number is rolled, he tries to build the smallest possible number. Players simultaneously turn over one card at a time and place it on their place-value strips in the desired positions. Once a card has been placed, it can't be moved. When all places on the place-value strips are filled, each player reads his number aloud. To make it easier to compare the numbers and identify the winner, players just align their strips!

Debbie Berris, Poinciana Day School, West Palm Beach, FL

Mix, Match, and Attach!
Equivalent fractions

Get students up and moving to find fractions of equal value. First, create sets of fraction cards by writing five different simple fractions on separate index cards. Label additional index cards each with a different equivalent fraction for one of the simple fractions. On the back of each card in a set, record the total number of cards in that set. Then give one card to each child. Have her move about the room, finding and locking arms with other members of her fraction group as they are found. When the number of students in each group matches the number on the backs of their cards, that group is complete and ready for you to check!

Miriam Krauss, Beth Jacob Day School, Brooklyn, NY

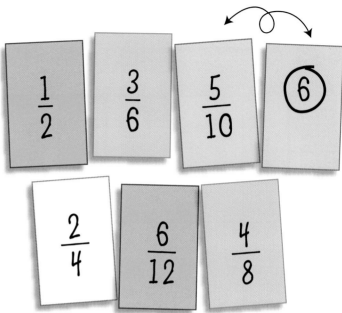

Dice Derby
Two-digit multiplication

A quick roll of the dice provides valuable multiplication practice in this game for two to four players. Each student numbers her paper from one to ten, leaving room to work the problems. Taking turns, each player rolls the dice, mentally multiplies the numbers, and then records the product on her paper. She repeats the process to get a second product. Next, she multiplies the two products and has a teammate check her answer with a calculator. When all players have had a turn, the products are compared, and the largest product is circled. The player with the most circled products after ten rounds wins the derby.

Arita Brody, Deer Park Elementary, New Port Richey, FL

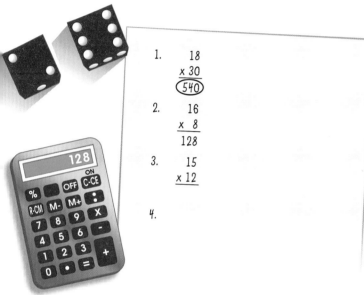

Five Apples—You Win!
Using coordinates

Use this partner game, similar to the Battleship game, to get your students graphing in a snap. Each student glues a sheet of graph paper to a sheet of construction paper and then folds it in half. On the top half, he creates a gameboard by outlining a 10 x 10 grid, numbering each axis from one to ten, and then drawing ten apples and ten worms at intersecting line segments. On the bottom half of the graph paper, he outlines another 10 x 10 grid on which to track his guesses about his opponent's gameboard. Player 1 positions his folded paper as shown; then he calls out a coordinate, such as (5, 4). His opponent reveals whether he has found an apple, a worm, or neither. Player 1 marks the outcome on his tracking grid. Play alternates until one player finds five worms. The player with more apples at that time wins.

Karen Slattery, St. Vincent's Elementary, Oakville, Ontario, Canada

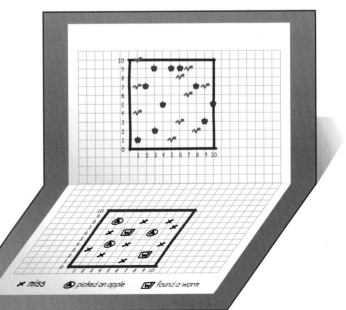

Place-Value Strip and Cards

Use with "It's in the Cards!" on page 240.

Millions			Thousands		
hundreds	tens	ones	hundreds	tens	ones
		,			,

Ones					
hundreds	tens	ones	tenths	hundredths	thousandths
		.			

Glue here.

0	1	2	3	4	5	6	7	8	9
TEC44026	TEC44026	TEC44026	TEC44026	TEC44026	TEC44026	TEC44026	TEC44026	TEC44026	TEC44026

0	1	2	3	4	5	6	7	8	9
TEC44026	TEC44026	TEC44026	TEC44026	TEC44026	TEC44026	TEC44026	TEC44026	TEC44026	TEC44026

Numbers from least to
greatest: 40, 73, 80, 87, 89,
93, 100, 100, 100, 100, 100

Range: 60
Mode: 100
Median: 93
Mean: 87

Stems	Leaves
4	0
7	3
8	0 7 9
9	3
10	0 0 0 0 0

| 73 | 100 | 100 | 87 | 100 | 80 | 100 | 93 | 40 | 100 | 89 | |

"Leaf" It to the Numbers
Ordering numbers, graphing

To complete this math activity, give each child an odd-numbered set of numbers. (A ready source is a page of grades copied from your record book and cut into strips.) Also give each child a colorful copy of the leaves pattern on page 245. On the left leaf, the student orders his set of numbers from least to greatest. Then he finds the range, mode, median, and mean of the numbers—rounding the mean to the nearest whole number, if necessary—and adds this data to the leaf. On the second leaf, he shows the numbers as a stem-and-leaf plot, recording the number of tens in each number (the stems) to the left of the dividing line and the corresponding ones place digits (the leaves) to the right of the dividing line.

Belinda Y. Anthony, Chukker Creek Elementary, Aiken, SC

Candy Corn Problem Solving
Making an organized list

This sweet activity has students finding all the possible color combinations of a popular seasonal candy! Give each child one piece of yellow, orange, and white candy corn. Ask students to identify the candy's three colors. Next, have each child use a letter code to make an organized list of all the possible color combinations her piece of candy could have. If she needs help visualizing the problem, encourage her to make colorful drawings. When she has the correct answer, she can eat her candy!

Brooke Beverly, Dudley Elementary, Dudley, MA

W, Y, O
W, O, Y
Y, W, O
Y, O, W
O, W, Y
O, Y, W

Roll 'n' Spin!
Multiplying by multiples of ten

To play this team game, Player A on Team 1 rolls two ten-sided dice and finds the sum of the numbers rolled. For a greater sum, have him use 12-sided or 20-sided dice. Next, he spins a spinner programmed with multiples of ten and then multiplies his sum by the number spun. Once Player A on Team 2 repeats the process, the player with the higher product earns a point. The team with more points after every player has had a turn wins. To practice estimation, have players round their sums to the nearest ten before they multiply. For a variation, have students multiply the numbers rolled instead of adding them!

Kristi Titus, Leesburg Elementary, Leesburg, VA

Wishful Shopping Spree
Number forms, decimals, and fractions

If a student had $100,000 to spend, what big-ticket items would she buy? Use this real-math project to find out! Gather a variety of catalogs and brochures; then make each child a packet of checks using the pattern on page 245. Allow each shopper to make a decorative check cover. Next, model how to write a check and track purchases. Then invite students to start their imaginary shopping sprees, providing each child with a recording form like the one shown. Your excited shoppers will be writing numbers in standard and word form as well as subtracting decimals and expressing cents as fractions!

Kristine Toland, Bayview Elementary, Belford, NJ

Check Number	Date	Person or Place Receiving Payment	Payment	Balance
				$100,000.00
1	Oct. 27	Circuit City	$4,999.99	$95,000.01
2	Oct. 27	High Point BMW	$42,795.00	$52,205.01

Leaves Pattern

Use with "'Leaf' It to the Numbers" on page 243.

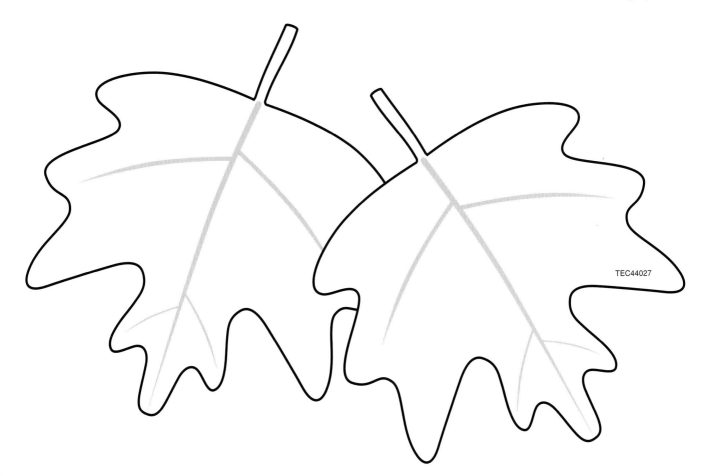

TEC44027

Check Pattern

Use with "Wishful Shopping Spree" on page 244.

Check Number _____

Date _____

Pay to the
order of

$ _____

_____

_____

_____ Dollars

_____

_____ memo   _____ signature

TEC44027

Math in a Box
Order of operations

Transform a pizza box into this small-group game! Draw a 7 x 7 grid on a piece of paper sized to fit the bottom of a pizza box. Color the grid; then program its 49 squares as follows: five each of the numbers 1, 6, 7, 8, and 9, and six each of the numbers 2, 3, 4, and 5. Laminate the grid for durability; then glue it to the bottom of the pizza box. Next, label 60 plastic discs or paper circles from 1 to 60 and put them in a small plastic bag. To play, one player draws a number from the bag and places it faceup. All players search the game tray for three adjacent numbers that equal the number drawn when they multiply the first two numbers together and then add the third to or subtract it from the product. The first player to record on paper and then point out a correct combination on the tray keeps the disc. The player with the most discs after an allotted time wins.

Ruth Menzer, Southwest Elementary, Pratt, KS

Dream a Little Dream
Adding, subtracting, and multiplying decimals

Invite each child to create a drawing of a new bedroom he would like to have as well as a budget for completing the project. Then allow him to scour catalogs and home improvement store flyers to price all the furniture and materials needed to complete the task. When he's finished, have him display the budget next to his drawing. He'll learn firsthand how quickly costs mount up!

Karen Slattery
Marie of the Incarnation School
Bradford, Ontario, Canada

Amount I Budgeted for My Bedroom:.............................$1,000

ITEM	COST
Rocket ship dresser	$350.00
Earth bed	$425.00
UFO rug	$54.95
Solar system bedspread	$74.99
Matching curtains	$49.99
2 gallons outer space-blue paint at $21.99 each........	$43.98
gallon galaxy-blue paint	$19.99
gallon starlight-white paint	$18.00
Total	$1,036.90

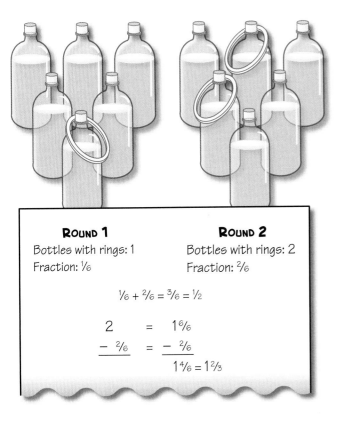

ROUND 1
Bottles with rings: 1
Fraction: 1/6

ROUND 2
Bottles with rings: 2
Fraction: 2/6

$$\tfrac{1}{6} + \tfrac{2}{6} = \tfrac{3}{6} = \tfrac{1}{2}$$

$$\begin{array}{rcl} 2 & = & 1\tfrac{6}{6} \\ -\ \tfrac{2}{6} & = & -\ \tfrac{2}{6} \\ \hline & & 1\tfrac{4}{6} = 1\tfrac{2}{3} \end{array}$$

Liter-Bottle Ring Toss
Adding and subtracting fractions

For this small-group game, arrange a number of two-liter bottles (filled with water and capped) equal to the denominator of the fraction you wish students to practice. Each player stands about four feet away from the bottles. He tosses six rings (cut from frozen-topping lids), one at a time, at the bottles, ringing as many bottles as possible. He records a fraction representing the bottles with rings. Then he plays another round, adds the two fractions together, and writes the sum in simplest terms. The player with the greatest sum after all players have a turn wins. To subtract fractions, each player subtracts one or both of his recorded fractions from a whole or mixed number greater than 1 that he draws from a prepared envelope. The player with the smallest difference wins!

Ann Fisher, Toledo, OH

CODE

yellow = Add a perpendicular line segment.
blue = Add an intersecting line segment.
green = Add a parallel line segment.
purple = Take two pieces from the pile.
orange = Lose a turn.

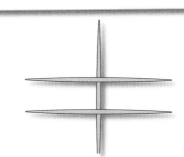

Six-and-Done Challenge
Parallel, perpendicular, and intersecting lines

Prepare for this two-to-four-player game by placing in a lunch bag five like objects: one yellow, one blue, one green, one purple, and one orange. Also put a copy of the code shown in a plastic bag with about 36 flat toothpicks, wooden skewers, or coffee stirrers. To play, each player takes six toothpicks. An additional toothpick is placed in the center of the playing area and the remaining toothpicks are stacked in a pile nearby. Then each player takes a turn drawing an object from the lunch bag, performing the action directed by the code, and returning the object to the bag. If the action involves adding a line segment, she adds one of her toothpicks to the toothpick in the center. The first player to use all six of her toothpicks wins.

Amber L. Barbee, Hutchinson Elementary, Richmond, TX

Great Catch!

Color the item green if the unit of measure is reasonable.
Color the item blue if the unit of measure is not reasonable.
Then cross out the unreasonable unit and write the correct unit next to it. Use the word bank for help.

1. fishing rod and reel

pounds

2. snowmobile

tons

3. two-foot-long northern pike

ounces

4. three-inch-long bluegill

pounds

5. peanut butter and jelly sandwich

pounds

6. fishing lure

ounces

7. thermos of coffee

gallons

8. empty tackle box

pounds

Word Bank

ounces	cups
pounds	quarts
tons	gallons

9. bag of chips

ounces

10. water cooler

quarts

©The Mailbox® • TEC44028 • Dec./Jan. 2006–7 • written by Jennifer Otter, Oak Ridge, NC • Key p. 313

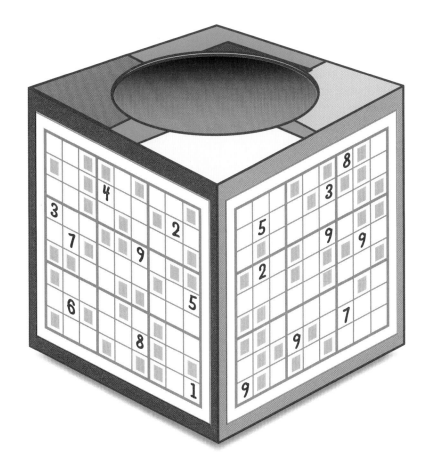

Sudoku Crazy
Problem solving

Use this easy-to-make center to help students think logically about numbers. Mount four different Sudoku puzzles (found free online or in newspapers and books) onto pieces of colorful paper that are the same size as the sides of a cube-shaped tissue box. Laminate the puzzles. Then glue them to different sides of the tissue box. Place inside the box each puzzle's solution and a wipe-off marker. To use the center, a student completes a puzzle and then uses the appropriate key to check his answers. When he's finished, he wipes the puzzle clean so it's ready for the next student. Replace the puzzle cube periodically with a new one to keep students' interest high.

Colleen Dabney, Williamsburg, VA

Fraction Interaction
Improper fractions, mixed numbers

To make this Go Fish! inspired game, divide students into small groups. Give each child eight index cards. Have her write a different mixed number on four separate cards and the corresponding improper fractions on the remaining cards. To play, have the students in each group combine their cards, deal each player three cards, and stack the remaining cards facedown. Next, players check their hands for matches and set those cards aside. Player 1 then converts (mentally or with paper and a pencil) a mixed number on one of her cards to an improper fraction (or vice versa). She asks another player if he has the matching card. If he does, he gives it to her and she sets those cards aside faceup. If not, she draws a card from the stack and Player 2 takes a turn. The first player to match all of her cards wins.

Melissa Bryan, West Chester, PA

Pass the Problem, Please!
Basic operations with whole numbers, decimals, or fractions

Begin this whole-class review by giving an index card to each student. Have him write on the card a problem of the type you announce. Collect the cards and number them sequentially; then instruct each child to number a sheet of paper for the total number of cards collected. Give each student a card. Have him solve the card's problem and then record its answer on his paper. After an appropriate amount of time, have each child pass his card to the next classmate and solve a new problem. Have students continue passing cards in this manner until each student has solved all the problems. Then check the answers together. Each time the activity is repeated, decrease the time allowed for solving the problems.

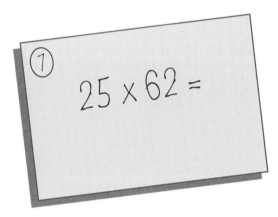

Make 'em Match!
Volume

Prepare for this partner game by giving each child ten index cards. On five of the cards, have her draw and label a different rectangular prism. On the other five cards, have her write the matching volume for each prism she drew. To play, each child then shuffles her cards with a partner's and arranges them in an array. The partners take turns turning over two cards at a time, trying to make a match. If the cards match, the player sets them aside and takes another turn. If they do not match, she turns the cards facedown again and her partner takes a turn. Play continues until all matches are made. The player with more matches wins.

Melissa Bryan

MATH MAILBAG

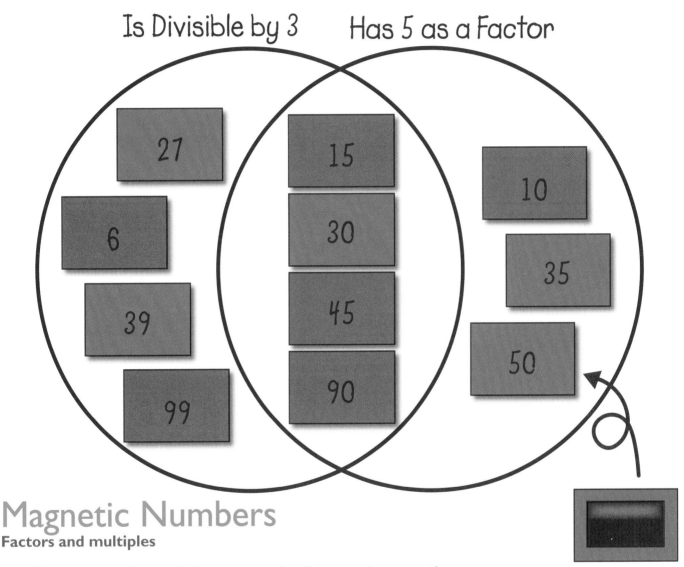

Is Divisible by 3   Has 5 as a Factor

27

6

39

99

15

30

45

90

10

35

50

Magnetic Numbers
Factors and multiples

This easy-to-adapt activity can make classifying numbers a routine part of your math class. Print two sets of numbers from 0 to 100 in a large font, using a different color of card stock for each set. Laminate the cards and cut them apart. Then affix a magnetic strip to the backs of the cards and store them in separate containers. Next, divide students into two teams and draw a large Venn diagram on the board. Label it with the skill(s) to be practiced. Have two players at a time (one per team) come up and place a number card on the diagram. The next player on a team can either place another number card or correct a teammate's mistake. To practice a different skill, just change the diagram's labels. To increase the difficulty level, use three circles instead of two!

Rebecca Blanchard, Harris Road Middle School, Concord, NC

Group Division
Game, math aid

Use this class game to review the steps of long division. Divide students into groups of four. Send two groups up to the board. Give each group the same problem to solve, but have each step completed by a different child. For the problem shown, the first student would divide 5 into 6, the second child would multiply the digit just written in the quotient by the divisor, the third child would subtract and bring down the next number, and the fourth child would start dividing again. Award the first group to solve the problem correctly a point; then call two new groups to the board. After continuing in this manner for a period of time, declare the group with the most points the winner. If students have difficulty remembering the steps, have them use glitter glue to write the mnemonic device _Dad_ (divide), _Mom_ (multiply), _Sister_ (subtract), _Brother_ (bring down) on an index card to keep as a reminder!

Clidean Epps, Mount Olive Elementary, Seale, AL
Carrie L. Greene, Oakfield-Alabama Elementary, Oakfield, NY

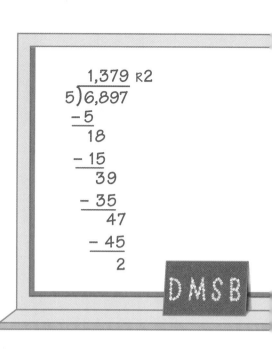

Matho
Probability

To help students discover which numbers on a die are most frequently rolled, make each child a 5 x 5 grid. Have him place his grid in a clear plastic sheet protector, and provide him with paper squares to use as game pieces. To play, each child uses a wipe-off marker to randomly program each square of the grid with a number from 2 to 12. Then roll two dice and have students cover the numbers rolled. The first player to cover five numbers in a row, column, or diagonal wins. To play again, students clean the sheet protectors and reprogram their grids. Once players discover that sixes, sevens, and eights are the most frequently rolled numbers, switch to three dice and have players program their grids from 3 to 18. For an even greater challenge, have students program their grids from 1 to 36 and, using two dice, multiply the numbers rolled!

Mary Backes, St. Mary School, Wilmington, NC

A Quest for Pi
Circumference, radius, and diameter

This hands-on exploration can help students understand that a circle's circumference is about three times its diameter. Have each child cut the circles from a copy of page 253 into wedges and tape them onto graph paper to form three approximate parallelograms as shown. Explain that the length of each created parallelogram equals one-half of the circle's circumference and that the height equals the circle's radius. Next, have students count and record the number of squares along the base and height of each glued figure and then divide the larger number by the smaller one. The quotient should be close to the value of pi (3.14). To see whether students can get their answers even closer to 3.14, have them average all three quotients!

Jeanette Griggs, Swartz Creek, MI

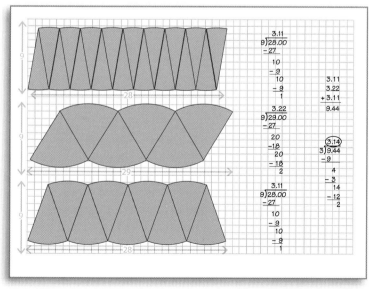

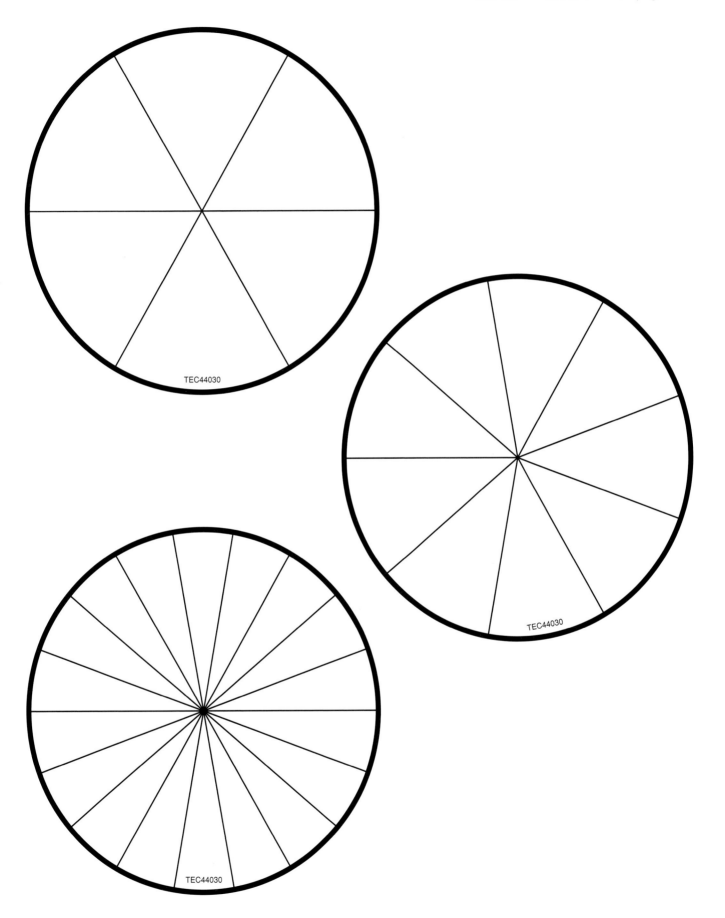

TEC44030

TEC44030

TEC44030

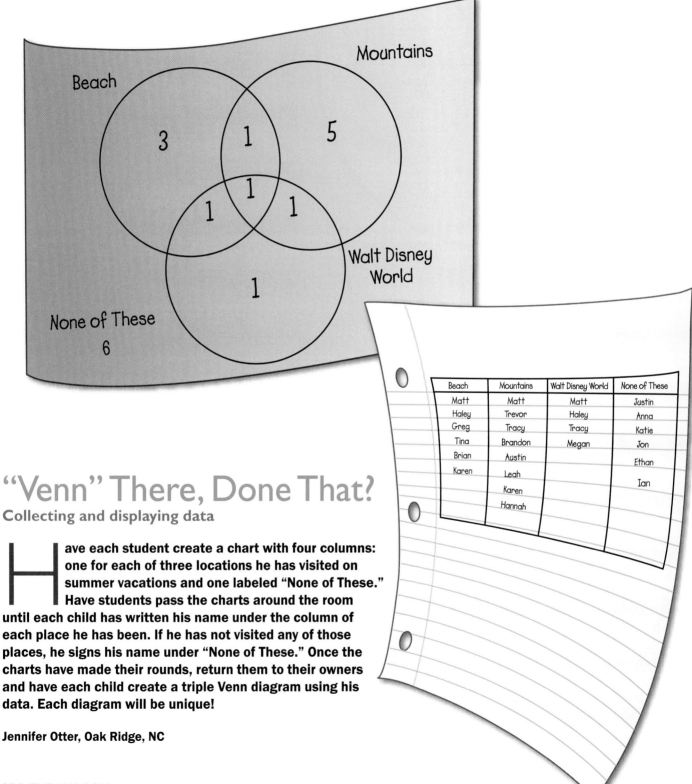

Beach	Mountains	Walt Disney World	None of These
Matt	Matt	Matt	Justin
Haley	Trevor	Haley	Anna
Greg	Tracy	Tracy	Katie
Tina	Brandon	Megan	Jon
Brian	Austin		Ethan
Karen	Leah		Ian
	Karen		
	Hannah		

"Venn" There, Done That?
Collecting and displaying data

Have each student create a chart with four columns: one for each of three locations he has visited on summer vacations and one labeled "None of These." Have students pass the charts around the room until each child has written his name under the column of each place he has been. If he has not visited any of those places, he signs his name under "None of These." Once the charts have made their rounds, return them to their owners and have each child create a triple Venn diagram using his data. Each diagram will be unique!

Jennifer Otter, Oak Ridge, NC

Musical Chairs Math
Problem solving

Gather enough index cards for each student plus three extra cards. Program each with a different review problem. Number the cards and place one card facedown on every child's desk and each extra card on an unoccupied desk. When the music starts, instruct students to walk around the room, with paper and pencil, in a path you direct. Since there are more cards than students, no child will need to rush for a chair when you stop the music. When the music stops, each student sits down at a desk, turns over the card, records its number on her paper, and solves the problem. After an appropriate amount of time, restart the music. Continue as time allows, reminding students not to sit in the same seat twice. To check answers at the end of the activity, have each child share the answer for the problem located on her desk. Then provide answers for the problems at the unoccupied desks.

Lynn Brown, Bell Creek Elementary, Bellbrook, OH

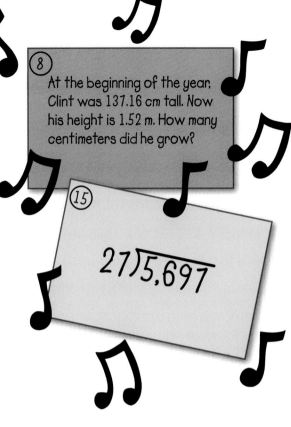

8 At the beginning of the year, Clint was 137.16 cm tall. Now his height is 1.52 m. How many centimeters did he grow?

15 $27\overline{)5,697}$

$1.00 ÷ $2.99 ≈ 0.33 ≈ 33% savings

SAVE $1.00

Hand Lotion $2.99

Sizzlin' Sales
Percentages

Obtain enough copies of an appropriate drugstore sales flyer for every two students. Ask the class to look through the flyer and select an item a mom or mother figure would buy. When an item has been selected, have students use calculators to determine the percentage of savings on the item's price when using a $1.00-off coupon. Repeat the steps, selecting items that a student, dad, sister, brother, grandpa, and grandma would buy!

Maria Jamell, Lincoln Middle School, Lincolnton, NC

Fantasy Farm
Geometry and measurement

Many math concepts can be assessed with this fun project. Give each child or pair of students a copy of page 256 and discuss the activity's directions. Then have the designers make a sketch, gather the needed materials, and create a model of a farm. To vary the project, change the items in the checklist and have students create a zoo or park instead!

Andrea Keith, Letford Elementary, Johnstown, CO

Fantasy Farm

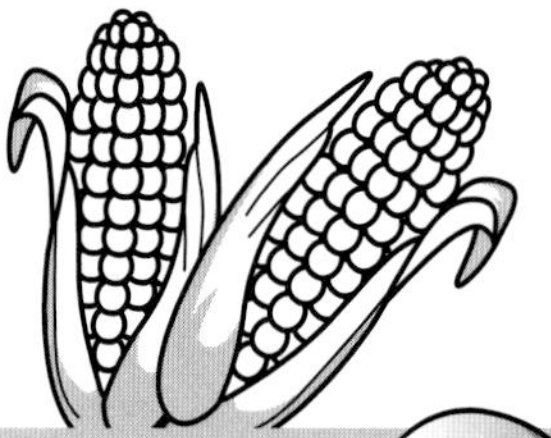

Design a model of a farm that includes the items listed below. Check the box as you complete each item. Try to earn 100 points! Then answer the questions.

Item and Description	Point Value
☐ field with an area of 60 square units	20
☐ barn that is a rectangular prism and has a square door	20
☐ weather vane made of perpendicular lines on top of the barn	10
☐ scarecrow with arms at right angles to the body and legs that form an acute or an obtuse angle	10
☐ fence	5
☐ ditch made of parallel lines next to the field	5
☐ pig made of cylinders	10
☐ horse with a quadrilateral as its body	5
☐ cow with a trapezoid as its body	5
☐ chicken with a hexagon as its body	5
☐ sheep with a triangle as its head	5

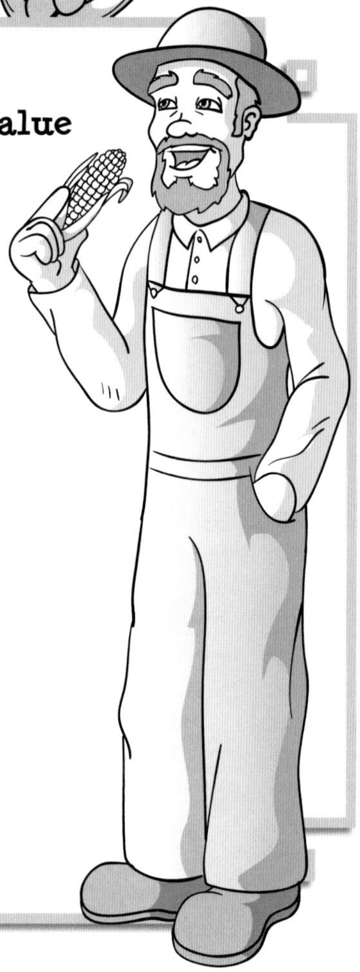

1. How long is the field? _____ How wide? _____ What is its area? _____
   Its perimeter? _____

2. How long is the barn? _____ How wide? _____ How tall? _____
   What is its volume? _____

3. How long is the ditch? _____

4. How many sides does the horse's body have? _____ The cow's body? _____
   The chicken's body? _____ The sheep's head? _____

5. Did you include any extra geometric features? If so, describe them. _____

   _____

   _____

WRITE ON!

WRITE ON!

Writing Racetrack

Fuel up.	Start your engine!	Rev up. VROOM	Make a pit stop.	Take the final lap.	Cross the finish line!
Prewriting	First Draft	Revising	Editing	Publishing	Sharing and Celebrating

Rayshad

Writing Racetrack
Tracking the writing process

Want to know at a glance which students are writing first drafts and which are editing? This visual tool will help! Divide a whiteboard into six sections and caption them as shown, adding illustrations if desired. (For patterns, go to themailboxcompanion.com.) Then have each child personalize a construction paper copy of the racecar pattern on page 58, affix a magnetic strip to the car's back, and position it at the prewriting line. Also give each writer a copy of page 260 to keep in his writing folder as a guide. Students can advance their cars along the track as they complete each step of their writing. Once a writer crosses the finish line, he selects a new topic and starts again!

Nikki Rodriguez, Trinity Elementary, Trinity, FL

Adventures Ahoy!
Narrative writing

Transform students into pirates for a writing activity they won't forget! Before Talk Like a Pirate Day on September 19, invite each child to bring in a bandana, an eye patch, or another appropriate pirate prop. On that day, allow students to wear their props and pretend to be pirates as they write an adventurous tale about something that happens to them on the high seas or an isolated island. Their imaginations will run wild!

Jaime Compton, Blessed Trinity School, Ocala, FL

Shiver Me Timbers!

No one should have to be alone on Goosebump Island. I am so happy to be back on a ship away from that eerie place. How I got there is quite a story.

The Perfect Desk
Descriptive writing

Student desks aren't the most comfortable places to sit. So challenge each child to design a desk that's both practical and comfy! To jump-start the activity, ask questions such as the following: What kind of shape should the perfect desk have? Should the chair have a padded seat? Next, have each child draw a picture of the desk she imagines and then write a paragraph describing it. Collect the paragraphs and drawings, labeling each illustration with a different letter of the alphabet and each description with a different number. Post the papers and challenge students to match each picture and paragraph. The better the descriptions are, the easier the task will be!

Meredith Allison, Gladwin, MI

Visual Cue
Expository writing

Informative paragraphs are easy for students to write if this eye-catching tool is in view! Create a giant ice-cream sundae from poster board and display it on a wall or bulletin board throughout the year. Use it to discuss with students what a good expository paragraph consists of. Invite each child to refer to the guide whenever he writes about any of the following: a retelling of something read in a science or social studies text, a problem that has one or more solutions, an event and its effects, a topic whose details need to be presented in a particular order, or the similarities and differences in two or more things. This visual reminder will make it much more likely that the writing you get is correctly organized!

Doreen Placko, Antioch, IL

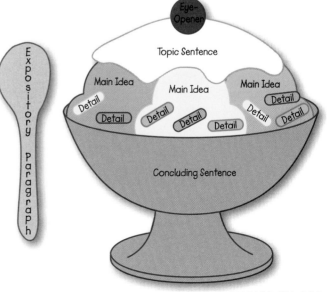

Expository paragraph

Eye-Opener

Topic Sentence

Main Idea   Main Idea   Main Idea

Detail   Detail   Detail   Detail   Detail   Detail

Concluding Sentence

STAYING ON TRACK

Prewriting

Fuel up.
- Gather ideas.
- Make a list, draw a web, or fill in a graphic organizer.

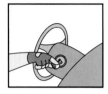

First Draft

Start your engine!
- Write your first draft. Remember to skip lines.

Revising

Rev up.
- Revise your writing, using these questions as a guide:

  ___ Did I stay focused on the topic?

  ___ Does the introduction hook the reader?

  ___ Did I include important details?

  ___ Did I use specific words and vivid verbs?

  ___ Did I vary the sentences?

  ___ Does the story have a beginning, a middle, and an end?

- Ask someone to read your work and suggest revisions.

Editing

Make a pit stop.
- Check your writing for grammar, spelling, punctuation, and capitalization.

Publishing

Take the final lap.
- Write your final draft.

Sharing and Celebrating

Cross the finish line!
- Read your work aloud to the class or share it with a partner.

©The Mailbox® • TEC44026 • Aug./Sept. 2006 • written by Nikki Rodriguez, Trinity, FL

See	Smell	Touch
green	sweet	slick
bumpy	vinegary	wet
long		
ridged		
yellow spots		

"Pickle-licious" Experience

Writing a detailed description

Students will call upon their senses to complete this nifty activity! Pull one pickle from a jar of pickles and display it on a paper towel. Allow students to pass the paper towel from child to child to get a closer view of the pickle. As it's being passed, ask, "How could you describe this pickle so it could be picked out from a group of four pickles?" Record the responses related to sight, smell, and touch on the board. Next, have students help you write a paragraph that describes the pickle so well that anyone who reads it could select the right pickle. Then invite the principal or another teacher to your class to read the paragraph and pick out which of four pickles is the one being described. If the right pickle is selected, reward the class with a special treat!

JoAnn Brandenburg, Hatcher Elementary, Ashland, KY

Hook 'em at the Beginning!
Writing introductory sentences

This ball-bouncing activity will guarantee that students' stories get off to a super start! Have students stand in a circle. Next, say a bare-bones sentence, such as "I went home." Then bounce a ball to one child. Have him add or change one word or phrase to improve the sentence. For example, he might say, "I sprinted home." He bounces the ball to another child in the circle, who adds or changes one more word or phrase. For example, she might say, "I sprinted toward home." That child bounces the ball to a third child, who adds or changes yet one more word or phrase. For example, he might say, "As the sun set, I sprinted toward home." The fourth student to catch the bouncing ball can either add to or change the existing sentence, or introduce a new bare-bones sentence. When everyone in the circle has had a turn, each child returns to his seat and writes five different interesting sentences. Post the completed sentences at a writing center to use as story starters!

Kim Minafo, Dillard Drive Elementary, Raleigh, NC

Story Starters

It was so quiet that we could hear a pin drop.

Standing beside the wet road was the dirtiest cat I'd ever seen.

It was a clear, windy October night.

Raindrops kept slamming against the window.

Dry leaves crunched under my feet as I crept up the steps of the abandoned house.

Writer's Café
Writing motivation

Autumn Adventure

The sound of rustling leaves,
Moved by a nighttime breeze
Whistling through the trees,
Never puts me at ease.

So stay with me, please,
As I get on my knees
And look for Mom's keys
That I dropped in the leaf pile when I sneezed!

Regularly enjoy stories, poems, and essays written by students by setting aside a special time just for that purpose. Once a month, invite each child to come to a designated area of the classroom and use a microphone to share something she's written during that month. If desired, allow listeners to sip and munch on seasonal beverages and light snacks provided by parents during this time. Knowing that written work could be shared in such a setting, students will be most eager to write!

April Chamberlain, Irondale Community School, Irondale, AL

Stretch It Out!
Elaboration

Jeff was speechless when Keshia stormed into the room and ripped the paper out of his hands.

Encourage students to add detail to their writing with some theatrics! First, write the following sentence on the board: "The student took the paper from the desk." Discuss with students the boring nature of this sentence. Then invite two students into the hall with you. Have one child return to the room, sit at his desk with a sheet of paper, and then react with shock when the other child rushes in and snatches his paper. After the scene plays out, have students write about what just occurred and then share their writing with the class. No doubt what is shared will be more detailed than the sentence on the board. If desired, repeat the activity, this time having one student gingerly slide the paper off the desk as the child at the desk growls and glares! For more practice, have each child complete a copy of page 263 as directed.

Cristina Heredia, Franklin Elementary, East Chicago, IN

Flesh 'em Out!

Add words to each bare-bones sentence to make it more detailed.
Use adjectives, adverbs, and prepositional phrases.

1. The driver honked the horn. _____

_____

2. A boy closed the door. _____

_____

3. I sat at my desk. _____

_____

4. Our team won. _____

_____

5. I forgot a book. _____

_____

6. We went to lunch. _____

_____

7. My pencil needs sharpening. _____

_____

8. The paper was written. _____

_____

9. I have homework. _____

_____

10. The day was warm. _____

_____

©The Mailbox® • TEC44027 • Oct./Nov. 2006 • written by Colleen Dabney, Williamsburg, VA

Note to the teacher: Use with "Stretch It Out!" on page 262.

WRITE ON!

Both
- The girls have the same number of mean family members.
- The girls are not allowed to do what they really want to do.
- The girls get help from someone other than a family member.
- The stories have happy endings.

Cinderella
- Cinderella has many chores to do.
- Cinderella's fairy godmother helps her.
- The prince looks for Cinderella.

The Biggest, Best Snowman
- Nell is not allowed to do chores because of her size.
- Nell's friends help her.
- Nell's family goes to look at the snowman.

The Superhero Snowman by Taylor

Book-Based Tales
Comparing and contrasting, narrative writing

Grab copies of *Cinderella* by Charles Perrault and *The Biggest, Best Snowman* by Margery Cuyler for a partner writing activity students won't forget! After reading the books aloud, ask students to share how the books are alike and different and record their remarks in a Venn diagram. Next, have each child use the tales' similarities to write a story with a different setting and characters. When he's finished, have him draw and color a snowman and cut it out to make a cover. He traces the cover on lined paper and cuts out the tracings. Then he copies his story onto the tracings and staples them behind the cover. After the stories have been shared, display them on a wintry bulletin board!

Natalie Hughes-Tanner, Ermel Elementary, Houston, TX

Check out the graphic organizer on page 266.

What Are They Saying?
Writing dialogue

Wordless books (or ones with very few words in them) are great for teaching students how to punctuate words spoken by characters. Ask your librarian to pull a selection of these books by authors such as Alexandra Day, Mercer Mayer, and David Wiesner. Share pages from some of the books so students can note the absence of text. Next, ask students how they know what a comic-strip character is saying. *(The words are usually in a speech bubble.)* Model how to write words from a speech bubble as a sentence with quotation marks. Then have pairs of students each choose a wordless book and create at least one sentence of dialogue for each page. After you check the papers, have partners copy the sentences correctly. When students share their work with the class, have one partner read the dialogue and the other show the matching page(s) of the actual book!

Shari Miller, Northeast Elementary, Arma, KS
Angela Ritter, Killough Middle School, Houston, TX

> What's this frog doing in our lunch basket?

The woman screamed, "What's this frog doing in our lunch basket?"

Colorfully Organized
Prewriting

A Trip to an Amusement Park

space roller coaster — Dad
mountain roller coaster — Sammi
penny toss — log ride
scared — hotdog
basketball shoot — thrilled
bumper cars — raft ride
Ferris wheel — bored
boats — train
excited — soda
ice cream — nervous
Mom

This bright idea makes grouping items for writing a colorful task! Have each writer record her writing topic at the top of her paper. Then have her brainstorm on the paper a list of everything she might include in a story about that topic. After creating a lengthy list, have her use colors to group like ideas together. If she is writing about a trip to an amusement park, she could circle or highlight in blue the water rides and the emotions she felt while riding them. She could use yellow for the nonwater rides and orange for all other activities. She could use pink for the food and drinks she had at the park and green for the people who went with her to the park. When it's time to write a draft, she just makes sure each set of like-colored items is in the same detailed paragraph!

Jennifer Gunerman, Klem Road North Elementary, Webster, NY

Writer's Resource Booklet
Student reference tool

Put tips for writing paragraphs, narratives, descriptions, expository essays, and more right at students' fingertips! Create a booklet for each child that includes samples and mini lessons about different types of writing, specific adjectives and strong verbs, writing dialogue, and anything else you think is helpful for developing good writers. You could even include a sample of your writing rubric, a list of tricky words, or a reminder about what to do when you are having a conference with another student. Have each child keep his book in his writing folder. Then collect the books at the end of the year to use with next year's class!

Sue Reed, Ebenezer Elementary, Lebanon, PA

What Every Writer Needs to Know

Roll 'em!

Write an event or detail in each film frame below to show the order in which you will include it in a story or an essay.

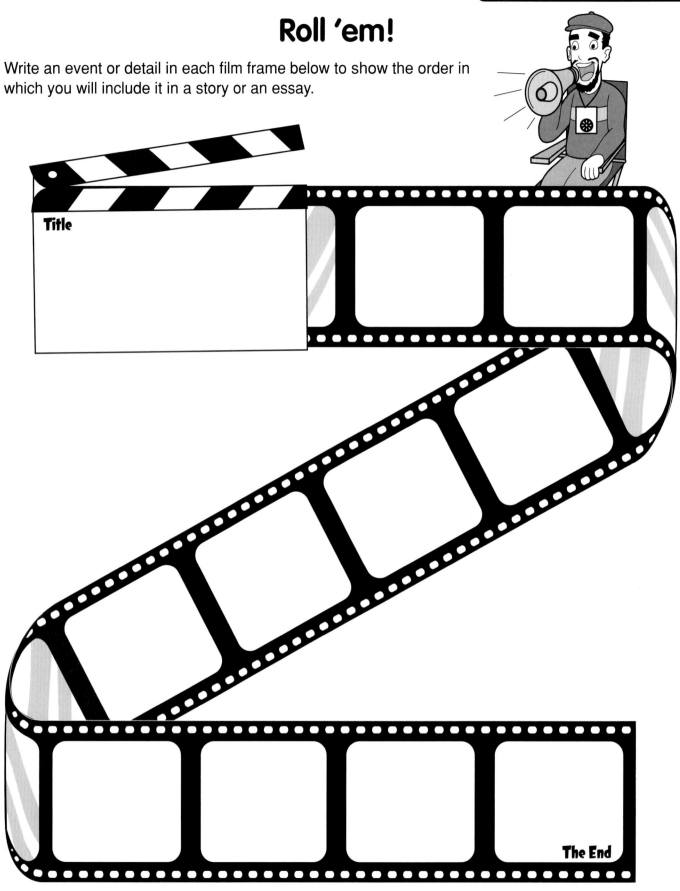

Title

The End

Note to the teacher: Have students use this as a planning page to sequence events when writing a narrative or to show the order in which important details will be presented in an expository essay.

WRITE ON!

How to Make Chocolate Fudge and See the World

by Ethan

Chocolate Fudge

2 tbsp. butter
²/₃ c. evaporated skim milk
1²/₃ c. sugar
¹/₂ tsp. salt
2 c. miniature marshmallows
1¹/₂ c. semisweet chocolate chips
1 tsp. vanilla

Combine butter, milk, sugar, and salt in a saucepan over medium heat. Bring to a boil. Cook four to five minutes, stirring constantly. Remove from heat. Stir in remaining ingredients and continue stirring until marshmallows melt. Pour into a buttered eight-inch square pan and cool. Cut fudge into squares.

A Recipe for Writing
Expository writing, research

Begin by having students bring in copies of their favorite recipes. Then, if possible, read aloud *How to Make an Apple Pie and See the World* by Marjorie Priceman, the story of a girl who travels the world to get ingredients for an apple pie because the market is closed. Next, have students find out from which states or countries each of their recipes' ingredients come. When the research is complete, have each child write his own how-to-see-the-world story, including the forms of transportation he uses to get to different destinations. For extra credit, have him label a world map to show where he traveled!

Amy Vagnoni, Frederick School, Grayslake, IL

To See or Not to See

Persuasive writing

Do your students want Punxsutawney Phil to see his shadow on Groundhog Day? To find out, have each child write a letter to Phil that includes three reasons why he does or does not want the animal to see his shadow. When the letters are finished, pretend to be Phil. Read each letter aloud and appear to give each writer's arguments serious thought. To repeat this activity at other holidays, just adapt the writing purpose and the role that you assume.

Cris Petro, Bailly Elementary, Chesterton, IN

Dear Phil,
There are three really important reasons why you shouldn't see your shadow on Groundhog Day. The biggest reason is so our new house can be finished. If you see your shadow, we'll have six more weeks of winter and the work crew won't be able to work outside as much. The second reason is so I can stop shoveling snow and ice. We need warmer temperatures, not colder ones! The third reason is that I'm tired of wearing a heavy coat everywhere I go. I want to put on a T-shirt and shorts instead. Please, just sleep all day on February 2!

Your friend,
Will

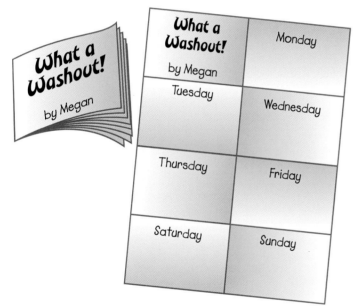

Big-Screen Edits

Proofreading

To gather stories for this review activity, have each child save on a disk a story she has written, protecting her identity as the author by using an assigned number or letter instead of her name. Next, display one of the stories on a TV screen connected to a computer. Then get students' editing input by reading the displayed story aloud and using prompts such as those shown. While you have students' attention, demonstrate how to correct any spelling, punctuation, or capitalization errors in the tale.

Dana Sanders, Kingston Elementary, Kingston, GA

How's the Weather?

Prewriting, narrative writing

Begin by having students brainstorm crazy or humorous things that could happen on a farm, in a neighborhood, or in a big city during a week of very windy weather. Then have each child think about what could happen in a different place or during a week of rainy weather. Have her create a storyboard to plan a picture book about such a tale by folding a sheet of drawing paper in half three times to make eight boxes. In the first box, she writes the title and her name. In each of the seven remaining boxes, she writes a different day of the week and what will happen on that day. Then have her edit her work and publish it using eight same-size sheets of paper. As a reward, allow her to share her book with a younger child at your school.

Diann Anderson, Kitty Hawk Elementary, Kitty Hawk, NC

- Tell about a part of the story you think is funny, exciting, or well written.

- Ask a question that you had as we read the story, or suggest a way the author could improve the story.

- Tell what you would like to see happen next.

> This object landed in my backyard last night. It sat in the yard for a few minutes. Then it opened and stood straight up. U-shaped people started to fly out of it one at a time. I captured the object and brought it in today so you could help me figure out what this thing is. What is it called? Where is it from? Who are these U-shaped people? What are they here to do?

You Must Be Mistaken!

Explanatory writing

For a memorable writing activity, invite students to look at ordinary classroom and household objects in a way they never have before! Hold up a familiar object such as a stapler. Without naming the object, ask students to tell you about it. After listening to explanations about its function, say, "You must be mistaken!" Then make up a creative use for the object (see the example) and have each child write about it. You'll be amazed at the explanations your writers come up with!

Jennifer Klipp, Taylors, SC

WRITE ON!

A Topic a Day
Journaling

Get students' help with generating the journal prompts they'll be writing about. Cut several file folders in half as shown. Then invite your writers to brainstorm interesting topics and corresponding prompts. Write a topic on the left side of a file-folder half and the corresponding prompts on the right. File the folder halves in an inexpensive plastic crate. Each day, when it is time to write a journal entry, a child can choose a topic from the file and write about a prompt of her choice!

Amber Barbee, Wharton, TX

Friends

Desserts

Animals

Prompts
1. Why do you think turtles move so slowly? Explain.
2. Suppose that monkeys could talk. Write about what you think they would say.
3. Pretend that you have found a tarantula in your sleeping bag on a camping trip. Explain what you will do.
4. What would you think if you saw a puppy riding a pony? Explain.
5. What is your least favorite animal? Why?

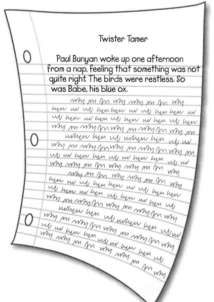

Twister Tamer

Paul Bunyan woke up one afternoon from a nap, feeling that something was not quite right. The birds were restless. So was Babe, his blue ox.

Pure Fiction?
Writing a legend, myth, or short story

To integrate story writing into any subject, have students weave some of the facts they are learning about a current topic into their next writing assignment. Imagine reading about Charlotte spinning a web of 3-D figures, Uncle Sam bragging about working out a system of checks and balances for the government, or Paul Bunyan taming a bigger-than-life weather system that is threatening to become a category 5 hurricane in the Atlantic or an F5 tornado in Kansas. Whether the heroic characters who emerge from the stories are legendary, mythical, or realistic, you'll get an idea of what students understand about a nonfiction topic!

Terry Healy, Manhattan, KS

It's Traditional!
Narrative writing

Traditions are not just for holidays. What about all the things that students do with their families every day, week, month, or year? Discuss such times with students, helping them understand what qualifies as a tradition and what does not. Next, have each child complete a copy of the planner on page 271 as directed and use it to write a narrative about a family tradition. Then have her publish her work by illustrating it and stapling it inside a decorated construction paper cover. The resulting "photo album" can even include photos brought from home if she wishes!

Peggy Morin Bruno, Squadron Line School, Simsbury, CT

Name _____

It's a Family Tradition!

Fill in the organizer based on something you do with your family every day, every week, every month, or every year.

WHAT	WHO
My favorite family tradition is	The people who are part of this tradition are

WHEN and WHERE
This tradition happens every	at

HOW	WHY
This is how our family tradition works	We started this tradition because

Nonholiday Traditions
- selecting the menu on your birthday
- trip to the beach every summer
- pizza before soccer practice every Wednesday
- Sunday dinner at Grandma's

It's a Family Tradition!

Fill in the organizer based on something you do with your family every day, every week, every month, or every year.

WHAT

My favorite family tradition is _____

_____

_____

_____.

WHO

The people who are part of this tradition are

_____

_____

_____.

WHEN AND WHERE

This tradition happens every _____

at _____

_____.

HOW

This is how our family tradition works:

_____

_____

_____

_____

_____

_____

_____

WHY

We started this tradition because

_____

_____

_____

_____

_____

_____.

Note to the teacher: Use with "It's Traditional!" on page 270.

THE MAILBOX **271**

WRITE ON!

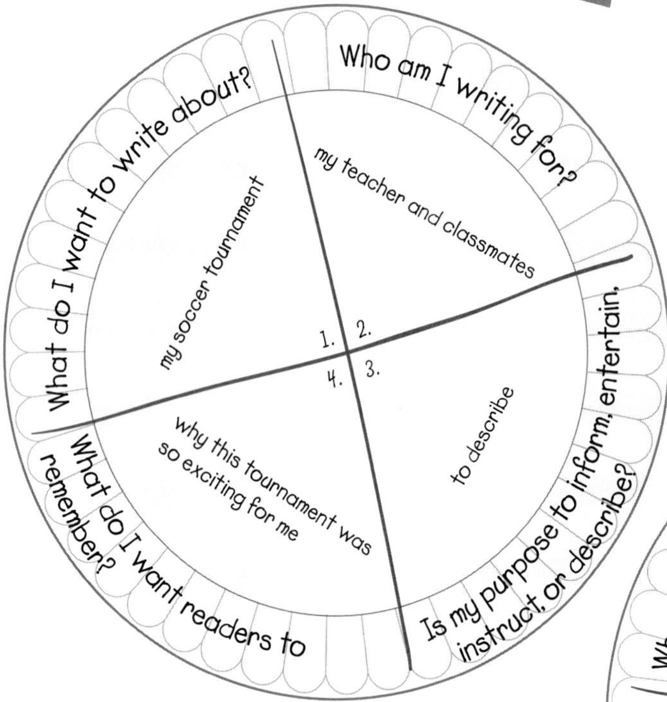

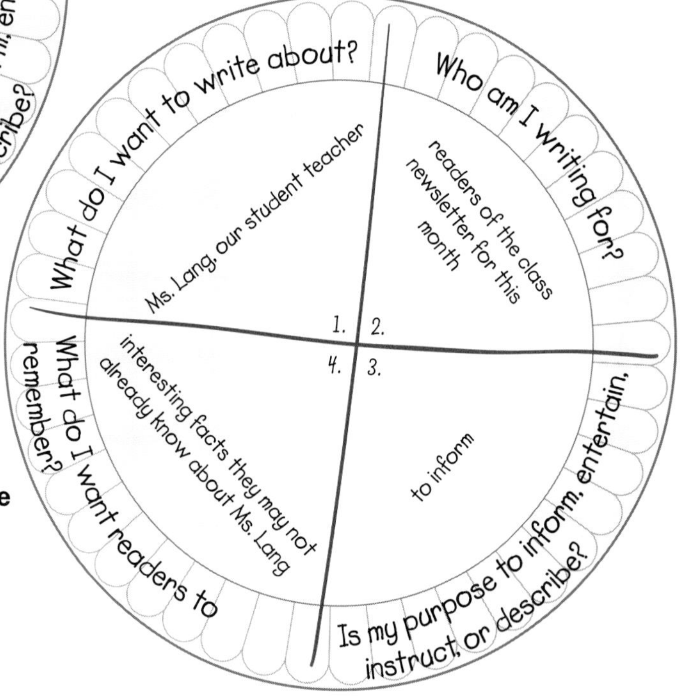

Writing Wheels

Prewriting

To help students develop their writing ideas before they put pencil to paper, have each child divide a paper plate into four sections as shown. Then have him label each quadrant with one of these numbered questions:

1. What do I want to write about?
2. Who am I writing for?
3. Is my purpose to inform, entertain, instruct, or describe?
4. What do I want readers to remember?

Have each student write his answers on his plate. Then divide the class into groups of four. As each student shares his wheel, encourage his group to make suggestions or ask questions that will help him narrow his topic or elaborate on it. After everyone has shared, provide time for each student to use his wheel to write a finished piece.

Terry Healy, Marlatt Elementary, Manhattan, KS

Do Details Matter?
Persuasive-writing warm-up

Use this partner activity to reinforce the importance of using supporting details when convincing someone to do something. Brainstorm with students ten silly actions, such as those shown. Next, divide the class into pairs. Direct Student A in each duo to choose an action and try to persuade her partner to do it. After three minutes, have Student B choose a different action and do the persuading. Students will quickly see how important supporting details are in persuasion. The next time you assign a persuasive-writing task, have partners complete a similar persuasion talk to make sure they have enough supporting details for their topics.

Shawna Miller, Wellington Elementary, Flower Mound, TX

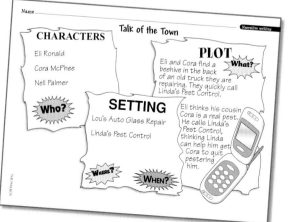

Ketchup on cereal? Yuck!

Silly Actions
Put ketchup on your cereal.
Wear socks on your hands.
Wear your shoes on the wrong feet.
Read a book from the end to the beginning.
Do a dance in the middle of a mall.
Sleep with your head at the foot of your bed.
Wash your hair with spaghetti sauce.
Serve kitty treats at your next party.
Paint your face green.
Unplug all the appliances in your house.

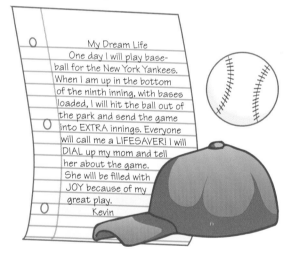

My Dream Life
One day I will play baseball for the New York Yankees. When I am up in the bottom of the ninth inning, with bases loaded, I will hit the ball out of the park and send the game into EXTRA innings. Everyone will call me a LIFESAVER! I will DIAL up my mom and tell her about the game. She will be filled with JOY because of my great play.
Kevin

My Dream Life
Personal narrative

In advance, collect a supply of grocery and drug store advertising circulars. Discuss with students dreams they have for their future. For example, does someone want to be a ballerina, a racecar driver, or the president of the United States? Next, give each student or pair of students one or more circulars and a highlighter. Have the student highlight brand names that are also common words (see the capitalized words shown). Then challenge each child to write a narrative piece using the highlighted words to describe an event that will happen in her future dream life.

Kim Minafo, Dillard Drive Elementary, Raleigh, NC

Talk of the Town
Narrative writing

For this ready-to-use activity, place a telephone book and copies of the organizer on page 274 at a writing center. A student randomly opens the phone book and finds a name for a character he can include in his story. He writes the name on a copy of the organizer and then continues flipping to different pages until he has listed three (or more) names. Next, the student turns to the business listings and finds two interesting locations to list in the organizer's "Setting" box. He concludes by listing one or more plot ideas that include at least two of the names and at least one of the settings. Have students use their completed organizers to write original narratives. If desired, display the stories on a bulletin board titled "Our Stories Are the Talk of the Town!"

Colleen Dabney, Williamsburg-JCC Schools, Williamsburg, VA

Name _____

CHARACTERS
Eli Ronald
Cora McPhee
Nell Palmer

Who?

Talk of the Town Narrative writing

PLOT **What?**
Eli and Cora find a beehive in the back of an old truck they are repairing. They quickly call Linda's Pest Control.

SETTING
Lou's Auto Glass Repair
Linda's Pest Control

Eli thinks his cousin Cora is a real pest. He calls Linda's Pest Control, thinking Linda can help him get Cora to quit pestering him.

Where? **When?**

Name _____

Talk of the Town

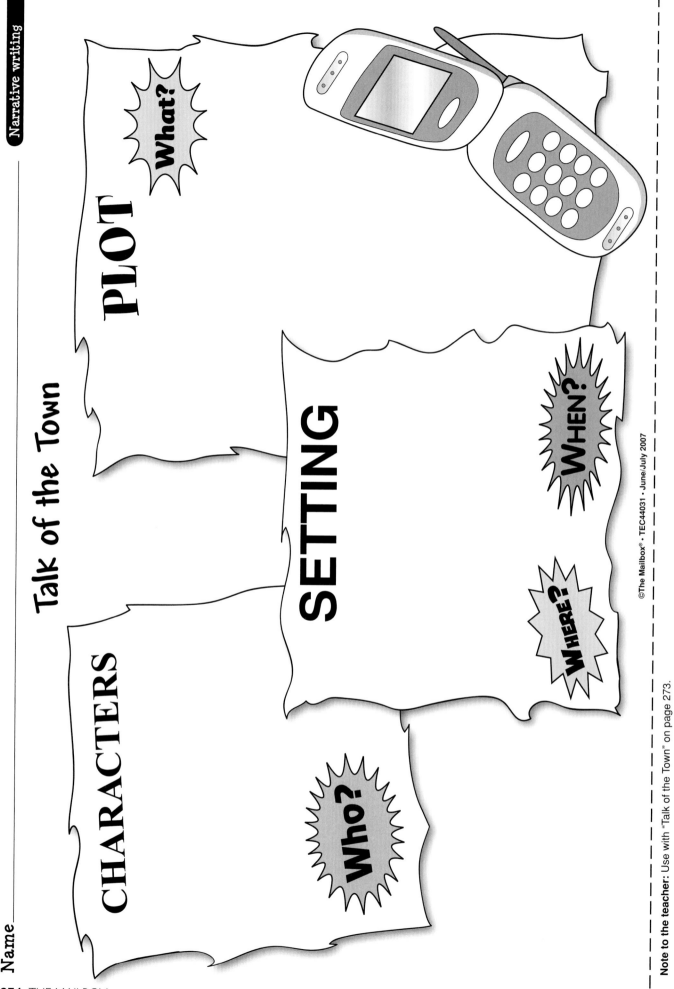

PLOT

What?

SETTING

When?

Where?

CHARACTERS

Who?

Note to the teacher: Use with "Talk of the Town" on page 273.

Language Arts Spotlight

Language Arts Spotlight
NOUNS

People

teacher	Mr. Walsh
secretary	Ms. Venezuela
~~pal~~	Ms. Halley
~~ian~~	

Places

library	Patrick Cox Library
bathroom	
cafeteria	
computer lab	Gateway Computer Lab
school	Hickory Day School

Things

desk	
book	<u>Little House on the Prairie</u>
dictionary	<u>The American Heritage Dictionary</u>
van	Ford Aerostar
flowers	

People
- teacher
- janitor
- principal
- parent
- bus driver
- cook
- secretary
- librarian
- best friend
- delivery man
- crossing guard
- vice principal
- grandmother
- sister
- brother
- nurse
- aide

Places
- library
- bathroom
- cafeteria
- computer lab
- school

Things
- desk
- book
- dictionary
- van
- flowers

Clipboard Quest
Identifying common and proper nouns

Supply small groups of students with a clipboard for this schoolwide search! Have each group label a sheet of paper "People," "Places," or "Things" and then head out into the school for a set amount of time to search for examples of common nouns that fit that category. To make the task more challenging, require that all nouns recorded start with a specific letter of the alphabet. When all groups have returned, list the collected examples on chart paper and have students suggest a proper noun for each common noun!

Kristin Priola, Hickory Day School, Hickory, NC
Jolene DiBrango, Mendon Center Elementary, Pittsford, NY

Name That Noun!
Identifying people, places, and things

Noun Category	First Letter	Answer	Points
Animal	F	fox	1
City	B	Baltimore	1
Country	M	Mexico	2
Famous Person	S		0
Book	D	dictionary	2

No answer = 0 points | Same answer as another student = 1 point | Unique answer = 2 points

Critical-thinking skills will be strengthened with this categorizing game. Write each letter of the alphabet on a separate slip of paper. Place the slips in a bag. Have the class select five different noun categories that each player then records in the first column of a copy of the game card on page 278. Next, draw five letters from the bag. Have each child record the letters, in the order called, in the game card's second column. Allow players three minutes to record in the third column a noun that matches each letter and category. When time is up, each child scores her card using the scale on the game card. The player with the most points wins!

Laurie Cappas, Kings Park, NY

Scrutinize It!
Identifying singular and plural nouns

Students will be eyeballing pictures for particular people, places, and things for this activity! Each child cuts out a detailed picture from a magazine and glues it to the center of a sheet of construction paper. To the left of the cutout, the student lists the letters A–M. To the right of the cutout, she lists the letters N–Z. For each letter listed, she tries to find one pictured noun and then records both its singular and plural form next to the letter as shown. As a challenge, students could include an adjective for the noun that starts with the same letter!

Joyce Hovanec, Glassport Elementary, Glassport, PA

A – apple, apples
B – bird, birds
C – candy, candies
D – dog, dogs
E – eye, eyes
F – foot, feet
G – grade, grades
H – hat, hats
I – instrument, instruments
J –
K – kid, kids
L – leaf, leaves
M –

note, notes – N
– O
path, paths – P
– Q
rabbit, rabbits – R
school, schools – S
toe, toes – T
– U
– V
window, windows – W
– X
yard, yards – Y
– Z

It's in the Bag!
Identifying singular and plural possessive nouns

The boys' bikes were parked by the school.

What belongs to whom will be clearer with this activity! Label two lunch bags as shown. Then make a copy of the cards on page 279. Cut the cards apart and place them in the "noun" bag. Write "singular possessive" and "plural possessive" on an equal number of paper slips and place them in the corresponding bag. Each child draws a slip from each bag and then writes and illustrates on unlined paper a sentence that uses that noun form correctly. After the projects have been shared with the class, display them on a colorful board to show that students really do have singular and plural possessive nouns in the bag!

Jenneane D. Snyder, Richmond, VA

Game Card Patterns

Use with "Name That Noun!" on page 277.

Name That Noun

Noun Category	First Letter	Answer	Points

No answer = 0 points   Same answer as another student = 1 point   Unique answer = 2 points

TEC44026

Name That Noun

Noun Category	First Letter	Answer	Points

No answer = 0 points   Same answer as another student = 1 point   Unique answer = 2 points

TEC44026

bag TEC44026	lady TEC44026	house TEC44026	DOG TEC44026
cat TEC44026	BOY TEC44026	book TEC44026	car TEC44026
student TEC44026	soda TEC44026	calculator TEC44026	toy TEC44026
DINNER TEC44026	telephone TEC44026	computer TEC44026	paper TEC44026
sister TEC44026	brother TEC44026	homework TEC44026	pencil TEC44026
CHEF TEC44026	school TEC44026	flower TEC44026	truck TEC44026

Language Arts Spotlight
WORD ANALYSIS

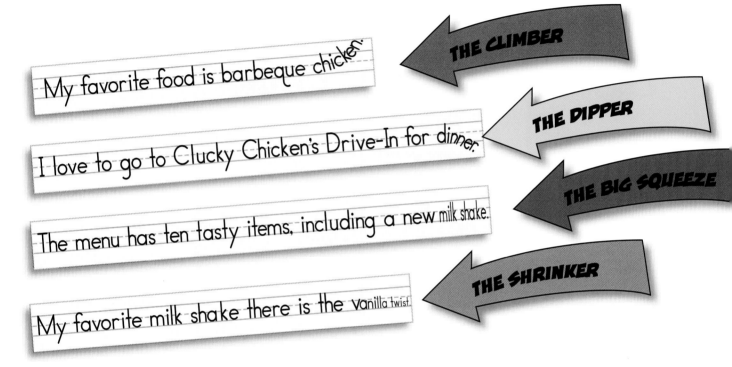

THE CLIMBER

My favorite food is barbeque chicken.

THE DIPPER

I love to go to Clucky Chicken's Drive-In for dinner.

THE BIG SQUEEZE

The menu has ten tasty items, including a new milk shake.

THE SHRINKER

My favorite milk shake there is the vanilla twist.

The Syllable Solution
Dividing words

Show students a practical reason for knowing how to separate a word into its parts. Program sentence strips demonstrating what students often do when the space on a writing line ends before a word is completely written. Next, create appropriate labels that describe the incorrect methods writers use to solve this problem. As you display each example, have the class match it to the correct label and discuss the corresponding rule for dividing the word. Share the tips shown about hyphenating words. Then have each child copy the sentences from the sentence strips onto a sheet of paper as a paragraph, hyphenating any words at the end of each writing line as needed.

Amy Vanderwaall, Deer Park Elementary, New Park Richey, FL

Hyphenation Don'ts

• Don't divide a one-syllable word.

• Don't separate a one-letter syllable from the rest of the word.

Language Arts Spotlight
WORD ANALYSIS

Rhythmic Reminder
Prefixes

Students won't forget that adding a prefix to a base word doesn't require a spelling change once they repeat the rhyme shown several times. To provide practice with the rule, first review different prefixes and their meanings with students.

Amy Vanderwaall, Deer Park Elementary, New Park Richey, FL

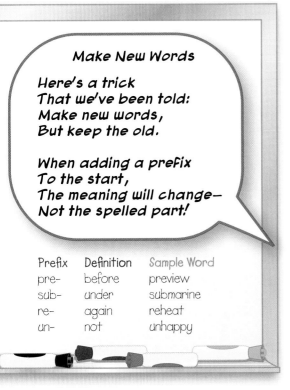

Make New Words

Here's a trick
That we've been told:
Make new words,
But keep the old.

When adding a prefix
To the start,
The meaning will change—
Not the spelled part!

Prefix	Definition	Sample Word
pre-	before	preview
sub-	under	submarine
re-	again	reheat
un-	not	unhappy

Sorted Servings
Compound words

This center helps students see that some multisyllable words are just a combination of two or more words that may or may not have a hyphen. Label the inside of each of four small bowls with a different one of the following labels: "One-Word Compound," "Hyphenated Compound," "Spaced Compound," and "Not a Compound." Write examples of these words on plastic spoons. On the bottom of each bowl, write the matching words with a permanent marker. To use the center, a student sorts the words by placing each spoon in the correct bowl. When he's finished, he lists the compound words on paper in groups and then turns over each bowl to check his answers.

One-Word Compound	Hyphenated Compound	Spaced Compound
wrongdoing	nitty-gritty	after all
nevertheless	toss-up	time line
aboveground	soft-spoken	every which way
mankind	life-size	vice president
ongoing	fund-raiser	work camp

nitty-gritty

fantastic

Hyphenated Compound

Not a Compound

Dissected Words
Using a resource to find meanings, pronunciations, and derivatives

Introduce key vocabulary for any unit with this adaptable activity. Outline on copy paper a shape that represents the topic, such as a beaker for a science unit on the states of matter. Give each child a copy of the shape. She cuts out the shape and then writes an assigned vocabulary word on it in black as shown. Below the word, she writes its pronunciation in red, its derivative and the derivative's meaning in blue, the word's definition in green, and a sample sentence in purple. Have each child color her cutout. Then collect the shapes and display them along a wall. Or bind them into a class booklet that can be used as a study aid!

Julia Ring Alarie, Pierce Memorial School, Huntington, VT

suspension

sə-ˈspen-shən

Latin: suspendere
(to hang)

the state of a substance when its particles are mixed with but undissolved in a fluid or solid

The brownie mix became a <u>suspension</u> when I added nuts to the batter.

Language Arts Spotlight
PARTS OF SPEECH

Feed the Pachyderms!

Answer Key

1. noun
2. adjective
3. verb
4. verb
5. preposition
6. adverb
7. preposition
8. noun
9. adjective
10. verb
11. noun
12. verb
13. adverb
14. adjective

Directions for two players:
1. The game cards are stacked facedown. Then each player chooses a color of game markers.
2. Player 1 draws a card, reads it aloud, and tells what part of speech the bold word is.
3. Player 2 checks the answer with the key. If correct, Player 1 "feeds" an elephant by covering it with a game marker. If incorrect, no elephant is covered. The game card is put at the bottom of the pile. Then Player 2 takes a turn.
4. Play continues until every elephant has been fed. The player who fed more elephants wins.

Feed the Pachyderms!
Center game

Make a copy of the game cards and answer key on page 285. Cut the cards apart and place them in a large resealable plastic bag along with the answer key and 28 paper squares (14 each of two different colors) to use as game markers. Then laminate a copy of the gameboard on page 284 onto a sheet of construction paper and add it to the bag. To play the game, a pair of students simply follows the directions on the gameboard.

Colleen Dabney, Williamsburg, VA

Pick a Sentence and a Word
Team game

Write several sentences on the board that each include the parts of speech you want students to review. Have two teams take turns choosing a sentence and identifying the part of speech of any word in that sentence. Award one point for a correct answer. Award two points if the answer is more specific. For example, if players say that *dog* is a noun, give them one point. If they say that *dog* is a singular noun, give them two points. Then cross out the identified word. The team with more points when all the words have been crossed out wins.

Debbie Ritsch, Mt. Calvary Lutheran School, Omaha, NE

Silly Sentences
Whole-class activity

Have each child cut a sheet of notebook paper into three long strips. At the top of one strip, have her write the name of a famous person or familiar book character. Next, have her fold the labeled part of the strip back so her answer cannot be seen. Then have her pass her strip to a classmate. Below the fold line on the new strip, have each child write the present-tense form of an action verb, fold the strip, and pass it on. Continue in this manner, instructing each student to write a different part of speech, fold her paper back, and pass it on until the sentence includes an adverb, a preposition, an article and an adjective, and a noun, or whatever parts of speech you wish to review. Collect the strips and read the silly sentences aloud. With each new round, be more specific with the parts of speech so there will be practice with singular and plural nouns, possessive nouns, verb tenses, and superlative forms of adjectives and adverbs as well!

Debra R. Cully, Naples Christian Academy, Naples, FL

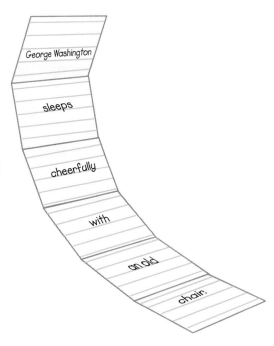

It's a Match!
Game for two to four players

Label a set of 52 index cards with examples of the different parts of speech you wish students to review. Also make a spinner and label it with the parts of speech included on the cards. To play, each player is dealt five cards (or seven if there are only two players). The remaining cards are stacked facedown in a pile. Players then take turns spinning to determine which type of card to discard faceup. If a player is not holding a card that matches the part of speech on the spinner, she draws from the pile until she finds a match. The first player to discard all of her cards wins.

Natalie Hughes-Tanner, Ermel Elementary, Houston, TX

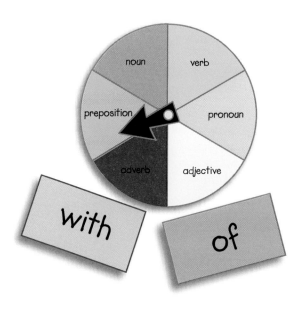

Feed the Pachyderms!

Place game cards here.

Directions for two players:
1. The game cards are stacked facedown. Then each player chooses a color of game markers.
2. Player 1 draws a card, reads it aloud, and tells what part of speech the bold word is.
3. Player 2 checks the answer with the key. If correct, Player 1 "feeds" an elephant by covering it with a game marker. If incorrect, no elephant is covered. The game card is put at the bottom of the pile. Then Player 2 takes a turn.
4. Play continues until every elephant has been fed. The player who fed more elephants wins.

Game Cards and Answer Key

Use with "Feed the Pachyderms!" on page 282.

1 Elephants touch **trunks** to greet each other.	**2** An elephant's tail is about **one** meter long.	**3** Elephants **eat** grass, leaves, and fruit.	**4** Elephants **are** the largest land animals.
TEC44028	TEC44028	TEC44028	TEC44028
5 An elephant's tusks are made **of** ivory.	**6** Elephants **really** love water.	**7** Elephants roll **in** mud to stay cool.	**8** Elephants are super **swimmers!**
TEC44028	TEC44028	TEC44028	TEC44028
9 Elephants are color-blind and have **poor** eyesight.	**10** Elephants **have** good hearing.	**11** **Elephants** have superb memories.	**12** Elephants can **live** about 65 years.
TEC44028	TEC44028	TEC44028	TEC44028
	13 Elephants are **very** fast learners.	**14** An elephant's skin is gray and **wrinkled**.	
	TEC44028	TEC44028	

Answer Key

1. noun
2. adjective
3. verb
4. verb
5. preposition
6. adverb
7. preposition
8. noun
9. adjective
10. verb
11. noun
12. verb
13. adverb
14. adjective

TEC44028

Language Arts Spotlight
LETTER WRITING

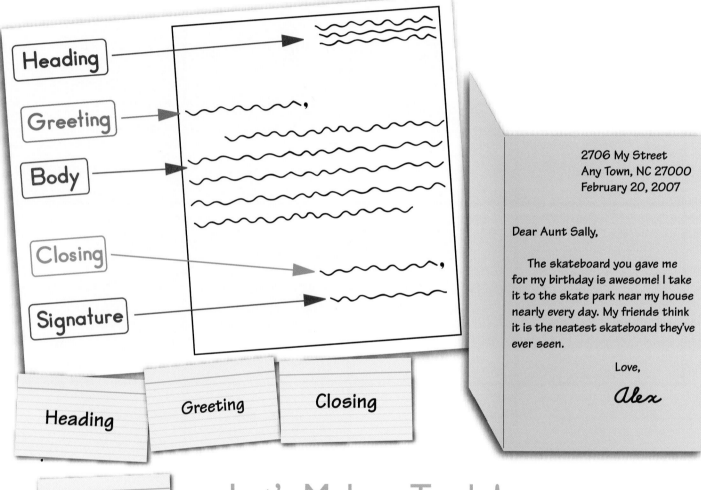

Heading

Greeting

Body

Closing

Signature

2706 My Street
Any Town, NC 27000
February 20, 2007

Dear Aunt Sally,

The skateboard you gave me for my birthday is awesome! I take it to the skate park near my house nearly every day. My friends think it is the neatest skateboard they've ever seen.

Love,

Alex

Heading

Greeting

Closing

Signature

Body

Let's Make a Trade!
Game, thank-you note

Begin by displaying a poster that shows the arrangement of the five parts of a friendly letter. To prepare game cards, have each student label five index cards as shown. Collect and shuffle the cards. Then deal each child five cards facedown. Allow students to trade cards one at a time by requesting the specific letter parts they need until each player has five different cards. For example, if two of a student's cards are headings and he needs a closing, he must say to a classmate, "I'll trade you a heading for a closing." If he forgets a part's name, he can look at the poster. Follow up by having each child use all five parts to write a thank-you note to a family member for a birthday gift he received.

Denise Neal, Northwest Middle School, Knoxville, TN

Cheerful Correspondence
Friendly letter

1706 My Street
Any Town, NC 27000
February 19, 2007

Dear Greg,
My teacher told me that you have leukemia. My cousin was a year younger than you when the doctors told him he had leukemia. While he was in the hospital, he liked having his family and friends visit him. When they couldn't be there, he listened to books on tape, played video games, and spent time with other kids on his floor. Now he's playing soccer again. I bet you'll be up and around soon just like him!

Sincerely,
Tony

The next time you hear about a child in your community who is seriously ill, have your class send him or her encouraging letters. Share appropriate information about the child's condition with students and discuss topics that might cheer up the child. Then invite each student to write an encouraging letter to the boy or girl. Once the letters have been revised and edited, students can address envelopes. If desired, place a fun sticker inside each envelope along with the letter. Then mail one letter a day so the recuperating child will get mail every day for as many days as you have students!

Susan Miyamoto, Founders Memorial School, Essex Junction, VT

Advice Needed
Friendly letter

Turn some of the crazy predicaments of familiar book characters into exciting letter-writing opportunities. Brainstorm with students several characters and problems, and list them on the board. Have each child write a letter from one of the characters to an advice columnist, asking for help. Then collect and randomly distribute the completed letters to different students, making sure that no one gets his own letter. Have each child answer the letter he is given with one that offers a solution to the character's problem. When the replies are finished, read the matching letters aloud without revealing the authors. You may hear some wise advice and creative solutions!

Debra Wilham, Mt. Pulaski Elementary, Mt. Pulaski, IL

4706 My Street
Any Town, NC 27000
March 5, 2007

Dear Abby,
I get into trouble a lot and make poor grades. I also tell lies. I'd like to be friends with Jeff, the new boy in my class who went into the girls' bathroom by mistake. What should I do?

Sincerely,
Bradley Chalkers

3706 My Street
Any Town, NC 27000
February 27, 2007

Customer Service Department
Super-Duper Backpack Company
1800 Backpack Street
Any Town, Any State 01234

Dear Customer Service Representative:
I am writing to let you know how disappointed I am that the backpack on wheels I ordered from your company broke after one use. Such an expensive backpack should have lasted longer than that. I had saved my allowance and babysitting money for months to buy it. You cannot imagine how I had looked forward to using it every day. I am returning the damaged backpack. Please send me a free replacement as soon as possible. In the meantime, I'll be using my old backpack with shoulder straps.

Yours truly,
Maggie Student

Getting Down to Business
Persuasive business letter

Begin this real-life activity by having each child write to a fictitious company about a product that broke or stopped working properly right after it was first used. In the letter, challenge her to convince the company's customer service representative to replace the item free of charge. Suggest that she mention the item's cost, when it was purchased, and even how devastated she was when it broke. Then read the completed letters aloud. Have the class act as the customer service person and decide by voting whether to replace an item based on each letter's persuasiveness.

Language Arts Spotlight
POETRY

Find a poem...
1. that makes you laugh
2. that does not rhyme
3. about a holiday
4. about food
5. about an animal
6. about nature
7. that has a shape
8. with personification
9. with a metaphor

Find a poem...
1. with alliteration
2. that tells a story
3. about a tree
4. about a season of the year
5. that has nonsense words
6. about a historical event
7. with a simile
8. about the weather
9. that asks one or more questions

CLASS Anthology

In Pursuit of Poems
Reviewing elements of poetry

Here's a scavenger hunt that turns identifying such things as rhyme, onomatopoeia, alliteration, similes, metaphors, and more into a fun project! Prepare several task cards such as those shown. Next, display poetry books gathered by your librarian. Then give each group a card and have students search through the books for nine brief poems, one to fit each category. When they find an appropriate poem, have them share it with the rest of the group and copy it on paper, adding an illustration if they like. Collect the poems and bind them into a class anthology. Then send each child off to create his own poem!

Cynthia Suvak and Tammy Pollock, St. Clement School, Lakewood, OH

How to Be an African Elephant

To be an African elephant, you must
Like having wrinkled gray skin,
Not mind weighing about four tons,
Like giving yourself a shower with your trunk,
Not mind having a nose that is about five feet long,
Like lifting up to 600-pound weights,
Not mind having poor sight,
Like not being able to jump,
Not mind having ears that are about four feet wide,
Like not being able to sweat,
Not mind having flies and mosquitoes bite your skin,
And like rolling in mud to stay cool!

To Be a What?
How-to poem

To prepare, first have your librarian gather simple nonfiction books about animals. Read one of the selections aloud. Afterward, have students brainstorm phrases that describe the selection's featured animal. Record the phrases on the board. Next, invite students to help you use the most informative phrases from the list to write a poem, beginning each line with a verb. When the poem is finished, have students read it aloud. Then have each child work with a partner to choose a book and write a similar poem featuring a different animal!

Christina Bryant, Huffman Middle School, Huffman, TX

Pix Rhyme
Picture poem

For a poem that can transform a dull topic into one that's definitely more interesting, challenge students to end a poem's lines with rhyming words that can be illustrated in a creative way (see the example). For even more fun, have each child write the poem on a shape that suggests the topic!

Val R. Cheatham, Wichita, KS

Rain

When the rain is
And the wind is
It's time to wear
And a plastic rain

Ten Little Lines

One line is a skinny flagpole.
Two lines will a mountain make.
Three lines form a little chair,
And four a useful garden rake.
Five lines make a nice, small house,
And six a ladder that's not too tall.
Seven make a sad winter tree,
And eight a puppy that's very small.
Nine lines will make
A playground swing,
And with all ten,
I can draw many, many things.
How about a man?

Give Me Ten!
Form poem

All students need to complement this cool form of poetry are simple stick drawings. Just have each child write a poem, using a format similar to the one shown, about what can be drawn by increasing the number of lines from one to ten!

Val R. Cheatham

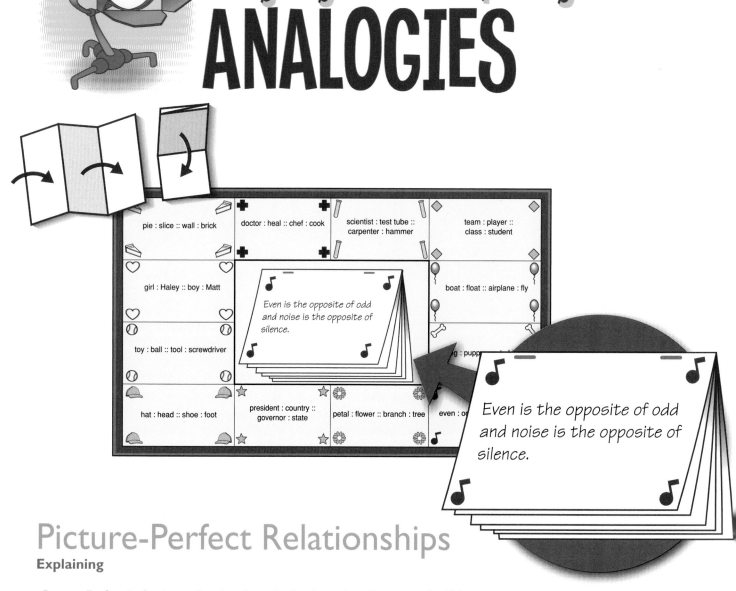

pie : slice :: wall : brick

doctor : heal :: chef : cook

scientist : test tube :: carpenter : hammer

team : player :: class : student

girl : Haley :: boy : Matt

Even is the opposite of odd and noise is the opposite of silence.

boat : float :: airplane : fly

toy : ball :: tool : screwdriver

hat : head :: shoe : foot

president : country :: governor : state

petal : flower :: branch : tree

even : o

Even is the opposite of odd and noise is the opposite of silence.

Picture-Perfect Relationships
Explaining

Help students understand analogies by using the reproducible on page 292 to frame their thinking. To begin, have each child fold a sheet of white paper into six sections and then trim about two inches from the unfolded edge. Have him unfold his paper, cut apart the six boxes, staple them together at the top, and use a small piece of Sticky-Tac to mount the resulting booklet on his copy of page 292 where indicated.

Next, direct each student to choose an analogy from a picture-frame section on page 292 and explain on his first booklet page the relationship between that analogy's pairs of words. Have him also draw on the page the symbol from the matching picture-frame section. Have students repeat for each remaining page, using a different analogy on each page. When everyone is finished, discuss why students chose the analogies they did and talk about their responses. Finally, have each child remove his booklet so he can replace it with a new one to repeat the activity as desired.

All-Star Matchups
Creating

For this practice activity, cut five stars each from red, blue, and yellow construction paper. Glue one star of each color to the outside of a brown paper lunch bag. Place the remaining stars in the bag. Then display an analogies chart like the one shown. After discussing with students the different types of analogies listed, have one child pull a star from the bag. Direct her to give an example of an analogy of the type that matches her star's color on the chart. Encourage other students to give additional examples. Then have another child draw a star from the bag and repeat the activity. Collect the stars at the end of the activity to use again when students need another review.

Red: Object to Action	Blue: Part to Whole	Yellow: Member to Group
boat : float :: airplane : fly	slice : pie :: brick : wall	player : team :: student : class
phone : ring :: bird : chirp	window : house :: lightbulb : lamp	actor : cast :: musician : band

chair : sit : | : bed : sleep

Analogies
bandage : blood :: dam : river
peel : apple :: shear : sheep
win : lose :: stop : go
chair : sit :: bed : sleep
hear : ear :: talk : mouth
5 : 10 :: 3 : 6
pretty : beautiful :: warm : hot
snow : cold :: sun : hot
she : her :: he : him
bear : den :: bee : hive
8 : 24 :: 9 : 27
glove : hand :: boot : foot
we : us :: they : them
paw : dog :: fin : fish
girl : mother :: boy : father

Finding Common Ground
Matching

Comprehending how the words in an analogy are related is the gist of this matching activity. Gather index cards of two colors (15 of each color). Write the first half of each analogy shown on a card of one color and the second half of each analogy on a card of the other color. Give each child a programmed card and challenge him to walk around the room and find the classmate with the matching half of his analogy. (Use only enough analogies for each student to get a card. Join in if you have an odd number of students.) If two students believe their cards make a match, have them sit together. When everyone is sitting, review the students' matches and make any corrections.

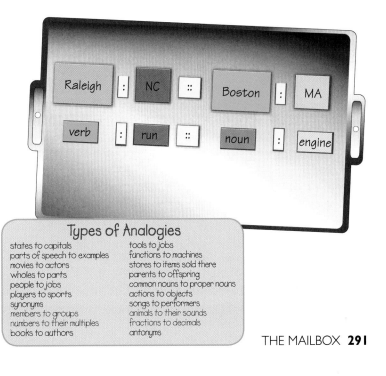

Types of Analogies
states to capitals
parts of speech to examples
movies to actors
wholes to parts
people to jobs
players to sports
synonyms
members to groups
numbers to their multiples
books to authors

tools to jobs
functions to machines
stores to items sold there
parents to offspring
common nouns to proper nouns
actions to objects
songs to performers
animals to their sounds
fractions to decimals
antonyms

Word-Tile Analogies
Forming

To prepare this center, program pieces of index cards with words, colons, and colon pairs that, when aligned, create analogies of the types shown. Affix a magnetic strip to the back of each card and then store the cards in a resealable plastic bag at a center along with a cookie sheet. Post up to ten types of analogies at the center. Students using the center arrange the magnetic tiles on the metallic sheet to form an analogy for each type you post. Periodically change the posting to keep students' interest high.

Name

Picture-Perfect Relationships

Follow your teacher's directions to complete the picture frame.

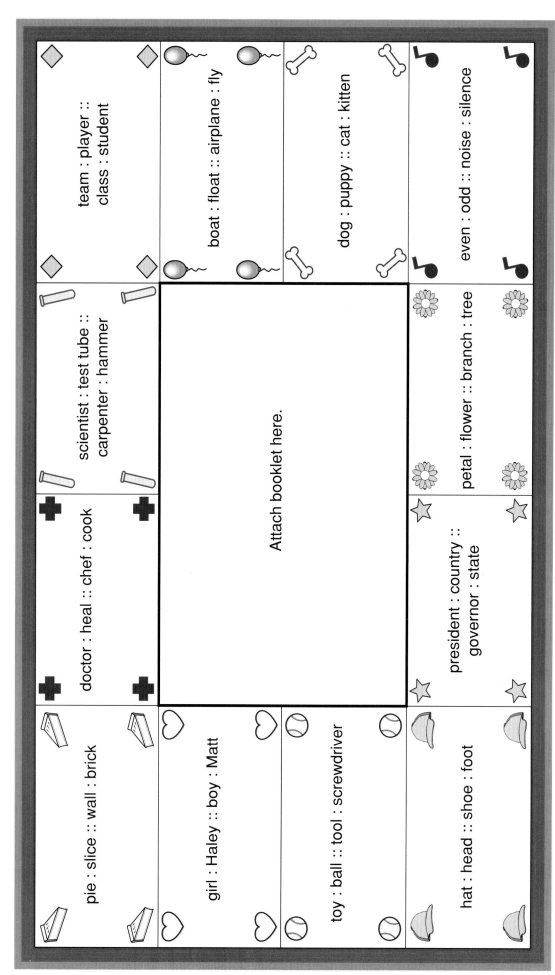

team : player ::
class : student

boat : float :: airplane : fly

dog : puppy :: cat : kitten

even : odd :: noise : silence

scientist : test tube ::
carpenter : hammer

Attach booklet here.

petal : flower :: branch : tree

doctor : heal :: chef : cook

president : country ::
governor : state

pie : slice :: wall : brick

girl : Haley :: boy : Matt

toy : ball :: tool : screwdriver

hat : head :: shoe : foot

©The Mailbox® · TEC44031 · June/July 2007

Note to the teacher: Use with "Picture-Perfect Relationships" on page 290.

MANAGEMENT TIPS
AND TIMESAVERS

Management Tips and Timesavers

A Seat for All

Get organized by creating and then laminating a versatile seating chart for each group you teach. Once the chart is made, you can use an overhead pen to mark daily information such as absences, homework grades, and discipline warnings. Then transfer any needed data to your record book before you wipe off the chart to use the next day. Not only will this tool keep you organized and your students accountable, but substitute teachers will appreciate it too!

Kristi Lovell, Marrington Middle, Goose Creek, SC

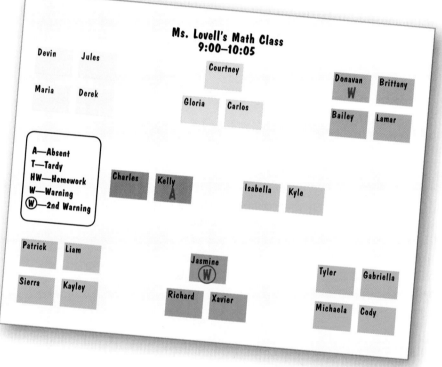

Ms. Lovell's Math Class
9:00–10:05

Devin   Jules

Maria   Derek

Courtney

Gloria   Carlos

Donavan **W**   Brittany

Bailey   Lamar

A—Absent
T—Tardy
HW—Homework
W—Warning
Ⓦ—2nd Warning

Charles   Kelly **A**

Isabella   Kyle

Patrick   Liam

Sierra   Kayley

Jasmine **Ⓦ**

Richard   Xavier

Tyler   Gabriella

Michaela   Cody

CAESAR

Stick-Up Cups

To keep a student's workspace tidy, grab a plastic cup and a self-adhesive Velcro circle or strip! Adhere the fastener's hook side to the cup and its loop side to the child's desk. Then have him store his office-type supplies in the cup. Whenever he needs to work in a different place, he just unfastens the cup and he's ready to go!

Jennifer Norman, Northeast School, Stamford, CT

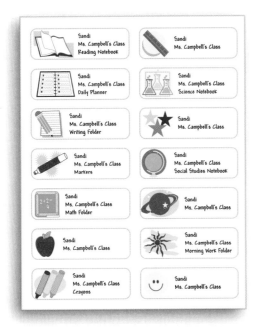

Labels Everywhere

Personalize students' belongings with this simple tip. Print a sheet of self-adhesive labels for each child. Have her affix an appropriate label to each school supply she brings to school, such as a notebook or a box of crayons or markers. Misplaced items can be identified quickly. Plus, the labels are neater and don't require a child to write her name over and over!

Amanda Campbell, Finley Elementary, Finley, TN

Front or Back?

Need a way to help students recognize the front of a binder? Use stickers! Have each child who confuses the front and back of a binder affix a green dot sticker (go) to the front of each notebook and a red dot sticker (stop) on the back. These visual reminders should lead to fewer mix-ups!

Goldie Eichorn, Yeshiva of Belle Harbor, Brooklyn, NY

Storage Freebies

If you need storage cartons, ask your local discount retailer to donate the cardboard boxes that hold pocket folders in the store's school supply section. Use the boxes, similar to magazine holders, to expand your filing system or to hold individual portfolios. What a creative and cost-free storage solution!

Karen Slattery, Marie of the Incarnation School Bradford, Ontario, Canada

Management Tips and Timesavers

Tidy Tote

Need a storage solution for all the overhead manipulatives scattered around your projector? Organize the pieces in an inexpensive fishing tackle box. The divided trays keep the items separated so they're easier to find. And with a snap of the lid, the pieces are portable!

Eric Hess, Johnson Elementary
Fort Collins, CO

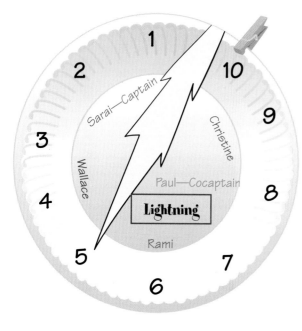

Cooperative Challenge

To encourage appropriate behavior and teamwork, divide students into small groups. Give each group a paper plate, markers, and a clothespin. The group chooses a team name and symbol and creates a unique design in the center of the plate. One group member writes the numbers 1–10 around the plate's rim and clips the clothespin to the number 10. Next, each group chooses a team captain and cocaptain and has each member sign the team plate. After the plate is attached to the captain's desk, students are challenged to stay on task and be on their best behavior throughout the day. As needed, team leaders remind individual group members to work quietly and cooperatively. If inappropriate behavior occurs, a team loses a point and its clothespin is moved to the next lower number. At the day's end, each team's points are tallied. The first team to reach 100 points earns a special treat; then the cycle begins again.

Gretchen Gottschalk, Brookridge Elementary, Brooklyn, OH

Supplies on the Go

Spend more time teaching and less time distributing student supplies with help from clear plastic boxes. Number a box for each child and fill it with needed supplies. Inside its lid, tape a list of the box's contents. Then assign a box to each child, informing him that he will be responsible for replacing any lost or depleted items. Since the containers are easy to stack, they can be stored in a convenient place until students need those particular materials. Plus, the sturdy boxes can be reused year after year!

Shonja Alexander, Highland Renaissance Academy, Charlotte, NC

Big Bucks

Reward students with play money for positive behavior. Give each child $20 to begin the week. Then pay her throughout the week a set amount for first-rate conduct and finished work. Charge her for negative behaviors, such as forgetting a pencil, losing homework, or misbehaving, so she'll also learn about consequences. Each Friday, allow her to choose how she'll spend her earnings, using her bucks to buy such things as a homework pass, a treasure box item, a school supply, or five minutes of extra recess. Getting paid for a job well done will make her feel like she's part of the real working world!

Brooke Blake, Wentworth Elementary, Wentworth, NH
Natalie McGregor, Grenada Upper Elementary, Grenada, MS

Big Bucks

You earn the following:

- $5 per day for completing homework/class work
- $5 per day for good behavior
- $1 if caught doing something good

You pay the following:

- $2 for a lost pencil
- $3 for missing homework or incomplete class work
- $1–$5 for misbehavior

$20

Homework PASS

$50

TREASURE CHEST $10 per item

File It Away!

To stay better organized, label a folder for each school day (and one for each week of a grading period). Keep the folders in a convenient location. Then, as you receive memos to send home and notes about upcoming meetings or have student worksheets to file, place the relevant paperwork in the corresponding folder. Not only will you be more organized, but the files will also be a huge help to a substitute when you're absent!

Kim Minafo, Dillard Drive Elementary, Raleigh, NC

Management Tips and Timesavers

Assignment Routing Slips

Quickly keep track of assignments with an idea borrowed from the business world. For each subject, collect a different-colored pocket folder. Then create a routing slip such as the one shown. Staple a supply of the slips on the front of each folder. When it's time to collect an assignment, pass the appropriate folder around the classroom. Each child places her completed work inside the folder, initials the slip, and then hands the folder to the next classmate. When you get the folder back, highlight the names of students who didn't turn in their work; then tear off the slip and keep it on your desk as a reminder of who owes you an assignment.

Tanya Johnson, St. Paul Lutheran School, Luxemburg, WI

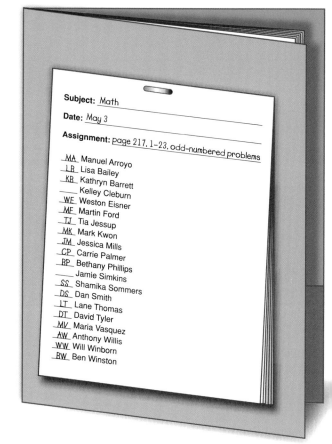

Subject: _Math_

Date: _May 3_

Assignment: _page 217, 1–23, odd-numbered problems_

_MA_ Manuel Arroyo
_LB_ Lisa Bailey
_KB_ Kathryn Barrett
____ Kelley Cleburn
_WE_ Weston Eisner
_MF_ Martin Ford
_TJ_ Tia Jessup
_MK_ Mark Kwon
_JM_ Jessica Mills
_CP_ Carrie Palmer
_BP_ Bethany Phillips
____ Jamie Simkins
_SS_ Shamika Sommers
_DS_ Dan Smith
_LT_ Lane Thomas
_DT_ David Tyler
_MV_ Maria Vasquez
_AW_ Anthony Willis
_WW_ Will Winborn
_BW_ Ben Winston

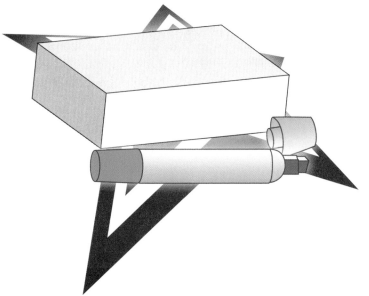

Come Clean!

Looking for a quick, easy, and inexpensive way to keep your dry-erase board sparkling clean? Try using a Mr. Clean Magic Eraser cleaning pad. This handy cleaning sponge will remove stains from your dry-erase board with ease, even without wetting it.

Sarah Lamb, Elliott R. Hughes Elementary, New Hartford, NY

Bookshelf Tip

Do you stock your classroom library with yard sale finds? If so, then you know these bargain books can smell musty. Combat this problem by placing several unwrapped bars of inexpensive soap along your book-shelves. Not only will your books smell fresher, but some kinds of soap can also keep pesky bugs at bay.

Jane Walsh, Sweetwater Elementary, Lithia Springs, GA

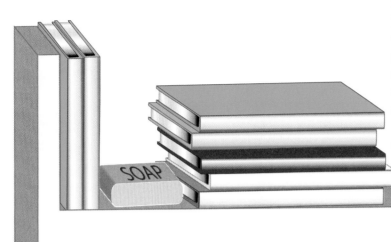

Computer Alert

If you've tried to teach students while they work at computers, you know it's virtually impossible to get through a lesson without technical difficulties. To cut down on inter-ruptions and calls for help that can disrupt your lesson, place a small red plastic cup at each computer. When a student has a question or problem, she simply places the cup upside down on top of her monitor. At a glance you'll see who needs a helping hand.

Dr. Brenda Tweed, Pigeon Forge Middle School, Pigeon Forge, TN

Distraction Mufflers

To keep easily distracted students more focused during inde-pendent work, collect several sets of old headphones (the kind often used in listening centers). Store the earphones in a basket, bundling each cord with a twist tie. Then encourage students who work better when it's quiet to don a pair when working at their seats or taking tests. The earphones will muffle classroom noise and help the students focus better.

Laura Tolbert, Bellwood Elementary, Richmond, VA

Silent Signal

Bring in an interesting, inexpensive lamp or motion light to give your classroom a homey feel and to control the noise level. When you need students to work silently, turn the light off. To allow whispering, turn it back on. The lamp can serve a dual purpose!

Terry Warner, Brookview Elementary, Jacksonville, FL

Blurt Alert

Do you have overeager students who blurt out answers during classroom discussions, leaving your more timid students fewer chances to contribute? Make several cards like the one shown. When a child has trouble remembering that she should raise her hand and wait to be called on before speaking, discretely slip her one of the cards. This quiet reminder will help her begin to monitor her own behavior and give her classmates a chance to speak up.

Brooke Beverly, Dudley Elementary, Oxford, MA

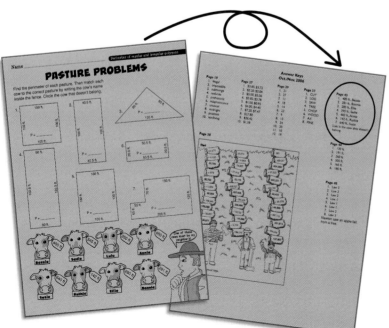

Multicolored Masters

If you need help keeping answer keys and matching copies of student reproducibles from *The Mailbox*® magazine or The Mailbox Companion® together, make colorful double-sided masters. Copy the page on one side and the corresponding answer key on the back. Not only will the master copies be easy to spot, but the answer keys will also be right at your fingertips!

Suzanne Darden, Carter Elementary, Strawberry Plains, TN

OUR READERS WRITE

If you would like to contribute an item to our classroom, please take a star and return the item with your child.

Thank you!

pocket folders

Wishes on a Star

Obtaining contributions of needed class-room materials is easy when I create a decorative display that doubles as a wish list! I post a large star character at open house and attach smaller black stars to it. To each small star, I affix a yellow sticky note labeled with the name of a different item. Then I add a speech bubble to the character, inviting interested parents, friends, and family members to participate!

Kathleen Butler, Meadows Elementary, Millbrae, CA

Postcard With a Plus

To recognize my students' birthdays, I present each child with a birthday note that becomes a homework pass. I make or purchase postcards that say "Happy Birthday" and label them, as shown, with an expiration date that is one month from their birthday. If a child has a summer birthday, she can redeem her pass in September or May. My students still want their birthdays acknowledged, just not in the same way as younger children!

Susan Bastian, Sylvania Franciscan Academy, Sylvania, OH

Abbie,
This card is good for one free homework assignment!

Happy birthday!
Ms. Bastian

Your birthday: September 27
Card's expiration date: October 27

Happy Birthday!

Classic Memories

Tops cut from cubed tissue boxes make perfect frames for my collection of digital class photos. I take photos throughout the year and display them on a board titled "Classic Memories Are Only a Click Away!" At the end of the year, each child takes home her favorite photo.

Colleen Dabney, Williamsburg, VA

Tablecloths to the Rescue

Instead of using paper for bulletin board backgrounds, I purchase inexpensive plastic tablecloths from a discount store. The colorful cloths don't fade, so I fold them up and use them year after year!

Teresa Campbell, Clark-Pleasant Middle School, Whiteland, IN

OUR READERS WRITE

New Prime Minister Elected

Current Events Geography

With help from a few news articles and a box of crayons, **finding countries and states on a map is a regular routine** in my classroom. I display a supersize copy of a world map and have students share weekly current event articles. Each presenter then locates, colors, and labels on the map the state or country of his article's origin. This motivates my students to search hard for articles about different places around the globe so more of the map can be colored. At the end of the school year, I draw one child's name and present the map to him as a memento.

Megan McNiel, Barstow School, Olathe, KS

Colorful Word Walls

To expand the use of my word wall, I reinforce key vocabulary for all subject areas. I assign each subject a different color and then write each vocabulary word on a different color-specific sentence strip. Students are quick to notice new additions to the word wall, which then signal each child to add these words and their definitions to her corresponding-subject notebook.

Shannon Hillis, Grove Park Elementary, Orange Park, FL

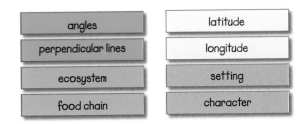

angles	latitude
perpendicular lines	longitude
ecosystem	setting
food chain	character

The BUG Club

I have a Brought-Up Grade (BUG) Club in my classroom to motivate students to improve their grades. At the end of each grading period, I compare each child's current grades to his previous ones and invite every student who brings up any grade five points or more to join the club. I also present him with a special certificate or treat and the opportunity to sign a BUG Club poster!

Amy Janak, Cypress Grove Intermediate, College Station, TX

Differentiation by Design

Here's how I individualize classwork assignments in a snap. I make a three-column chart, affix a different-colored sticker above each column, and then laminate the chart. Below each sticker, I record with an overhead marker a daily assignment for each group. Then I place a coordinating sticker on each child's notebook to specify which column of work she should complete. Simple!

Cheryl Fowler
Crofton Meadows
   Elementary
Crofton, MD

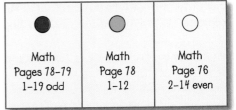

| ● | ● | ○ |
| Math Pages 78–79 1–19 odd | Math Page 78 1–12 | Math Page 76 2–14 even |

OUR READERS WRITE

Audio Books

During silent-reading time, I often found my struggling readers off task because of a lack of low-level reading material or the embarrassment of reading a book below grade level. In my search for a solution, I discovered that a tape player and headphones could meet their needs. I began buying books on tape so these students could enjoy a good read. I also borrow sets from my local library!

Joyce Hovanec
Glassport Elementary
Glassport, PA

No Missing Rubrics

When scoring student work, I print the rubric on large mailing labels and affix a label to each child's paper. The label stays attached to the work whether I file it or send it home for a parent to review!

Valerie Canady
Boulevard Elementary
Kokomo, IN

Snappy Displays

To show off students' good work, I cut a 10" x 13" piece of poster board for each child and glue two spring-type clothespins at the top. I write the student's name on the poster board between the clothespins. Then I tape the individual boards to the wall and clip each child's latest story, essay, or poem to the matching board. Or I display student work by attaching a clear page protector to the back of a construction paper frame. The papers are easy to remove and replace no matter which method I use!

Patti Etchison, Living Word Academy, Yorktown, VA
Jennifer Hoff, Edison Elementary, Stickney, IL
Holly Robinson, Santa Clarita Elementary, Saugus, CA

Authentic Writing

My students actually write for a real audience. When? Each time we update our class Web page! I have small groups write articles of interest to parents to keep them informed about school events and happenings. My writers peer-edit the articles; then I proofread them before they're posted. Because my students are the ones doing the writing, I'm free to spend my time on other teaching tasks!

Terry Healy, Marlatt Elementary, Manhattan, KS

OUR READERS WRITE

Royal Geography

My students use this time-filling game to learn countries' locations. To begin, I display a large world map, and each child finds the world map in her social studies book. To play, I announce the name of a country and each student tries to locate it on the map in her book. When she finds it, she stands beside her desk. I ask the first child who stood to come to the front and point out the country on the large map. If correct, she earns one point. If incorrect, she chooses someone else who's standing to come up and point out the country. Attempts continue until the correct response is given. The student with the most points at the end is crowned Geography King or Queen.

Nan Burger
Our Redeemer
   Lutheran School
Wauwatosa, WI

Which One Wins?

This variation of the rock-paper-scissors game gives my students a quick way to reinforce three important symbols used in geometry. Students choose a partner and then play using either the signals shown or individual wipe-off boards. If the partners use wipe-off boards, they each secretly draw one of three symbols—ray, line segment, or line—and then simultaneously display their boards to determine a winner.

Karin Wellington
Ballard East Elementary
Cambridge, IA

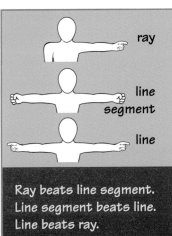

Ray beats line segment.
Line segment beats line.
Line beats ray.

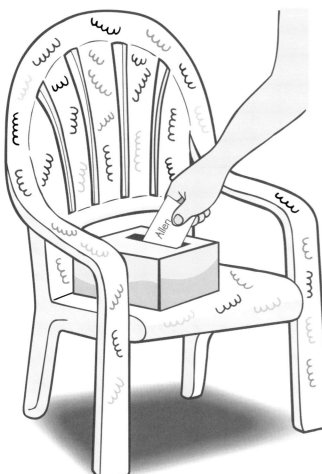

The Autograph Chair

To motivate students to read throughout the year, I allow each student to sign an inexpensive plastic chair with a colorful permanent marker each time he completes a book. At the same time, he also writes his name on a small piece of paper and drops it in a box. When the chair is covered with signatures, I draw a name from the box and the student whose name is drawn gets to keep the chair!

Pam Morrow, Callisburg Elementary, Gainesville, TX

Positive Pillowcase

May this pillowcase give you plenty of rest So that you'll do well on your proficiency test!

I help ease **test-taking anxiety** with this make-and-take project! A few days before the test, I have each student bring in a clean, white pillowcase from home. Then I have the child use a fabric marker or paint to write on the pillowcase a message such as the one shown. (Substitute the name of your state-wide test for the word *proficiency*.) Students then take their pillowcases home and sleep on them to help them feel more relaxed about the test.

Taryn Miley, Crissey Elementary, Holland, OH

Highlighting Dialogue

To improve narrative writing, I use this colorful strategy. After students finish their rough drafts, I have each child use two different colors of highlighters—one to highlight any dialogue in his story and the other to highlight anything that is not. Once this is done, I have him decide whether he used too little, too much, or just enough dialogue in his story. Then I have him revise his work accordingly. Students soon realize how important it is to have a good balance between the dialogue and the details needed to develop a story's setting, characters, and plot!

Dana Johansen, Greenwich Academy, Greenwich, CT

Sticks and Stickers

I use craft sticks, dot stickers, and poster board to review points, lines, rays, and angles. I begin by posting a list of geometric vocabulary similar to the one shown. Then I challenge pairs of students to create and label on a sheet of poster board a visual representation of each term. I display the completed projects around the room as ready references.

Christine Cooley, C. C. Meneley Elementary, Gardnerville, NV

point
line segment
line
ray
parallel lines
intersecting lines
perpendicular lines
right angle
acute angle
obtuse angle

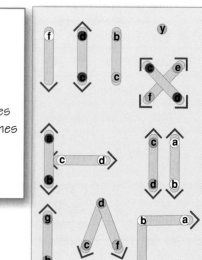

OUR READERS WRITE

Build a Book Report Sandwich!

First bread slice (white): Title, author, and your name
Tomato slice (red): Setting
Lettuce leaf (green): Main characters
Cheese slice (yellow): Main problem and its solution
Meat slice (tan): Summary of plot
Second bread slice (white): Opinion about book

Title:
A Year Down Yonder

Author:
Richard Peck

Kel

Appetizing Reports

For an engaging **book report project,** my students build their own book sandwiches! After going over the guidelines shown, I provide students with access to construction paper (in the colors noted) and other art supplies. Each student completes each sandwich part and then staples the parts together at the top to make a sandwich. I display the projects on a bulletin board covered with a red-checkered tablecloth.

Sandra Huber, Cornwall Elementary, Cornwall, PA

Give Me Three!

To stretch vocabulary skills, I announce a category, such as sea creatures, and three sequential letters, such as *r, s,* and *t.* I challenge students to list three words that fit the category and start with the selected letters (such as *rays, starfish,* and *turtles*). Sometimes I divide the class into teams and award one point for each correct word that isn't listed by another team.

Isobel Livingstone, Rahway, NJ

Category	Letter	Word
Sea creatures	r	rays
	s	starfish
	t	turtles

End-of-Year Keepsake

At the end of the school year, I give my students a memento that uses the classroom photos I've taken throughout the year. I take the photos to a videographer, who makes a DVD (including music) featuring the photos. About a month before school is out, I mail a letter home asking that each parent secretly donate two or three dollars for a special keepsake for students. I then have an assistant help me make copies of the DVD so I can give one to each child as a goodbye gift.

Angie Regan, Brandon, MS

A Memorable School Year

Answer Keys

Page 10
Declarative—2, 3, 10, 12
Interrogative—1, 6, 8, 13
Imperative—4, 7, 9
Exclamatory—5, 11, 14

Bonus Box: Answers will vary.

Page 11

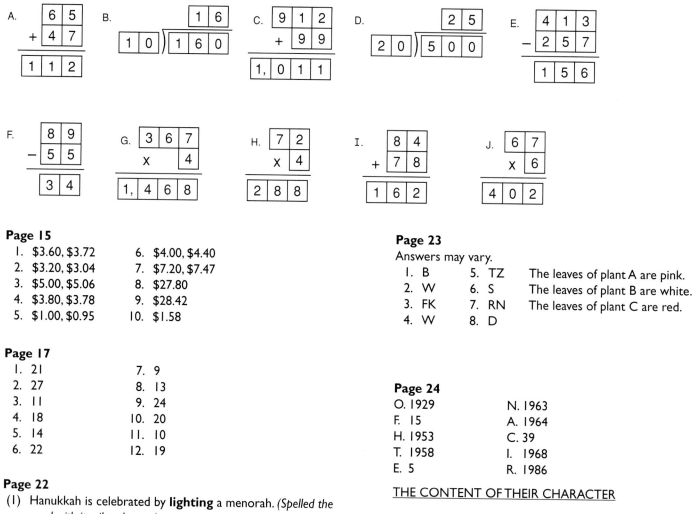

Page 15

1. $3.60, $3.72	6. $4.00, $4.40
2. $3.20, $3.04	7. $7.20, $7.47
3. $5.00, $5.06	8. $27.80
4. $3.80, $3.78	9. $28.42
5. $1.00, $0.95	10. $1.58

Page 17

1. 21	7. 9
2. 27	8. 13
3. 11	9. 24
4. 18	10. 20
5. 14	11. 10
6. 22	12. 19

Page 22
(1) Hanukkah is celebrated by **lighting** a menorah. *(Spelled the word with its silent letters.)*
(2) This candleholder **has** places for nine candles. *(Changed the verb to present tense.)*
(3) Eight of the candles stand for the number of **days** the oil burned. *(Changed the homophone.)*
(4) The ninth candle, or **shammes,** is used to light the other eight candles. *(Added comma for the appositive.)*
(5) *Shammes* means "servant" in **Yiddish.** *(Capitalized the proper noun.)*
(6) Many **families** celebrate by gathering to eat foods made with oil. *(Spelled the plural noun correctly.)*
(7) Kids play with dreidels, and presents **are** exchanged. *(Made the subject and verb agree.)*
(8) Some kids receive gelt, or **money.** *(Used lowercase for the common noun.)*
(9) If only the celebrations **could last** longer than eight days! *(Corrected the past participle.)*

Page 23
Answers may vary.

1. B	5. TZ	The leaves of plant A are pink.
2. W	6. S	The leaves of plant B are white.
3. FK	7. RN	The leaves of plant C are red.
4. W	8. D	

Page 24

O. 1929	N. 1963
F. 15	A. 1964
H. 1953	C. 39
T. 1958	I. 1968
E. 5	R. 1986

THE CONTENT OF THEIR CHARACTER

Page 28

1. E	6. E
2. H	7. Y
3. C	8. L
4. T	9. C
5. O	10. N

"THE CYCLONE"

Page 29

1. A
2. Y
3. M
4. B
5. U
6. O
7. E
8. Y
9. T
10. I

IT MAY BE YOU!

Page 30

1. some
2. all
3. none
4. all
5. some
6. some
7. some
8. all
9. some
10. some
11. none
12. none
13. lizard; The rest are types of snakes.
14. offensive odor; The rest are ways snakes defend themselves.
15. fur; The rest are characteristics of snakes.

Page 35

A. 8
B. 9
C. 21
D. 24
E. 180
F. 7
G. 96
H. 2
I. 80
J. 64,000

Glass—H; Metal—B; Paper—A, C, D, E, F; Other—G, I, J

Page 36

1. I
2. We
3. me
4. our
5. her
6. my
7. us
8. him
9. he
10. them

Page 37

1. A
2. D
3. E
4. I
5. N
6. O
7. R
8. T
9. C
10. Y

DECORATION DAY

Page 41

1. Betsy Ross had the chance to create the first American flag.
2. The flag Betsy Ross created had 13 stars and 13 stripes.
3. The American flag with 13 white stars on a blue field and 13 alternating red and white stripes became official.
4. Some people began to think this day should be observed every year.
5. Flag Day is observed on June 14 every year.
6. Today our flag has 50 stars.

Page 42

Order of answers may vary.

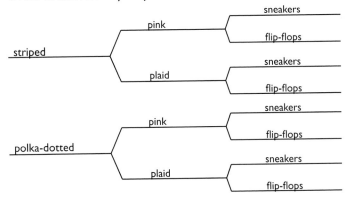

1. eight combinations
2. striped shorts, pink shirt, sneakers
   striped shorts, pink shirt, flip-flops
   striped shorts, plaid shirt, sneakers
   striped shorts, plaid shirt, flip-flops

   polka-dotted shorts, pink shirt, sneakers
   polka-dotted shorts, pink shirt, flip-flops
   polka-dotted shorts, plaid shirt, sneakers
   polka-dotted shorts, plaid shirt, flip-flops

Page 43

The first day of the Wilson <u>family's</u> vacation was finally here. Jan, Jerry, Jim, Jill, and Jack had been waiting many <u>months</u> to go on this trip. They had packed two <u>weeks'</u> worth of clothes. Each <u>person's</u> clothes had filled two <u>suitcases</u>.

Soon the Wilson <u>family</u> loaded into a van. There was barely enough room to squeeze in the luggage around all the people!

Jim asked, "Dad, where are we going?"

"Please tell us!" exclaimed all the <u>kids</u> at once.

"We are driving to the airport," Dad answered. "Then we are going to get on one of those big <u>airplanes</u> and fly to London!"

<u>Squeals</u> of joy erupted.

"I have just one question," said Jill. "Will the airplane be big enough to hold all our <u>suitcases</u>?"

Page 44
1. San Francisco Bay
2. Walt Disney World
3. Hollywood, CA, and Austin, TX
4. Hollywood, CA; Austin, TX; and Pike's Peak for west of the Mississippi or Washington, DC; New York City, NY; and Colonial Williamsburg for east of the Mississippi
5. eight people
6. New York City, NY
7. the one at Niagara Falls
8. Washington, DC, and New York City, NY
9. 58 people
10. four people

Page 69
1. B
2. D
3. C
4. C
5. Answers will vary. Possible answer:
   Jason loves to do tricks on his skateboard.

Page 97
1. Jim is a police officer.
2. Answers will vary.
3. Jan is going to exchange a shirt.
4. Answers will vary.
5. Jon is excited.
6. Answers will vary.
7. Jamie is at a movie theater.
8. Answers will vary.

Page 100
Memoir: Personal record of an event
Biography: True account of a person's life written by someone else
Autobiography: True story written by a person about his or her own life
Informational: Facts and ideas about real topics
Realistic Fiction: Story about things that could really happen
Fantasy: Story that can include imaginary events and talking animals
Traditional Literature: Stories—including folktales, fables, fairy tales, myths, and legends—that have been shared from person to person throughout history
Historical Fiction: Imaginary story based on a real event or time from the past
Science Fiction: Special type of fantasy that includes or is based on scientific principles

Page 115
Answers may vary.
1. C
2. C
3. B
4. A
5. D
6. C or D
7. A
8. C
9. A or D

Page 129
1. Scrammers
2. Dashers
3. Racers
4. Scooters
5. Zoomers
6. Bustlers
7. Trackers
8. Speeders
9. Darters
10. Movers
11. Fliers
12. Sprinters
13. 726,190
14. 7,004,500
15. 23,077
16. 4,035,512
17. 23,867
18. 4,005,050
19. 7,040,100
20. 726,019
21. 23,768
22. 4,050,501
23. 7,400,001
24. 727,036

Page 130
1. 57.080
2. 56.99
3. 57.8
4. 128.05
5. 128.4
6. 92.841
7. 129.026
8. 57.081
Running Shoes: 92.841
Running Socks: 57.8
Running Shorts: 128.4
Running Shirts: 57.081
Runners' Safety Vests: 57.080
Hoodies: 128.05
Running Pants: 56.99
Running Jackets: 129.026

Bonus Box: 56.99, 57.080, 57.081, 57.8, 92.841, 128.05, 128.4, 129.026

Page 135
1. a
2. b
3. c
4. a
5. c
6. b

Bonus Box: TOM and MIT

Page 139
1. CUT
2. LOG
3. SAW
4. TREE
5. CHOP
6. WOOD
7. AX
8. PINE

Page 144

1. 400 ft., Bessie
2. 281 ft., Bonnie
3. 280 ft., Ellie
4. 345 ft., Sadie
5. 460 ft., Annie
6. 142 ft., Ruthie
7. 640 ft., Susie

Lulu is the cow that doesn't belong.

Page 145

1. 130 ft.
2. 191 ft.
3. 260 ft.
4. 305 ft.
5. 165 ft.
6. 180 ft.

Page 148

1. ¹/₁₂
2. ¹/₁₆
3. ²/₂₈ = ¹/₁₄

Page 149

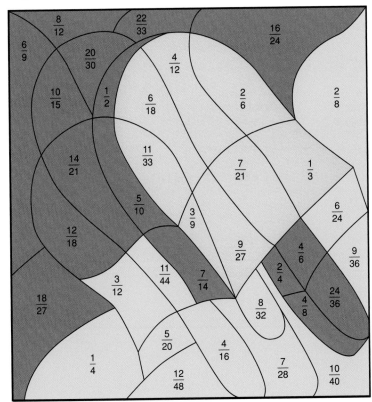

Page 153

1. 50°
2. 75°
3. 125°
4. 50°
5. 40°
6. 90°
7. 135°
8. 50°
9. 185°
10. 50°
11. 60°
12. 110°
13. 105°
14. 10°
15. 115°
16. 85°
17. 120°
18. 205°

To control speed, a skier can do a <u>SNOWPLOW</u>.

Page 158

P. 0.9, 90%, blue
O. 0.25, 25%, yellow
H. 0.7, 70%, blue
C. 0.08, 8%, green
U. 0.05, 5%, green
D. 0.01, 1%, green
K. 0.1, 10%, green
E. 0.8, 80%, blue
T. 0.4, 40%, yellow
S. 0.6, 60%, yellow

They were a <u>DUCK</u>, a <u>ROOSTER</u>, and a <u>SHEEP</u>.

Page 163

1. mean = 15
   median = ~~18~~ 14
   mode = 18
   range = ~~7~~ 8

2. mean = ~~51~~ 52
   median = ~~52~~ 50
   mode = 54
   range = 23

3. mean = ~~7~~ 6
   median = 6
   mode = ~~7~~ 6
   range = 8

4. mean = 20
   median = ~~16~~ 18
   mode = ~~16~~ 18
   range = 36

5. mean = 27
   median = 24
   mode = ~~25~~ 24
   range = ~~15~~ 14

They are <u>BOTH IN A BAD MODE</u>!

Page 168

Table 1: 2.76
Table 2: 5.092; 5.09
Table 3: 16.200; 16.20
Table 4: 6.11
Table 5: 7.44
$2.76 + $5.09 + $16.20 + $6.11 + $7.44 = $37.60

Page 169
1. $\frac{1}{10}$, I
2. $\frac{2}{9}$, A
3. $\frac{3}{20}$, E
4. $\frac{4}{9}$, M
5. $\frac{3}{16}$, P
6. $\frac{5}{18}$, H
7. $\frac{4}{21}$, W
8. $\frac{4}{15}$, O
9. $\frac{3}{8}$, S
10. $\frac{7}{10}$, T

WITH TOMATO PASTE!

Page 172
1. $5 + n$
2. $n - 8$
3. $n + 2$
4. $n - 5$
5. $6 - n$
6. $n - 4$
7. $n + 1$
8. $n - 9$
9. $n - 16$
10. $12 - n$
11. $15 + n$
12. $0 + n$
13. $n - 7$
14. $n + 10$
15. $n - 0$
16. $2 - n$
17. $13 + n$
18. $1 + n$
19. $11 - n$
20. $14 - n$
21. $6 + n$

Those that are being RIDDEN.

Page 173

6	4	5	7	0
1	9	12	2	14
10	3	17	16	20
11	15	18	8	19

24¢

Page 177
A. 86
B. 95
C. 32
D. 50
E. 59
F. 77
G. 68
H. 41

CHILE

Page 182
1. ROAD MAP
2. LUGGAGE
3. CAMERA

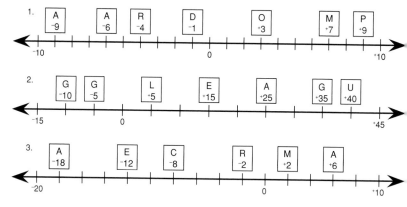

Page 187
Answers may vary.
1. high-fiber solid foods that take longer to digest
2. low-fiber solid foods that take less time to digest
3. the stomach's digestive juices
4. the stomach
5. digestion in the stomach
6. the half teaspoon of sugar; It is less dense.

Page 191
1. Law 3
2. Law 3
3. Law 2
4. Law 1
5. Law 1
6. Law 1
7. Law 2
8. Law 3

Newton saw an apple fall from a tree.

Page 195
Answers may vary.

Substance	Color	Shape	Texture	Water Test	Vinegar Test	Iodine Test	Heat Test
A. flour	white	dotlike particles	soft, smooth	mixes	no change	**turns purple**	yellows
B. sugar	white	odd-shaped crystals	hard	dissolves	no change	does not turn purple	**melts**
C. salt	white	**cubed crystals**	hard	dissolves	no change	does not turn purple	no change
D. baking soda	white	small particles	coarse	mixes	**fizzes, bubbles**	does not turn purple	may yellow

Bag 1 contains flour and salt.
Bag 2 contains baking soda and flour.
Bag 3 contains sugar, salt, and flour.
Bag 4 contains salt and baking soda.

Page 199

Answers may vary.

1. The climate during the first few years was probably warm and wet, promoting fast growth, but the climate in the later years may have been drier.
2. The climate from about year seven to about year 22 allowed for fast growth. There may have been more rainfall during this period.
3. The climate must have been good for growth because the growth pattern is consistent. There were no major climate changes.

Page 208

Answers may vary.

1. The cotton balls represent flowers. The powdered drink mix represents the pollen on a flower. Each cotton swab represents the hairy body of a bee visiting a flower.
2. When a bee lands on a flower, pollen attaches itself to the bee's hairy body and can be carried to another flower.
3. Answers may include other insects, hummingbirds, wind, and water.

Page 213

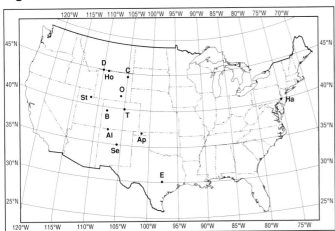

Bonus Box: the western part; All but one location is in that half of the country.

Page 214

1. gastropod
2. southeast
3. hills; Brachiopods have not been found in the plains, only in the hills.
4. Fossil Valley
5. three
6. five miles
7. Paleo Plains and Fossil Valley
8.

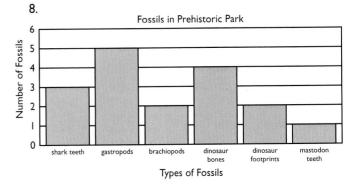

Page 222

Missouri Compromise, 1820—This plan kept a balance between free and slave states. Slavery was banned in the northern Louisiana Purchase area except in Missouri.

Nat Turner's Rebellion, 1831—This event made the Virginia General Assembly think about ending slavery.

Compromise of 1850—California came into the Union as a free state. Settlers of New Mexico and Utah were allowed to decide about slavery for themselves.

Kansas-Nebraska Act, 1854—This law ended the Missouri Compromise. Settlers of two new territories could decide for themselves whether to be free or slave states.

Dred Scott Decision, 1857—The Supreme Court ruled that no African American could be a U.S. citizen and that Congress could not ban slavery in a U.S. territory.

Lincoln's Election, 1860—The Southern states began to secede, or withdraw, from the Union.

Shots Fired at Fort Sumter, 1861—The Civil War began.

Page 248

1. green
2. blue, pounds
3. blue, pounds
4. blue, ounces
5. blue, ounces
6. green
7. blue, cups
8. green
9. green
10. blue, gallons

INDEX

ISBN-13: 978-156234813-7
ISBN-10: 156234813-2

9 781562 348137